They Did Not Dwell Alone

They Did Not Dwell Alone

Jewish Emigration from the Soviet Union
1967–1990

PETRUS BUWALDA

THE WOODROW WILSON CENTER PRESS
Washington, D.C.

THE JOHNS HOPKINS UNIVERSITY PRESS
Baltimore and London

Editorial offices:

The Woodrow Wilson Center Press

370 L'Enfant Promenade, S.W., Suite 704

Washington, D.C. 20024-2518

Telephone 202-287-3000, ext. 218

Order from:

The Johns Hopkins University Press

2715 N. Charles Street

Baltimore, Maryland 21218-4319

Telephone 1-800-537-5487

2 4 6 8 9 7 5 3 1

Library of Congress Cataloging-in-Publication Data

Buwalda, Piet, 1925–
They did not dwell alone : Jewish emigration from the Soviet
Union, 1967–1990 / Petrus Buwalda.
p.   cm.
Includes bibliographical references and index.
ISBN 0-8018-5616-7 (cloth : alk. paper)
1. Jews—Soviet Union—History.   2. Jews—Soviet Union—
Migrations.   3. Jews—Persecutions—Soviet Union.   4. Refuseniks.
5. Soviet Union—Emigration and immigration—Government policy.
6. Israel—Emigration and immigration.   7. Netherlands. Ambassade
(Soviet Union)   I. Title.
DS135.R92B89   1997
947'.004927—dc21   96-29951
                                                                                      CIP

To the Refuseniks

Contents

Preface and Acknowledgments

The problem of the Jewish emigration played an important role right from the start of my assignment to Moscow which began in 1986 and was to last until 1990. Mikhail Gorbachev had just launched his policy of *perestroika* (restructuring), and the monthly numbers of Jews allowed to leave the Soviet Union soon became a test for its sincerity. The Netherlands embassy represented the Israeli interests in Moscow and therefore had to issue the visa that practically every Jew needed to depart. This task made it both desirable and possible to follow closely the fate of those who applied for emigration and to keep contact with those who were not allowed to go—the Refuseniks. Many of them had burned their bridges behind them to such an extent that they dared receive a foreign ambassador and his wife in their home; some have become friends for life.

From this close involvement with the problem and with its victims stems this book. Its focus is Soviet Jewish emigration during the years in which the Netherlands embassy in Moscow represented Israeli interests. My intention was not—except for a brief prologue—to deal with the history of the Jews in Russia; others, more qualified than I, have already done that. Nor have I examined the fate of the emigrants once they left, except insofar as that fate influenced the flow of the emigration. On the other hand, I have paid much attention to the motivations of the Jews who wanted to leave and to the internal and external reasons for Soviet authorities to allow them to go. The Jewish emigration from the Soviet Union did not occur in a vacuum: it was influenced not only by internal political and economic factors but by the political and economic relationship between East and West, as that relationship was, in turn, influenced by the problem of Jewish emigration.

The Six-Day War in the Middle East in June 1967 induced the Soviet Union to break its diplomatic relations with Israel and to halt completely the very limited emigration of elderly Soviet Jews to that country. This emigration recommenced a year later, and the Netherlands embassy began issuing visas for Israel. Twenty-three years later, in November 1990, a meeting of the Conference on Security and Cooperation in Europe in Paris marked the end of the cold war; Soviet-Israeli relations were resumed on January 3, 1991, terminating the task of the Netherlands embassy. Finally on May 20, 1991, a new Soviet emigration law was adopted, removing most of the restrictions that had thwarted the Jewish emigration for so long. From then on, Jewish emigration was subject to normal international rules and no longer a bone of contention in East-West relations.

I must face, of course, the question of my objectivity, having been involved myself for almost four years in discussions about Jewish emigration with the Jews themselves, with my own authorities in the Netherlands, and with authorities of the Soviet Union, Israel, and even the United States. There was never a serious conflict, but differences of opinion were bound to occur. Under these circumstances total objectivity is probably unobtainable, but I have done my utmost to present the various points of view as fairly as possible.

I am grateful to the governments both of Israel and of the Netherlands, which have allowed me access to the documentation regarding the representation of Israeli interests by the Netherlands embassy in Moscow. The Office for Public Access to Government Information and the assistants in the archives of the Ministry of Foreign Affairs in The Hague have been particularly helpful in this respect. Both Israeli and Netherlands authorities have perused the manuscript and informed me that they have no objections to my publishing the present text. Of course, responsibility for the contents rests with me alone.

The Woodrow Wilson International Center for Scholars provided me with a visiting scholarship that enabled me to carry out research in the United States. It included a stipend for a four-month stay, office space and equipment, a research assistant, every conceivable help and encouragement, and a stimulating and inspiring intellectual atmosphere. I am deeply grateful to the Center for its marvelous assistance, and especially to its director, Charles Blitzer, and its deputy director Samuel Wells. I also thank Ambassador Max Kampelman in Washington for his early support.

The Office of Freedom of Information, Privacy and Classification Review of the U.S. Department of State in Washington, D.C., was very helpful in tracing, declassifying, and releasing to me documents relevant to my research.

In Israel I have received much help and information from Lishka in Tel Aviv. Furthermore, the Van Leer Foundation, statutorily not permitted to support my research financially, extended hospitality and much good advice in the Van Leer Institute in Jerusalem. I am most grateful to both institutions.

The bureau of the U.S. Union of Councils for Soviet Jews in Washington gave me much help, while its Moscow Center for Human Rights provided valuable information and contacts for my research in the Russian capital. My thanks go to both of them.

In the Netherlands, the Foundation Levi Lassen in The Hague was the first to support my project, financially and with constant encouragement. My research has also been supported by a grant from the Netherlands Organization for Scientific Research (NWO). I express my sincere thanks to both institutions.

Professor P. M. E. Volten and Professor A. H. Huussen of the University of Groningen have given me a great deal of help by shaping my manuscript and by critically following the drafting of the text. My two oldest friends, W. R. H. Koops and Professor M. G. Buist, lent much practical assistance.

Thanks also go to my research assistants Shaun M. Gummere in Washington, Victoria Melnik in Moscow, and Tatiana Kouvchinova in Leiden.

Very many people have given me their time to be interviewed, providing relevant information about my subject. I cannot mention them all here, but their names have been gratefully listed in the back of the book. Allow me to make four exceptions: our good friends Natasha and Leonid Stonov and Tanya and Yuri Zieman have all spent many hours recounting the events and ordeals, but also the joys and satisfactions of demonstrations or protest actions experienced during the long years they were not allowed to leave the Soviet Union. To them, and to all the other courageous Refuseniks, this book is dedicated.

And, last but not least, my deep gratitude goes to my wife, Vilma, for her constant encouragement and forbearance.

Introduction

Between 1967 and the end of 1990, the period covered by this book, more than a quarter of the Jews who, according to the census of 1959, had lived in what was then the Soviet Union left their country. By the end of 1995 about 1.2 million Jews, or about 50 percent, had emigrated. This exodus is comparable only to the first large-scale Jewish emigration from the Russian empire, between 1881 and 1914, when some 2 million left.

In this second exodus there were two main waves. During the first, in the 1970s, about 220,000 Jews were allowed to go. A record year was 1979, with over 50,000 emigrants. The second wave began in 1987. Between that year and January 1, 1991, more than 300,000 Jews emigrated, more than 184,000 in 1990 alone. The yearly totals varied a great deal, however. Before 1971 and during the early 1980s there were years in which fewer than 1,000 Jews received permission to leave.

The Jewish desire to emigrate from the Soviet Union was prompted as much by a distaste for the "living in dishonesty," forced upon them by the communist state, as by antisemitism, as much by a general sense of hopelessness regarding their future in their country as by anti-Jewish discrimination. It was enormously stimulated by the founding of a Jewish state in Israel, especially after that state had prevailed in the Six-Day War of 1967. The Jews themselves then began to stir and to demand their right to leave.

Permission to emigrate was not normally granted to a Soviet citizen. The communists claimed they had created a workers' and peasants' paradise; it was considered treason to presume to want to leave it. The Soviet Union abstained when the United Nations Universal Declaration on Human Rights was adopted in 1948, proclaiming that each person had the right to leave his or her country. In 1973 the Soviets did ratify, however, the International Covenant on Civil and Political Rights, which incorporated the provisions of the UN Universal Declaration. They also signed the Helsinki Final Act of 1975, which reconfirmed and strengthened that declaration. But the Soviet authorities never intended to fully carry out their international obligations in this respect. They would usually reject any reminder of those obligations with a reference to a different provision of those agreements, which prohibited interference in the internal affairs of one country by another. Many Jews (and some other Soviet citizens) were harassed, fired from their jobs, and sometimes jailed, for trying—or even for just applying—to get out. So why did Leonid Brezhnev in 1971, or Mikhail Gorbachev in 1987, suddenly decide to let more and more Jews go?

One school of thought holds that permission for the Jews to emigrate from the Soviet Union was granted largely as a result of foreign policy considerations, that it was mainly, if not exclusively, foreign pressure which induced Soviet authorities to allow Jews to go. It will be called the external theory in my analysis. What will be called the internal theory says that, on the contrary, the decisions to allow emigration were made independent of external forces and were due to considerations internal to the Soviet Union and to the pressure of the Soviet Jews themselves.

A third theory will be proposed in this study: the interaction theory. It holds that external pressure did play a large role in urging or even forcing Soviet leaders to allow Jews to emigrate. But that foreign pressure did not spring up by itself; it had to be evoked first by pressure from inside the country. The urgent desire of many Jews to emigrate stood at the basis of their exodus. The constant refusal of the Soviet authorities to allow large-scale emigration, the harassment of applicants, and the maltreatment and persecution of those who were refused permission (the Refuseniks), in turn, generated pressure from the West. The conclusion will be, however, that this pressure proved to be effective only when internal considerations induced the Soviet leadership to accommodate it. Those considerations were, although the wish to remove "unreformable" citizens and the intention to "decapitate" the Jewish dissident movement played a role, mainly of an economic nature.

The reasons for the behavior of the Soviet leadership regarding Jewish emigration in the 1970s and in 1980s must, in other words, be sought in the interaction of internal and external factors, not in either of them alone.

Other elements influenced Jewish emigration. The help extended to the migrating Jews by foreign Jewish organizations and by foreign governments was important. The emigrants' choice of final destination—Israel or elsewhere—led in later years to increasing conflicts. Both will be discussed.

The interaction worked both ways. Jewish emigration frequently influenced international politics. It played a role in Henry Kissinger's "linkage" policies, caused the Jackson-Vanik Amendment to be adopted in the U.S. Congress and a Soviet-American trade agreement to be rejected, influenced the Helsinki discussions, and hung over many of Gorbachev's summit meetings with his American counterparts. All these, in turn, had their effect on the number of Jews allowed to emigrate in various periods.

This study is to a considerable extent based on the reporting of the Netherlands embassy in Moscow and the experiences of the Dutch diplomats there, since it was that embassy which represented the Israeli interests in the Soviet Union after diplomatic relations with Israel were broken by the Soviets during the Six-Day War in 1967. The Netherlands embassy placed the final stamp on the exit permit of practically every Jew leaving the Soviet Union, and on the exit permits of many non-Jews as well. Between 1967 and the end of 1990 the Netherlands embassy issued Israeli visas for some 570,000 persons.[1]

It should be emphasized, however, that this book is not only about diplomatic activities, relations between governments and their actions and decisions, theories and statistics. It intends also to be an account of an often dramatic historic episode—and of the people who lived through it:

— people of the Soviet Union, mostly Jewish, who had to make the agonizing decision whether or not to leave their country, whether to risk their jobs and perhaps jail just for applying for an exit permit;

— people who were refused such a permit and then had to cope with harassment, the loss of their jobs, a pariah status, and the decision whether to keep quiet or "make noise";

— people who fought the refusals, protested, and demonstrated, risked jail and health, and suffered in prison;

— people in Western Jewish and non-Jewish organizations who gave assistance and, with the help of courageous men and women "tourists," opened up and maintained communications with the Refuseniks in the Soviet Union;

— people in the governments of Israel, the United States, and other Western countries who agonized over whether to exercise pressure by "quiet diplomacy" or to protest openly and mention victims by name;

— people in the Dutch foreign service who during twenty-three years gave their best efforts to help the emigrants where they could and to ease their emigration.

In short, this book is about people who at all costs wanted to exercise their right to leave their country and people who made sure that those who tried "did not dwell alone."

They Did Not Dwell Alone

*Our government will sell Jews or not sell Jews,
will let them go or not, depending on what it gets in return.
Jews are a card in the political game.*

—Natasha Rapoport

Prologue

From where did the Jews come who lived in the territories of what later became the Russian empire? In the southern parts they may well have arrived much earlier than the Russians themselves. Even before the Christian era Jews are said to have migrated from ancient Babylonia and Persia through the Caucasus to the north.[1] Later they came from Palestine through Asia Minor and Greece to live in Greek colonies around the Black Sea. Still later Jews fled from Christian persecution in the Byzantine empire, again to colonies on the Black Sea and to the Khazars, a seminomadic tribe living in what is now southern Russia, especially after the Khazars took the Crimea. The Khazar king even adopted the Jewish faith in 740 to escape domination by the Muslims from Baghdad or the Christians from Byzantium.[2] Kiev was originally founded by Khazars and later had two Jewish colonies, one of Khazari Jews and one of Jews who had come from the West—the Ashkenazi. After the Genovese founded a colony in the Crimea, a large Jewish community also sprang up there. But the population of Kiev and the Crimea, including the Jews, was almost totally wiped out by Tatar invasions in the thirteenth century. Jews fled east to Volhynia and Galicia and north toward Lithuania. Only in the mountains of the Caucasus did some Jewish colonies survive, a few even into the present—only to disappear before our eyes.

According to most authors, however, the origin of most of the present Russian Jews lies not in the south but in the West.[3] In 1939 the non-Ashkenazi constituted not more than 3 percent of the Jewish population of the Soviet Union.

In Poland, Jews who fled persecutions in the West had been welcomed in the fourteenth century. In contrast to the local peasants they could read and write and were therefore engaged in estate management and tax and toll collecting for the feudal landowners, the king and the nobility, who preferred to stay in the cities. They also excelled in moneylending and trade. Because the Jews were the intermediate agents used by landowners to extract surplus from the peasantry, they were deeply despised in rural Poland (not unlike the half-casts later who performed the same functions in the British and Dutch colonies). But they also constituted a threat to the monopolies of the guilds in the cities, and Polish antisemitism was caused as much by the fear of competition in the cities as by the hatred of the oppressed peasantry.

The period from the beginning of the sixteenth century to the middle of the seventeenth century has been described as a golden age for the Jews in Poland. Their numbers increased from 10,000–12,000 in 1500 to 150,000–170,000 in 1650 both by natural growth and by further immigration, and they had their own judicial, administrative, and educational institutions.[4]

It was not until the sixteenth century that Polish and Czech Jews settled in larger numbers in Lithuania and White Russia. A homogenous group of Russo-Polish Jews was then formed from two elements: Jews who had fled from Western Europe, especially from Germany, and Jews who originated from old Kiev and Khazaria, including Khazars who had adopted the Jewish faith.[5] Up till the end of the seventeenth century, Jews were forbidden to enter Russia proper.

Jews under the Czars

Czar Peter the Great (reigned 1682–1725), although anti-Jewish, permitted Jewish bankers to settle in Moscow and other Jews in border areas. His wife Czarina Catherine I who succeeded him (reigned 1725–27) rescinded the measure, and his daughter Elizabeth (reigned 1741–62) declared that the Jews "shall henceforward not be admitted to our Empire for any purpose."[6] Catherine II, who took the throne in 1762, was more liberal, but she had to tread carefully at first against the opposition of the Orthodox Church. In 1772 the first partition of Poland took place, and Russia received most of what is now Belarus.[7] Catherine then ordered the governor of that territory to issue a decree granting the Jews "freedom of religious worship and sanctity and integrity of the property of each and all."[8] The second and third Polish partitions in 1793 and 1795 brought the eastern part of what was left of Poland,

Courland, and Lithuania under Russian sovereignty—and with it a large part of the Polish and Lithuanian Jews.

But in the meantime the czarina had been deeply shocked by the French Revolution, which had also led to the adoption of a liberal constitution in Poland, duly crushed by the Prussian and Russian armies. At the end of 1791 she sent an edict to the Senate stating: "Jews have no right to register as merchants in the towns and internal harbors of Russia and only by our express command have they been permitted to enjoy civil and urban rights in Byelorussia."[9] The edict marked the beginning of a much harsher regime that, with many ups and downs, essentially lasted untill 1917. Some scholars see this edict as the first indication of a *cherta*, or Pale of Settlement.[10] Others rather believe the Pale was established in 1804 with an edict of Czar Alexander I that ordered Jews to leave their villages by January 1, 1807 (only partially carried out), and extended from Astrakhan to the Caucasus.[11]

The Pale of Settlement was an area enclosing the Russian parts of Poland and the western provinces of Russia where in principle all Jews had to live and which they were not allowed to leave without special permission. It was in fact a huge ghetto.[12] The mercantile and handicraft classes of Russia proper, especially, had insisted that the Jews be confined in this way to their provinces of origin.[13] The Jews constituted about 10 percent of the population of the area, but since they were usually not allowed to live in the larger cities and frequently driven out of the villages, they were heavily concentrated, often overcrowded, in the smaller townships (*shtetlekh*).

Sometimes Jews were forced to work on the land and forbidden to enter the cities; then again they were driven from the villages and forced to find employment in trades and handicrafts. At one time they were heavily involved in the production of alcohol; then the czar revoked the right of the Jews to brew and sell spirits in order to maintain the income of the state alcohol monopoly. At one time Jews were not allowed to serve in the army; then the army established conscription quotas for Jews that were three times higher than those of other people.

Very important for the Jews was the opening of schools and universities to them in 1804, during the reign of Alexander I.[14] The Jewish youth, already more literate than others, flocked to take advantage of the new opportunities. Their numbers later prompted the establishment of a *numerus clausus*, a limitation of the number of Jews who could attend any given institution. But even the *numerus clausus* could not reverse the fact that Russian Jews were, on the whole, more highly educated than the rest of the population.

Czar Nicholas I ruled with a harsher hand, promulgating the Jewish Regulations of May 31, 1835, which became a sort of Jewish constitution on which, until the Russian Revolution of 1917, all legislation was based. The regulations affirmed the special status of Jews. They regulated Jewish marriages, for example, and decreed that Jews leaving Russia without permission would forfeit their Russian citizenship and not be permitted to return—just as Soviet authorities were to decree in 1967. They also more precisely delineated and reduced the Pale of Settlement, which henceforth encompassed 362,000 square miles. In three additional edicts Nicholas tried to prohibit traditional Jewish dress, but finally only the long-skirted coat and the headgear remained forbidden.[15]

Nicholas's son Alexander II was certainly no liberal, but he realized that drastic reforms were necessary.[16] In the same year that he freed the serfs—1861—he also permitted Jews to enter government service and to settle anywhere if they were doctors of medicine or surgery, or holders of master's or bachelor's degrees. This right was later extended to artisans, mechanics, distillers of wines and spirits, and soldiers who had served in the Russian army. But all these measures affected only a small part of the Jewish population; the Jews remained *inorodtsi*, people "of other birth,"[17] somewhere between foreigners and citizens, until 1881.

In that year the position of the Jews worsened following the murder of Alexander II and the beginning of the pogroms, the outrages and massacres committed by peasants against local Jews. Pogroms were undoubtedly organized by such societies as the Sacred Hand and at least tolerated, if not sometimes instigated, by the central authorities, perhaps even the new Czar Alexander III himself. Those authorities saw the pogroms as a useful canalization of peasant unrest toward the increasingly intractable Jewish problem.[18]

Jewish homes were pillaged and burned; Jews were beaten and often killed. From 1881, Jews were regarded as aliens and, until 1905, were the victims of an extreme anti-Jewish policy. In 1881, the czar expelled 86 percent of the Jewish population from Moscow, and many expulsions followed thereafter. Civil rights were restricted, admission to state service and the officer's corps was denied, and in 1887 the *numerus clausus* was introduced in higher education. By the end of the nineteenth century the Jews were in effect barred from Russia proper except for a few rich Jews; barred in the Pale from the countryside and from major cities like Kiev; excluded from agriculture, civil service, and military office; and restricted

than the population in general. Although some 500,000 served in the army, Jews were still not trusted. And since they were considered unreliable, some 600,000 of them were expelled from the western parts of the Pale.[27] When the consequent overcrowding in the eastern part became intolerable, Jews were finally allowed to cross the border eastward in 1916. The exodus signified the effective end of the Pale, although it was not officially abolished until 1917, by the Kerensky government.

Jews and the Bolshevik Revolution

In view of the terrible conditions under which most Jews in Russia lived, and the severe restrictions on their civil rights, education, choice of employment, and mobility, it is hardly surprising that the rise of new and often secret political movements found a ready response among younger Jews, who sought to "shatter their own chains."[28] On the one hand, they flocked to Zionist movements that ranged from orthodox to liberal to socialist. The Zionists believed that Russia would never give the Jews the political, social, and economic rights that would ensure their security; they therefore agitated for a free Jewish life in their biblical homeland, Palestine. Russian Zionist organizations had more than 300,000 members, in 1,200 local units, in October 1917.[29]

In the non-Jewish socialist parties Jews were less numerous, but individual Jews played important roles in the Bolshevik, Menshevik, and Social Revolutionary Parties. Last but not least there was an important purely Jewish socialist party—the Bund, founded in 1897 on a Marxist basis. Originally the Bund was part of the Russian Social Democratic Workers Party, but it clashed with V. I. Lenin, especially over its demand for Jewish cultural-national autonomy. The Bund promoted extraterritorial autonomy, the idea of full national autonomy regardless of the territory in which the people in question lived, as first proposed by Austrian socialists. In December 1917 it had 33,700 members.[30]

The national question—the problem of cultural or national autonomy for the many different peoples, or nationalities, in the enormous Russian empire—preoccupied the communist leaders of the Soviet Union from its beginning to its end. In fact, the national question, never resolved, proved to be one of the main causes of that end.

Lenin sent Josef Stalin to Vienna to gather material for essays he was preparing on this question. Stalin's research resulted (with help from Nikolai Bukharin) in an article in a party journal in 1913 entitled

"Marxism and the National and Colonial Question."[31] Stalin defined a nation as a "historically evolved stable community of language, territory, economic life and psychological make-up, manifested in a community of culture." Only when all these characteristics were present could there be a nation. He rejected the autonomy promoted by the Austrian socialists, believing it would only increase national differences by creating artificial communities within each state. By definition, a Jewish nationality was thus excluded. Stalin added: "What . . . national cohesion can there be . . . between the Georgian, Daghestanian, Russian and American Jew? How can it be seriously maintained that petrified religious rites and fading psychological relics affect the 'fate' of these Jews more powerfully than the living . . . environment that surrounds them?"[32] He accused the Bund of retarding the natural process of assimilation, which he thought desirable and in the end inevitable. Although opposed to all manifestations of antisemitism, Lenin also denied the existence of a Jewish nationality, calling it a reactionary Zionist idea. And Zionism, he said, was counterrevolutionary. It was inconceivable to him that a people should exist without a territory of its own or a common language. To him the Jews were nothing but a sect. [33]

After the czar resigned on March 2, 1917, the government of Alexander Kerensky granted cultural-national autonomy to all national minorities, including Jews. It also withdrew all the restrictive laws Jews had endured and officially eliminated the Pale.[34] Jewish political and cultural life suddenly blossomed, and Zionism was greatly strengthened by the Balfour Declaration of November 2, 1917. "His Majesty's Government," it said, "view with favour the establishment in Palestine of a national home for the Jewish people."[35]

The October Revolution (in fact a *coup d'état* carried out by a small minority) brought Lenin and his Bolshevik Party to power on October 25, 1917 (November 7 on the new calendar). Lenin continued to denounce Zionism as counterrevolutionary and to advocate the assimilation of the Jews. Yet he hinted that the Jews might develop as a separate nationality, although he remained unalterably opposed to "Jewish bourgeois nationalism."[36] Stalin became people's commissar for nationalities, a post he would occupy until 1922. Born a Georgian but now an assimilated Russian, Stalin also continued to demand complete assimilation of the Jews.[37] But first the new regime had to establish itself. The civil war lasted well into 1920, and, as so often in troubled times in Russia, the Jews suffered terribly. Massacres were not uncommon, especially in the

Ukraine, and it was estimated that between fifty thousand and sixty thousand Jews were killed.[38] As a result, many Jews turned to the communists for protection. Nevertheless, the Jewish masses in general did not support the new regime.[39]

In 1918 a Jewish section was created in the Communist Party, the Evsektsya, which tried to win over the Jews to communism while denouncing the "counterrevolutionary essence" of Zionism. Its efforts were not without success: while only 1,000 Jews were members of the Bolshevik Party in 1917, Jews constituted 5.1 percent of all party members in 1922. Their motives must have been mixed, as usual, but besides protection the party offered Jews an end to discrimination and an outlet for their revolutionary drive while it allowed them to become part of the society surrounding them.[40] The party, moreover, offered well-paid jobs in difficult times. Jews were also well represented in the Central Committee of the party and later, until the mid-1930s, in the Politburo. All came from assimilated families. However, as one scholar has explained, "the large masses of the Jews were shocked and bewildered by the swift and brutal Bolshevik measures which destroyed their property, their religious and national culture and often their livelihood. The freedom and political efflorescence of the brief March Revolution was extinguished— an immense loss especially for Jews."[41]

It soon became clear that in a communist state there was no place for separate Jewish political parties or for Jewish religion or traditional Jewish life. While all religions were attacked, the Jewish religion seemed especially hard hit. All central synagogues were closed by the Evsektsya, only smaller ones remaining open. Jewish religious schools were also closed. Jewish political parties, including the Bund, were taken over by the Evsektsya and, in the early 1920s, incorporated into the Bolshevik Party. The campaign against Jewish traditional life was waged to a large extent by communist Jews. Zionism and Hebrew culture had to be "cleansed." The Jewish youth movement was closed down, and Zionists were arrested. The last Hebrew publication appeared in 1926.[42]

In that same year Stalin began a confrontation with a so-called bloc in the party led by Leon Trotsky, Grigori Zinoviev, and Lev Kamenev,[43] all of whom were of Jewish descent. Stalin's antisemitism got a new impetus. Trotsky was exiled in 1929 and later murdered, on Stalin's orders, in Mexico. The other two were expelled from the party in 1934, arrested the next year, and condemned to death and executed in August 1936. The only Jew left on the Politburo for many more years was Lazar Kaganovich.[44]

Throughout the Soviet period Soviet officials both condemned and encouraged the concept of Jewish nationality, depending on which domestic and foreign policy considerations were at the forefront. The early "checkered, contradictory, unpredictable pattern of decisions affecting Jews" was repeated later.[45] If the czars "never quite knew what to do with their Jews," the Soviet commissars didn't either. In the mid-1920s the Jewish section of the party, although now manned mostly by former members of the Bund, realized that for the Jewish nationality to survive under the rules created by Stalin it would need a territorial base. Declared longtime Soviet president M. I. Kalinin in November 1926:

> The Jewish people faces a great task—to preserve its nationality, and for this end a large part of the Jewish population, hundreds of thousands at least, must be turned into agricultural peasants, settled in a continuous area. Only in those conditions can the Jewish masses hope to preserve the continued existence of the Jewish nationality.[46]

And so the Evsektsya set out to establish a Jewish republic somewhere on the territory of the Soviet Union. In the early 1920s it was thought that the Crimea could serve that purpose. Some Jewish agricultural colonies were actually established there, with the help of a Western Jewish organization—the Joint Distribution Committee, founded at the beginning of the First World War to provide aid to "Jews in need wherever they are."[47] But by 1932 only 5,000 families had been resettled, and in any case Stalin vetoed the plan, probably because he was uneasy about a concentration of Jews in such a strategic area.

Then came Birobidzhan.[48] It was an improbable choice—a territory slightly larger than Belgium with some natural resources but a most inhospitable climate, on the border with China, very sparsely populated and thousands of miles from the centers where Jewish populations were concentrated. The decision by the Central Committee in March 1928 that a Jewish republic was to be established there obviously had nothing to do with the interest of the Jews. Indeed it was even opposed by the Evsektsya and was probably, once again, dictated mostly by strategic considerations, in this case to provide a buffer against Chinese infiltration. The Russian state was supposed to make all the necessary investment in infrastructure and subsidize settlers on collective farms. Foreign aid was requested and, indeed, provided by American sources. Authorities in Moscow tried to promote Birobidzhan as an alternative to Palestine: "For the first time in the history of the Jewish people their desire for own national statehood has been fulfilled." But it was a failure. Between 1928 till 1934 less than 20,000 Jews moved to Birobidzhan and 60 percent of those soon left it again. Birobidzhan received the status of autonomous region in 1934, but in 1936 only 18,000 Jews lived in the territory, constituting a meager 23 percent of the population.[49] When the Jewish leadership in Birobidzhan was exterminated by the purges of 1936–38, it was clear that the Jews were not going to create a republic in this faraway and hostile land with which they had no emotional, historical, or national bond.

Stalin's Policies on the Jews

Between 1929 and 1939, the very survival of Jewish religion,[50] education, literature, press, and theater was threatened. This period was Stalin's Iron Age. The Jewish organizations in the United States then faced a question that would torment them many times afterward: Should they protest Stalin's policies publicly, or would such action endanger the Soviet Jews and destroy whatever fragile contacts they had with them and with Soviet authorities? The American Jewish Congress did call a conference in 1930 to protest the persecution of the Jewish and other religions, and it succeeded in obtaining the release of some rabbis who had been arrested.[51]

Meanwhile in January 1930 the Central Committee had ordered a reorganization of the Communist Party and abolished all national sections, including the Evsektsya. In February 1931 so-called work certificates were introduced, and on December 27, 1932, the infamous internal passport of the czars was revived for all urban residents age sixteen and older. Besides the usual identification data, the document listed the nationality of the bearer. Jews were now marked as *Yevrei*. This document had to be shown everywhere, even to obtain permission for ordinary travel in the interior. It impeded not only emigration but also settlement in another city.

The years 1936–38 brought the horrors of the Stalinist purges. Thousands of intellectuals, leaders of the state apparatus, the army, and last but not least the Communist Party were arrested in massive waves, usually on the most ludicrous charges, and either liquidated or exiled. A great many Jews perished in these purges. Some historians discern "a conspicuous anti-Jewish thrust" and a "disproportional suffering of the Jews."[52] Another historian asserts that Jews were overrepresented in the central administration and the military commands in relation to their share of the population and were not necessarily liquidated because they were Jews.[53] In any case, practically all Jews were expelled from the state apparatus, the diplomatic service, the Central Committee of the Communist Party, and even Stalin's personal secretariat. Furthermore the destruction of all cadres of Jewish cultural workers and agencies dealt an irreparable blow to any identifiable Jewish life. A whole generation of Jewish communists involved in Jewish affairs was liquidated, including the leadership of the Evsektsya and in Birobidzhan.[54]

One can hardly meet a Russian Jewish family that does not have a tale to tell of the horrors of the purges and of close relatives who were murdered or disappeared for many years in labor camps or internal exile. In such cases all other members of the family would suffer: they often became nonpersons who could not get jobs or educations. It is a story of random persecution and suffering that ended only with the outbreak of the Second World War.

Just before that war began in the West, Stalin authorized his foreign minister V. M. Molotov to conclude an agreement with his German counterpart Joachim von Ribbentrop. This Nazi-Soviet Pact was signed on August 23, 1939. It delineated spheres of influence in Eastern Europe and in fact allowed the Soviet Union to annex parts of Poland and Rumania as well as all the Baltic states. As a result, an estimated 1.88 million Jews came under Soviet rule, bringing the Jewish population of the Soviet Union up to 5.2 million—curiously enough the same number estimated to have lived in czarist Russia in 1914, before the First World War.[55]

Many Jews in the Soviet-occupied zone of Poland who refused to accept Soviet passports were deported to Siberia. A large percentage of them succumbed under the inhuman circumstances there, but possibly as many as 200,000 survived[56] and later spread over Central Asia.

Nazi Germany attacked the Soviet Union on June 22, 1941, and within four months German armies were standing before Moscow and Leningrad. The entire territory that had once been the Pale of Settlement, where 37 percent of Soviet Jews still lived,[57] was now in Nazi hands, including many cities with large Jewish populations such as Kiev, Vilna (Vilnius), Minsk, and Odessa. Perhaps as many as 1.5 million Jewish factory workers from the industrial areas in the western Soviet Union were evacuated when their factories relocated to the Urals and Siberia. Most of the Jews who remained behind were not aware of what the Germans had already done to the Jews in their own country and in the German-occupied part of Poland, because after the Nazi-Soviet Pact of 1939 the Soviet media had stopped reporting Nazi atrocities. There was, as one scholar has reported, "ignorance, incredulousness, and confusion." Special SS-Einsatzgruppen were soon sent to the occupied parts of the Soviet Union to eradicate the Jews. Hundreds of thousands were murdered within the first few months.[58] Then trains began to deport the remaining Jews to the extermination camps that had meanwhile been readied in Poland. The Holocaust raged over the Soviet Union for more than three years. Outside Nazi-occupied zones there were also many victims among the Jews, both civilian and military. It is believed, for example, that the percentage of Jewish soldiers killed during the war was higher than that of Russian soldiers or of any other nationality. Altogether it has been estimated that between 2.5 and 3.3 million Jews died; that is, half the Jews living in the Soviet Union in 1941 were dead by the end of the war[59]—an inconceivable slaughter.

Soon after the German invasion Stalin realized that to defend his country he would have to gain the support of all elements, not just the Communist Party but also the Orthodox Church and every nationality, including the Jews. Besides, the leadership clearly thought that badly needed foreign aid, particularly from the United States, would be easier to obtain with the help of connections the Jews could make with Jews in the West. The Jewish Antifascist Committee, established in April 1942 as part of the Bureau of Information, constituted the first more or less representative body of the Soviet Jews since the demise of the Evsektsya in 1930. A famous actor, Shlomo Mikhoels, was named chairman, and soon he was allowed to broadcast to the Jews all over the world that he represented "that part of the Jewish people that is living in the USSR." This enormous departure from previous Soviet policy for a time raised Jewish hopes both in the Soviet Union and in the West. But it was "an opportunistic departure,"[60] and it was not going to last much beyond the war's end. Even during the war Soviet propaganda largely ignored the plight of the Jews, notwithstanding the existence of the Jewish Antifascist Committee. The mass murders in Babi Yar, near Kiev, for instance, were reported without mention of the fact that the overwhelming majority of the victims were Jews.

After the Germans capitulated in 1945, the alliance between the Western nations and the Soviet Union began to fall apart. Whatever some revisionist historians have asserted, it is now clear that Stalin's insecurity, his distrust of his allies, his imperial ambitions intermixed with envy of American power and economic growth, his disregard for the agreements concluded at Yalta and Potsdam, his xenophobia, and eventually his paranoia all made continuation of the wartime collaboration impossible. Stalin's paranoia came to the surface most clearly in his treatment of the Jews.

The Jews who had survived in the east were allowed to return to their former homes but discouraged by the Soviet authorities to do so. If they did, they often found that their possessions were not returned to them and that they faced a heightened antisemitism. Although Jews were admitted to economic, educational, and art institutions, they were barred from political or security posts and removed from positions in the government apparatus, especially those relating to foreign affairs, foreign trade, the military, and internal security.[61] While some Yiddish publications were still appearing, Yiddish schools were not allowed to reopen. As early as 1947 Jewish writers were criticized for "slandering Soviet man and Soviet reality" instead of stressing "class conflict." In addition to his habitual antisemitism Stalin was beginning to believe in a traitorous Jewish "cosmopolitanism."

On the other hand, up to 1951 the Soviets allowed Jews living in their Eastern European satellites to emigrate to Palestine. These included Jews who had returned to Poland after an accord had been reached between the Polish and Soviet governments concerning the repatriation of Polish citizens from Soviet territory. But the emigration of Soviet citizens remained practically impossible.

The Soviet Union and the State of Israel

At midnight on May 14, 1948, David Ben-Gurion proclaimed the State of Israel. Four days later the first full *de jure* recognition of the new state was extended by the Soviet Union.

At the end of a book on Soviet relations with the State of Israel, an Israeli author concludes that "The Soviet Union's original decision to sanction the creation of Israel at the cost of alienating the more than 35 million Arabs is still not fully comprehensible."[62] It was indeed a surprise, the more so since the Soviet support in the United Nations was the decisive factor for the adoption of the so-called Two States Resolution of November 29, 1947, which provided for the possibility of a Jewish and an Arab state within the territory of the former British mandate of Palestine. To this time almost automatic support for Arab causes had been standard Soviet policy.

Andrei Gromyko, deputy foreign minister and permanent representative of the Soviet Union at the United Nations, initiated the change in Soviet attitude toward a possible Israeli state in May 1947.[63] In a special session of the UN General Assembly devoted to the Palestinian problem, Gromyko declared, on May 14, that his country still preferred a joint Arab-Israeli government for Palestine but would support separate Arab and Jewish states in Palestine as a second choice.[64] In a session of the assembly on November 26, Gromyko professed two reasons for the new Soviet policy: "The Jewish people has been closely linked with Palestine for a considerable period in history," and "We must not overlook the position in which the Jewish people found themselves as a result of the recent world war."[65] The Two States Resolution was passed by a vote of 33 to 13 on November 29, 1947.

The reasons Gromyko offered for his vote were obviously not the real ones. The Soviet Union had never before recognized the Jewish links with Palestine; indeed it had offered Birobidzhan as a better choice for the settlement of Jews. A few months before, Soviet propaganda had still referred to Zionists as "bourgeois lackeys of British imperialism." Nor had recognition of the suffering of the Jews in the Holocaust ever been part of Soviet postwar policy. The real reason must be sought elsewhere.

It now seems most likely that the Soviet government had hoped an Israeli state could become an anti-British foothold in the Middle East.[66] The Soviet government had repeatedly been disappointed in the results of its support for Arab causes and may well have believed the assurances of "relatively important, though left-wing, individuals who might have risen to prominent positions in the future Israeli Government"[67] that Israel could become a socialist state and thus a Soviet client in the Middle East. The satellite countries in Eastern Europe, in particular Czechoslovakia, became the main suppliers for arms to the fledgling Jewish state. Stalin's disappointment at British Prime Minister Clement Atlee's decision in the autumn of 1946 to invite the Americans to share responsibility in the Middle East may also have played a role. He wanted to keep the Americans out of that part of the world at all costs.[68]

It turned out to be a major miscalculation. True, Ben-Gurion at first maintained a policy of nonidentification with either East or West and tried to maintain stable relations with the Soviet Union. On May 11, 1949, Israel was admitted to the United Nations with Soviet support.[69] However, Ben-Gurion was a social democrat, far from a communist, and the small Israeli Communist Party never gained any influence. Israel naturally kept the possibility of emigration of Soviet Jews in mind when dealing with the Soviet Union, but Ben-Gurion in 1950 clearly stated that Russia's lever of restricted emigration would never force Israel into the Eastern camp.[70] When Israel supported the resolution on the UN intervention against the North Korean invasion of South Korea in 1951, it was clear that, on the contrary, it had begun to enter the Western camp. Jewish emigration from the Soviet satellite countries virtually stopped, and only a few older Soviet citizens—by exception—received permission to join their families in Israel.[71]

The Soviets probably did not fully realize the effect that the founding of the State of Israel would have on Soviet Jews, although they must have had some doubts. Gromyko declared blandly, "The Soviet Union is not directly interested in the Palestine problem from the point of view of the emigration of Jews to Palestine, since the Jewish population of the Soviet Union does not show any interest."[72]

Golda Meyerson (later, Meir) arrived on September 3, 1948, as the first Israeli minister in Moscow. Shortly after her arrival the Jewish author Ilya Ehrenburg was made to write in *Pravda:* "Let there be no mistake about it. The state of Israel has nothing to do with the Jews of the Soviet Union, where there is no Jewish problem and therefore no need for Israel." But when a few weeks later Rosh Hashanah, the Jewish New Year, was celebrated and Meir and her legation staff went to the Moscow synagogue, "thousands upon thousands of Jews came . . . to be with us, to demonstrate their sense of kinship, and to celebrate the establishment of the state of Israel."[73] The Soviet reaction was one of surprise and disbelief, and it soon became clear that the Jews would have to pay a heavy price for the welcome they had given Golda Meir. Soviet authorities took measures to ensure the "lack of interest" of their Jews for Israel.

Antisemitism under Stalin and Khrushchev

The murder of Shlomo Mikhoels, the head of the Jewish Antifascist Committee, on January 13, 1948,[74] ushered in a period of extreme antisemitism often disguised as anti-Zionism. In the autumn of that year the last Yiddish magazine was closed down, as was the Yiddish theater. Beginning in December 1948, almost all the members of the Jewish Antifascist Committee were arrested, as were at least 430 Jewish writers, painters, actors, engineers, musicians, and public figures. All Committee members except Ilya Ehrenburg and Lena Stern were condemned. Many were among the twenty-five Jewish writers and public figures who were executed on August 12, 1952; most of the others perished in labor camps.[75] Obviously Stalin had decided to eradicate Jewish culture out of his fear for the imagined dangers of "cosmopolitan Zionism." He told his daughter, Svetlana Alleluyeva, who was then married to a Jew: "You don't understand. The entire older generation is contaminated with Zionism and now they're teaching the young people too." She concluded that there was no use arguing with him.[76]

Worse may have been in store for the Jewish population as a whole. On January 13, 1953, an article in the party newspaper *Pravda* informed the world of the so-called Doctors' Plot. Medical practitioners—most of them Jews—who had treated Stalin himself and many other members of the Communist *Nomenclatura*,[77] were accused of plotting to murder Soviet leaders in collaboration with Western Jewish organizations such as the Joint Distribution Committee.[78] These accusations were the cue for one of the worst periods of antisemitism ever. There are indications that Stalin planned to deport the whole Jewish population of the european part of the Soviet Union to Siberia.[79]

Stalin's death on March 5, 1953, may therefore have saved not only the doctors—except for several who had succumbed under the interrogation of the Committee for State Security (Komitet Gosudarstvenoy Bezopasnosti, KGB)—but also the Jewish population as a whole. By April 4 the new rulers acknowledged that the accusations of a plot had been "without any legal ground" and the arrests had been made without justification.[80]

The Doctors' Plot had in the meantime led to a worsening of the relations between the Soviet Union and Israel. The Israeli public naturally became incensed by the preposterous accusations against respectable Jewish medical practitioners. That was not an excuse, however, for the fact that on February 9, 1953, a bomb was exploded in the courtyard of the Soviet legation in Tel Aviv. The attack was immediately denounced by Prime Minister Ben-Gurion and the Knesset, but the Soviet government decided to break its diplomatic relations with Israel anyway. The Netherlands consented to represent Israeli interests in the Soviet Union. Israeli foreign minister Moshe Sharet considered this arrangement an act of special friendship. "We greatly value the warm relations between Israel and the Netherlands," he stated.[81] One of the few tasks the Netherlands embassy performed for Israel during this first break in Soviet-Israeli diplomatic relations was to convey Israeli condolences at the death of Stalin.

Stalin's death may have enabled his successors to return to a more normal Soviet policy in foreign affairs as well. In June the Polish envoy in Bulgaria told his Israeli counterpart (the Soviet satellites had not broken off their relations with Israel) that an Israeli request to the Soviet Union to restore relations would be well received in Moscow.[82] On July 20, 1953, diplomatic relations were officially restored. Not until November, however, did the Israeli minister return to Moscow; the Netherlands representation of the Israeli interests ended on December 1, 1953.[83] The Soviets then went even further in improving relations: on June 17, 1954, the legations were upgraded to embassies, and Jerusalem was recognized as the capital of Israel.[84] However, the hope that the Soviet Union would now also be prepared to grant exit permits to Jewish emigrants proved idle.[85]

During the confusion in the leadership of the Communist Party after Stalin's death, antisemitism subsided. Nikita Khrushchev came to power as secretary general in 1955. His speech to the Twentieth Party Congress in 1956 denouncing Stalin's methods was a turning point in the policies of the Communist Party. But Khrushchev was a traditional antisemite[86] and did not mention Stalin's crimes against the Jews. He also thought it necessary to adopt a stricter antireligious policy. At first the situation for the Jewish religion improved a little: the Moscow rabbi was allowed to visit Paris in 1956, and for the first time since the establishment of the Soviet regime a *yeshivah*, a Jewish theological school, was opened in Moscow. But in November 1958 the Central Committee of the party adopted a resolution to launch a concerted campaign against religions. Although the Orthodox Church was the main target,[87] the Jewish religion also suffered greatly during the next five years. More than fifty synagogues were closed.[88]

The war in the Middle East in 1956 did not lead to a break in diplomatic relations; this time the Soviet government only recalled its ambassador from Tel Aviv (where the embassy had remained despite recognition of Jerusalem as the capital) for about two months. But the war obviously did not improve the relations, and emigration remained practically impossible. It was not until 1962 that the number of exit permits granted increased to several hundred for the year.[89]

Khrushchev was deposed as secretary general in 1964 and initially replaced by a quartet: Leonid Breshnev, Alexei Kosygin, Nikolai Podgorny, and Mikhail Suslov. At a press conference in Paris on December 3, 1966, Kosygin stated in answer to a question that he saw no objection to "family reunion" of Jews who had been separated from relatives. This statement was published in the Soviet daily *Izvestia* two days later and gave hope to many Jews.[90] Breshnev gradually took sole power, but he was not yet completely in charge of Soviet foreign policy when a new war broke out in the Middle East in 1967.

The Netherlands' Representation of Israeli Interests

On June 5, 1967, war broke out once again between Israel and Egypt. The Soviet Union, closely allied to Egypt's leader Gamal Abdul Nasser, strongly condemned Israel, and whereas it had only recalled its ambassador in the aftermath of the 1956 war in the Middle East, it now decided to completely break its relations with Israel, as it had in 1953.

On June, 10 the Netherlands ambassador in Jerusalem informed his ministry in The Hague by cable that he had just had a phone call from the director general of the Israeli Ministry of Foreign Affairs: Would the Netherlands please represent the Israeli interests in the Soviet Union? The records do not show that there was much hesitation or even discussion about this request in The Hague. A positive reply was dispatched the same day, and the Netherlands embassy in Moscow was instructed to inform the Soviet authorities and ask for their approval. A note was handed to the Soviet Ministry of Foreign Affairs on June 11, and the approval was given by phone the next day.[91]

The Netherlands' speedy acceptance of the Israeli request was routine. Not only had the Netherlands embassy already performed the same task in 1953, but international courtesy alone would have demanded that the request be honored.[92] As to why Israel chose the Netherlands to represent it, the answer is that in 1967 the Netherlands, next to the United States, was Israel's best friend. The founding of the State of Israel had been warmly supported in the Netherlands, for reasons that were complex. First, there was undoubtedly an element of repentance in the Dutch attitude. Some 75 percent of the Jews who lived in the country in 1940 had perished in the Holocaust. Too many were delivered into the hands of the Germans by collaborating Dutch bureaucrats, policemen, and traitors. Many others were helped to go into hiding, but much more could have been done.[93]

There were also more positive reasons. Many Dutch Calvinists welcomed the founding of a Jewish state in Palestine as the fulfillment of biblical prophecies. Other Dutch people simply felt sympathy for this small democratic state struggling for survival. That sympathy was found in all circles; in 1973 the pro-Israeli attitude of the Netherlands government caused the Netherlands to be the only target, besides the United States and Israel, of the Arab oil boycott.

The Netherlands embassy in Moscow did not expect that the representation of Israeli interests would create much work. The main task would be issuing visas to emigrants going to Israel. The Israeli embassy had delivered no more than a few hundred per year between 1954 and 1964. There had been an increase to 891 in 1965 and even 2,046 in 1966,[94] but Soviet authorities had formally decided not to issue any more exit permits after the break in relations.[95]

The first duty of the Dutch was to help their Israeli colleagues return home with their belongings. Often when diplomatic relations are broken the "receiving" government allows a few nationals of the "sending" state to remain in the embassy of the "protecting power" to help with the new duties. Such help would have been very welcome to the Dutch, especially when Jewish emigration from the Soviet Union increased rapidly in the 1970s. But the Soviets did not allow any Israeli nationals to stay on, and so all of them left. Soviet customs at first declared that the Israelis had lost their diplomatic immunity and refused to pass their luggage without inspection. Fortunately the Soviet Ministry of Foreign Affairs (Ministerstvo Innostrannikh Del, MID) showed better understanding for its treaty obligations in this respect.[96]

The Israeli embassy building also had to be taken care of. Like most embassies in Moscow, it was rented from the Soviet authorities, who told the Dutch that they would not need it "for the time being," and it was sealed. It was not until much later that the Netherlands embassy demanded protection of the building on the basis of the Vienna Convention on Diplomatic Relations. Perhaps because the Netherlands itself was not yet a party to that convention, the embassy seems to have been unaware of the fact that the Soviet Union was bound by its provisions, which clearly state that the premises of an embassy shall remain inviolable even after a break in relations.[97]

Finally, the financing of the Dutch operation on behalf of Israel had to be organized. As is customary in these circumstances, the work of the Netherlands officials was provided free of charge, but Israel had to refund the salaries of the Russian personnel working exclusively for the interest section, the rent of their former building (which was thereafter paid by the Dutch during all the twenty-three years of the representation), the loans to be extended to emigrants, and some other expenses. Fortunately, Soviet authorities soon authorized the Netherlands embassy to make use of funds in the Israeli bank account in Moscow, which thereafter were replenished whenever needed. Financial statements were sent at regular intervals by the ministry in The Hague to Jerusalem. During the entire period of interest representation, there were no financial problems between the two countries.

Before the departure of Israeli officials from Moscow, the Netherlands consul discussed with them the provisions for the issuance of Israeli visas. Together they proposed the following to Jerusalem:

— No application forms would be required.
— Antecedents of applicants would not be checked. (Thus anyone showing a Soviet exit permit valid for emigration to Israel would be given a visa. Very few exceptions were made to this principle during the entire period of interest representation.)
— The number of the Soviet exit permits would be noted in the visa register. (Beginning April 1, 1967, passports were no longer issued by the Soviet authorities to Soviet citizens wanting to emigrate to Israel.)
— Visas would be valid for twelve months.
— Emigrants would be advised to travel to Vienna, where "an Israeli committee" (the Jewish Agency of Israel) would receive them.
— There would be no charge for the visa.
— Loans could be granted to Jewish emigrants to a maximum of the cost of a one-way trip by air to Vienna.[98] (The Israeli ambassador authorized the Netherlands embassy to extend such loans just before he left.)

Israeli authorities responded that application forms would be required, and blanks of the Israeli forms sent to Moscow shortly afterward and remained in use throughout the period of representation. All the other provisions were accepted and remained in force almost until the end of the interest representation.

The Netherlands embassy was able to issue to a few emigrants visas for Israel almost immediately after the break in relations because, after a few days of hesitation, Soviet authorities decided to honor exit permits that had already been granted. There were not many. The embassy issued 62 visas during the first ten days, but then the number tapered off. A total of 113 had been issued by July 11, a month after the Netherlands embassy took over the representation of Israeli interests, and only 3 more by August 8.[99]

Worried by the decision of the Soviets not to grant any new exit permits, the Israeli government on August 15 asked the foreign ministry in The Hague to emphasize to the Netherlands embassy in Moscow that "The Israeli government considers continuation of emigration of Soviet citizens to Israel of the utmost importance and regards this question as one of the most essential elements in the representation of Israeli interests by the Netherlands."[100] The ambassador was instructed to ask MID for a clarification of current Soviet emigration policy. The ambassador's response was clear but not encouraging:

> There is no chance to restart emigration. One should realize that for the Russians permission to emigrate is a great concession, because a Soviet citizen is in principle a serf who is not allowed to leave his country. At the moment the circumstances are not such that this serfdom can be removed in favor of those who want to go to Israel, because the State of Israel is acting in contradiction to the role which Soviet policy assigns to it.

The ambassador would, he said, continue to plead for special cases, although up till now he had had no success. He mentioned in this respect the case of two daughters left behind by their parents because of mixed-up emigration papers.[101]

The ambassador had no more success with the first diplomatic task with which the Israeli government entrusted him. The Soviet government had sent a sharply critical note about the Middle Eastern conflict to Jerusalem through the Finnish embassy, which was representing Soviet interests in Israel. The Netherlands ambassador was now instructed to present the Israeli answer to MID: "The allegations contained in your message are unfounded." On June 20, 1967, the Netherlands ambassador duly did so, only to have the note returned the next day: the Soviets had declared it "unacceptable."[102] Israeli diplomatic notes sent to the Soviet authorities through the Netherlands embassy were scarce after that. The issuance of visas for Israel, on the other hand, was to engage and sometimes to overwhelm the small Consular Section of the embassy for the next twenty-three years.

PART I
THE 1970s

I

The Second Exodus, the First Wave

In September 1968 the Netherlands embassy in Moscow reported that the Visa Office of the Soviet Ministry of Internal Affairs (Otdel Viz I Registracii Inostrannykh Grazdan, OVIR) had made it possible again for Jews to obtain exit permits—but only for the purpose of reuniting families. In general only elderly people were eligible or those who had received exit permits before the diplomatic relations with Israel were broken but did not, or could not, use them.[1] Thereafter, visas for Israel were issued by the Netherlands embassy. In 1969, 2,808 visas were issued, but in 1970 the number fell to about 1,000 (see Table 1, page 221, for a yearly account of visas issued; Table 2, pp. 222–23, is an accounting by month).

That rate changed suddenly in March 1971. By the end of April the embassy was handling several hundred applications per week, and the ambassador spoke of a "flood." The total number of Jewish emigrants that year was to exceed 13,000. The first wave of the second exodus had begun.

The Jews Begin to Stir

When Joseph Stalin died in 1953, the position of the Jews in the Soviet Union was seriously threatened. While the fiction of the Doctors' Plot was being developed by the KGB, a mass deportation of Jews may well have been planned. Then, with the rise to power of Nikita Khrushchev, the doctors were exonerated and Stalin's terror methods condemned. It seemed possible that living conditions for Jews would improve. But Khrushchev was also a traditional antisemite;[2] he repressed all religions, and the Jewish religion in particular. No Jewish institutions were allowed; no Jewish cultural center, school, or publishing house was reopened. Jewish cultural life, which had blossomed in the 1920s and early 1930s and briefly during the Second World War, could not be restored.[3] Antisemitism and an all-pervasive discrimination against Jews constantly reminded even highly assimilated Jews of their Jewishness. The birth of a Jewish state gave additional impetus to the idea of emigration.

The founding of Israel and the arrival in Moscow of the first Israeli minister, Golda Meir, in 1948 had stimulated the feeling of Jewish awareness in Moscow and elsewhere. But at that time mass emigration to the Jewish homeland remained no more than a faraway dream (see Prologue). Yet the birth of "their own" state and the relative relaxation of political pressures in the Khrushchev era emboldened some Jews to begin to think seriously about that faraway dream, and they continued to do so even after Khrushchev was replaced and the oppression of Jews worsened again. A young Jew in Kiev, Boris Kochubyevski, became the first hero of the Jewish movement in the Soviet Union. His case led the Netherlands embassy for the first time to report on a "Refusenik"— although that term for a Jew who was denied an exit permit was not coined until much later.

Boris Kochubyevski wrote in 1967:

> Why is it that the most active sector of Jewish youth, raised and educated in the USSR still retains a feeling of Jewish national unity and national identity? Thanks for that, in a large measure, can be given to anti-Semitism, the new brand which was implanted from above . . . and the old one which is still alive among the more backward sectors of Soviet society. . . .
>
> [Furthermore there is] the absence of Jewish schools, religious persecution, [discrimination] when we are looking for jobs or applying to institutes of higher learning.

Kochubyevski applied for an exit permit to emigrate to Israel, declaring: "I am a Jew and I want to live in the Jewish state."[4] Although he was first informed that his request had been granted, it was subsequently denied. When he continued his agitation, he was dismissed from his job, his wife was not allowed to continue her studies, and finally in December 1968 he was arrested and condemned to three years' imprisonment "for slander of the Soviet Union."[5]

In the meantime a twenty-year-old student, Yasha Kazakov, renounced his Soviet citizenship on June 13, 1967, in response to the Soviet government's vitriolic campaign against the State of Israel. "I am a Jew and consider Israel my fatherland," he declared.[6] Others had renounced their citizenship before him, but his statement was circulated in *samizdat* (literally, "self-publishing," the Russian name for underground publications) and then published in the West. Kazakov was given an exit permit the same year; Soviet authorities clearly thought they would be better off without such a troublemaker.

In 1969 more Jews decided to openly demand the right to emigrate. On August 6, eighteen families in Georgia addressed a letter to the UN Commission on Human Rights.[7] It was sent to the Netherlands embassy with a note addressed to "A friend of Anna Frank" asking the embassy to forward the letter to Golda Meir, who had by then become prime minister of Israel. The Georgians wanted their letter to be read on the Israeli radio. This letter became, as we shall see later, an important signal for public actions in the West.

In September 1969, ten Jews sent a letter to "World Jewry." It was followed by a letter, signed by twenty-five Jews, to UN Secretary General U Thant. For the first time a Jewish magazine appeared in *samizdat*. Fashioned after the *Chronicle of Current Events*, the famous magazine Russians had been issuing in *samizdat* for some time, it was called *Iskhod* (*Exodus*) and was written by a non-Jew, Fedosoyev, who was married to a Jew.

On June 15, 1970, the Netherlands embassy reported to The Hague that there had been an attempt to hijack a plane at Leningrad airport that day. One week later it informed the ministry that three men had been arrested for the crime and that eight others, all Jews, had been detained in connection with it.[8] These reports were, as always, passed on to the Israeli embassy in The Hague immediately. Although in the beginning many people in the West doubted that a hijacking in Leningrad had really been attempted, it became clear from later statements by the participants that a group of Jews from Riga had indeed planned a hijacking as a demonstration of their desperation to be allowed to emigrate to Israel.[9]

Just after the arrests in Leningrad, the militia unit guarding the Netherlands embassy in Moscow was increased from one to three men.[10] Apparently the KGB, now even more than before, wanted to prevent any unauthorized person from entering the embassy. It was generally believed in the West that the KGB had had advance knowledge of the hijacking

plan and allowed it to be developed with the express purpose of eliminating much of the leadership of the Jewish activist movement.[11]

Ultimately thirty-four men and women, two of them non-Jews, stood
trial in December 1970 in what came to be known as the Leningrad
Trial. The charge was "betrayal of the fatherland" (high treason). The
sentences were pronounced on Christmas Eve 1970: two of the accused
were sentenced to death, two to fifteen years in prison, and the others to
from five to fourteen years in prison.

In Moscow a non-Jewish dissident, Vladimir Bukovsky, sprang into
action. He has been called the "conductor of the whole human rights
orchestra."[12] He translated texts, telephoned foreign journalists, and
urged maximum publicity for the information he provided. This he got.
The Western press paid ample attention and diplomatic demarches were
carried out by many countries and by the Socialist International. The
Netherlands ambassador had already carried out a demarche at MID just
before the sentences were pronounced in Leningrad. The ambassador
cautiously stated that he did not want to interfere in internal Soviet
affairs, let alone the judiciary, but did want to point out that there was
anxiety in the Netherlands over the case and to express a hope for
clemency if death sentences were to be pronounced. He reported back
that the Soviet reaction, "as expected," had been totally negative. "Interference," "not suitable," "had to be rejected," "contrary to the wish to
promote good relations" the Soviet interlocutor had said—in what was
to become the standard response from MID to such demarches.[13] More
damaging for the Soviets than the diplomatic reactions was that for the
first time several Communist Parties, including those of France and Italy,
the two largest ones in the Western world, joined the protests. The
worldwide reaction must have startled the Kremlin by its intensity. The
Soviet Supreme Court met six days after the end of the first trial and
reduced all the sentences, the two death penalties to fifteen years.[14]

But the Jewish movement for emigration was not broken. There were
public demonstrations by Jews and even a sit-down strike at the Supreme
Soviet in the Kremlin in March 1971.[15] It may have been at this moment
that the authorities decided to allow a greater number of Jews to emigrate.[16] If so, it would seem that a two-pronged approach was decided
upon. Many leaders and the most committed Zionists would be allowed
to leave, apparently in the hope that their departure would reduce and
eventually exhaust future demand. At the same time, expectations that a
more relaxed policy regarding emigration would be forthcoming were
strongly discouraged, and a number of obstacles were set up to make the

emigration process difficult.[17] In May and June 1971 other trials took place in Leningrad, Riga, and Kishinev.

But the embassy did report that between March 3 and 10, 1971, an unusually high number of visas—135—had been issued. It was thought that among those given exit permits were the Jews from Riga who had staged the sit-down at the reception hall of the Supreme Soviet in the Kremlin.[18] It was the first, but not the last, time that the Soviet authorities tried to weed out the "unruly elements" in the hope of subduing the others. On April 2 the embassy added that a Scandinavian diplomat had been told by a *Pravda* journalist that the authorities had decided to let 30,000 Jews emigrate within two years, beginning with the "unruly elements." The ambassador noted that there had indeed been an increase in visa applications in the past month; thus the "Scandinavian" information might prove to be correct.[19] For some reason the ambassador did not report that the secretary in charge of his consulate had received similar information. The Soviet journalist Victor Louis, who later became notorious for passing on KGB messages and was generally believed to be working for that organization, visited the embassy to warn that visa applications would triple in the coming year.[20] They almost did.

Why Did They Want to Go?

It is obvious that the Jewish emigration from the Soviet Union would never have grown into the world issue it later became if there had not been strong pressure toward emigration among the Soviet Jews themselves. What drove them?

When that question was put to former Refusenik leaders now in Israel or the United States, their first reaction, without exception, was that they could no longer live under the regime that was ruling the Soviet Union at that time, that they could no longer tolerate the system. One said: "More and more I began to feel that something was wrong in the society in which I had grown up and in which you could not even be apolitical, you were forced to participate. That was unbearable for me. I hated that system, the antihumanism of it more than its antisemitism."[21] Another explained: "We really were not given an opportunity to be honest, not allowed a modicum of professional integrity."[22] So the main reason was not antisemitism? "Oh yes, that too, of course. We lived with that most of our lives, although personally . . ."[23] It was not that you ever got used to antisemitism. It was there when your son or daughter was not accepted at the university, the conservatory, or the scientific institute because of the *numerus clausus*, the quota for Jews that was applied under the communist regime just as strictly as it had been under the Czars. "The only difference is that under the Czars the number was known, now it is secret," said one Jewish professor.[24] It was there in your workplace where you would never quite reach the position you thought you were entitled to. It was there when you did not get the permission to travel abroad that your colleagues did receive. But you tried to adapt, to find another university or a correspondence course for the children, an institute for yourself that did accept Jews. One had learned to live with that—but not with a regime that allowed no civil rights or personal freedom, was patently dishonest, and forced you to participate in that dishonesty, even frequently trying to recruit you to spy on your friends and co-workers.[25]

Admittedly these opinions were voiced by intellectuals who had been able to obtain academic degrees and to reach comfortable positions. By the 1970s many Jews were relatively well off, at least according to Soviet standards. They overwhelmingly lived in the largest cities, and the Jewish share of white-collar jobs had increased since the Second World War. In the early 1970s the proportion of Jews with a secondary or postsecondary education was almost 2.5 times greater than that of the general urban population; the proportion of college-educated Jews (nearly a quarter of them physicians), 3.5 times.[26] They often held good positions, especially in the medical profession, scientific institutes, the art world, law offices, trade firms, and the lower echelons of the bureaucracy. Often both husband and wife worked, and together they earned an income that enabled them to live fairly well. Many had three-room apartments, holidays on the Black Sea or the Baltic, and even sometimes, after many years of waiting, the great luxury—a car. All that they had to give up to go to an unknown future in a faraway country.

Other Jews were less well placed, such as the ones who had been evacuated to Siberia and stayed there (see Prologue). Other Jewish colonies, sometimes very old, continued to exist in Central Asia and the Caucasus. The Jews in these areas had a range of motives to emigrate that were different from the motives of those in the cities. For them poverty would play a role, and antisemitism might be more direct. There was discrimination and fear that their children would not get an education or a good job. Sometimes they even feared pogroms, the dreaded anti-Jewish riots that occurred at the end of the nineteenth and the beginning of the twentieth century. When asked, very few Jews would say they *really* thought that pogroms could be repeated, but nevertheless the fear, fed by rumors, was often widespread.

Inability to exercise their religion seems to have been a motive for only a small percentage of the emigrants.[27] The Zionists, on the other hand, dedicated to the ideal of building a Jewish state and believing in the obligation of all Jews to participate in that endeavor, were in the vanguard of emigration in the early 1970s. But they were never a very large group, and by 1973 most of them had left.[28] Many others longed to fully experience their Jewishness or at least to live in a country where they would belong and not be a minority. But most Jews knew little about Israel, and that little was often colored by hostile communist propaganda. Inability to live their own lives and develop their own culture was a common motive. Elie Wiesel remarked in his famous book *The Jews of Silence*:

> By preventing the Jews from developing their own culture . . . the Kremlin seems to force them in the direction of complete assimilation; this process is held back by the difficulties which every Jew encounters when he tries to integrate in the Russian society. . . . The Jew cannot be a Jew but neither can he be a non-Jew.[29]

What finally tipped the balance for many Jews was the lack of hope. They saw no future for a Jew in their country and no improvement for their children: it was hopeless.[30] And so they decided, first by the hundreds then by the thousands, to try to legally leave the country where their forebears had lived for generations. In the early 1970s there was for them as yet only one destination—Israel.

Reactions in Israel

It can be assumed that the letter of the Georgians, as well as other individual or collective letters from Soviet Jews, generally became available to the Israeli government quite quickly. Were they transmitted through the Netherlands embassy? There is no evidence to that effect. On the contrary, there are indications that the ministry in The Hague at that time did not consider transmitting private letters from Soviet citizens to the Israeli government by diplomatic pouch as part of the representation of Israeli interests (see Chapter 5). But there were sufficient other channels: foreign journalists, businessmen, casual visitors, or the private pockets of diplomats going on leave. The letters undoubtedly reached Jerusalem in this way, but until the end of 1969 neither the letter of the Georgians nor the contents of *Iskhod* or any of the other letters were acknowledged, let alone published by the Israelis. There was a well-established policy against publication.[31]

The origin of this policy lay with an office in Tel Aviv that was the continuation of Mossad le-Aliyah Bet (Institute for Aliyah B) and a sister organization of the foreign intelligence service, the Mossad. Before 1948 the Mossad le-Aliyah Bet had handled the illegal immigration under British rule (Operation Gideon), the *Bet* having been added to distinguish it from the legal immigration. It was an amazing organization, built around a massive undercover travel agency, owning more than sixty ships and airplanes and countless trucks, all coordinated by a worldwide network of quasi-legal radio transmitters. This office succeeded in smuggling hundreds of thousands of Jews out of Arab and communist countries. "Bribery and secret diplomacy were crafts learned early on by Aliyah B."[32]

In 1952 the secret organizations were reorganized and the Mossad le-Aliyah Bet, apparently considerably reduced, became the office in Tel Aviv that for a long time was known as the "Office without a Name." Later it was given the name of Liaison Bureau of the Ministry of Foreign Affairs, although it was not a part of the administrative hierarchy of that ministry at all, but was responsible only to the prime minister. From then on it was usually called Lishka, an abbreviation of the Hebrew for "bureau of liaison," Lishkat Hakesher. After the State of Israel had been established, immigration was perfectly legal, but it was decided that immigration from "open" countries would be handled by the Jewish Agency and immigration from Iron Curtain countries by the new Lishka office.[33] Its first head was Shaul Avigur, who had organized Operation Gideon and was a confidant of President Ben-Gurion. Avigur retired in 1969 at age seventy, and was succeeded by Nehamiah Levanon in January 1970.[34]

In view of the origins of the office, it is not surprising that Avigur sought personal anonymity and insisted that any project in which he participated be tightly controlled and free from public inquiry. His office was clearly committed to the principle that any work done to help Jews to leave the Soviet Union would be achieved under strict military censorship, with responsibility only to the head of government. It seems that Avigur continued to exercise influence on Golda Meir after his retirement and believed that Russian Jews should be freed from the Soviet

Union through secret negotiation, as had been the case in Rumania, Bulgaria, and Poland.[35]

After she received the letter of the Georgians, Golda Meir therefore decided to try "quiet diplomacy" first. On October 7, 1969, the Netherlands ambassador in Moscow was instructed (via The Hague) to make a special demarche to MID to plead for the emigration of Georgian Jews, "many thousands of whom want to leave the USSR."[36] On October 16 the ambassador reported back that he had discussed the question in MID—only with the deputy of a vice-minister, apparently the highest official willing to receive him—but without any result.[37] Only then did the Israeli prime minister decide that she had to "go public."

It must have been a difficult decision for Meir to make against the advice of a trusted adviser like Avigur. She had to face, at this early stage, the dilemma that was eventually faced by everyone involved with Jewish dissidents and Refuseniks—or indeed with other dissidents—up to the very end of the Soviet state: Would it harm them if their letters and petitions were published, if journalists and diplomats had open contacts with them? Or would it, on the contrary, help and to a certain extent protect them?

Later experience proved that it was generally helpful to a dissident or a Refusenik to make as much noise as possible and to have as many foreign contacts as he could. The better known a Refusenik became, the better his chances to avoid arrest and to eventually obtain permission to leave as one of the "unruly ones." It was therefore better for him if his plight was published in the West and underscored by diplomatic actions. But this strategy was not as clear in 1969 as it is, with hindsight, now.[38]

Meir courageously decided in favor of publicity,[39] and on November 19, 1969, she read the Georgian appeal in the Knesset and requested the Israeli representative to the United Nations to have it circulated among all members. Soviet radio called the letter a forgery, but in April 1971 all the signers and many other Georgians were given exit permits. It has been called "a quirk of history that one of the most remote and least educated segments of Soviet Jewry should have captured the imagination of their fellow Jews and forced the government to some action. A miracle of Jewish survival."[40]

Lishka then also changed its policy and decided that public action was more effective than silence. Its representatives were attached to the Israeli embassies in Washington, London, Paris and elsewhere with explicit instructions to make as much noise as possible. They were successful in drawing the attention of scientists, lawyers, and many others to the plight of their colleagues in the Soviet Union, and they contributed significantly to the establishment of contacts between the Refuseniks inside the Soviet Union and activists in the West. Lishka also provided the information for a small magazine called *Jews in the Soviet Union* published for many years by the Institute of Jewish Affairs in London, which printed information and stories about Soviet Jews and even pictures of Refuseniks and their families, who were not afraid to allow it.

Reactions in the West

When in 1966 Elie Wiesel published *The Jews of Silence,* the title applied equally to Jews in the Soviet Union and to most Jews in the West. There was a feeling that nothing could be done to alter the course of events in the Soviet Union.[41] But in the United States groups such as the Student Struggle for Soviet Jewry, founded by Jacob Birnbaum, and the Cleveland Committee against Soviet Anti-Semitism, founded by Lou Rosenblum, were beginning to prepare public activities. The latter was the nucleus around which the Union of Councils for Soviet Jews, a movement of grass-roots activists, was formed. An Academic Committee on Soviet Jewry was founded in April 1967.

These groups organized public activities, especially at UN Headquarters in New York. There was also a large demonstration in Ottawa when Soviet prime minister Kosygin visited Canada. A rally was organized in Madison Square Garden in New York, in collaboration with forty American Jewish organizations. Petitions and cables were sent to the Soviet Union.[42] These activities were patterned after the peaceful actions of the civil rights movement, which during the 1960s had made open protest and civil disobedience respectable means of effecting change. But these activities were not appreciated by the Jewish establishment at the time. Jacob Birnbaum recalled that the Jewish establishment "did not want to 'rock the boat' and thought that these actions might be dangerous for the Jews in the Soviet Union and that public protest might be counterproductive and could embarrass the Jewish community in the United States."[43] And it might be added that protesting against the policies of the U.S. administration could harm the Israeli relations with the United States, so essential to the survival of the Jewish state. The Israeli ambassador had refused to appear before the American Council on Soviet Jewry, set up in April 1964, and Nahum Goldman, then president of the World Jewish Congress, in turn expressed doubt as to the wisdom of the leaders of that council seeing President Lyndon Johnson and wrote, "Demagogic speeches and exaggerated resolutions may do a lot of harm." But the conference of the American Council went forward, and three of its leaders were received by President Johnson and Secretary of State Dean Rusk.[44] After this meeting the council, however, remained inactive.

Mainstream Jews in the United States were further discomforted by the actions of Meir Kahane, a member of the Student Struggle for Soviet Jewry who in 1967 split off to form the Jewish Defense League. This group organized violent demonstrations, including an attack on the office of the Soviet mission to the United Nations.

The established Jewish organizations in the United States were thus faced with the same dilemma as were the Israeli leaders: Should they work through quiet diplomacy, or through public action, including open protests and demonstrations? While the Israelis, as we have seen, began mixing quiet diplomacy with public pronouncement in 1969, Nahum Goldman consistently denounced the public campaigns: "It is wrong to generate too much activity on behalf of Russian Jewry, because this could endanger the very existence of three million Jews." To which Wiesel answered: "How can we be sure that our complaints and protests will not have harmful results for them? . . . Only the Russian Jews themselves can answer that question and they do: 'Keep calling! Awaken public opinion!' "[45] The American Jewish establishment remained on the sidelines until the early 1970s, when the National Conference on Soviet Jewry was set up and the Jackson-Vanik Amendment supported (see Chapter 6).

About the same time, the U.S. administration began listening more closely to the signals from the Soviet Jews. In a statement before the Subcommittee on Europe of the Senate Committee on Foreign Relations, Assistant Secretary Davies stated:

> The rebirth of Jewish consciousness and pride, especially among Jewish youth, has been dramatic since 1967. Jews have been in the forefront of a nascent civil rights movement that only a decade ago would have been both unthinkable and impermissible in the Soviet Union. . . . In sum, Soviet Jews remain disadvantaged compared to most other major religious and ethnic groups, but their position has not perceptively worsened in recent years. What has changed is the new mood of militancy and expectancy among Soviet Jews and the corresponding echo evoked among Jews and men and women

of good will outside the USSR by the expression of this new
mood. Thousands [in the United States] now publicly demonstrate pride in their heritage.[46]

In the beginning there was a lack of knowledge in the West about
Soviet Jews as well as a lack of contact with them. No one knew how
many wanted to emigrate.[47] In 1970 a small European Conference on
Soviet Jews was convened in Paris at the initiative of the local Lishka representative. It prepared for the first World Conference on Soviet Jewry,
held in Brussels, February 23–25, 1971. The conference encountered
some difficulties, and Soviet authorities exerted a lot of pressure on the
Belgian authorities to prohibit it, but the Belgians stood firm. Kahane
unsuccessfully sought to attend; Ben-Gurion gave a short speech. A
World Presidium for Soviet Jewry began meeting twice a year in London,
or sometimes in Geneva, and drafted lists of "Prisoners of Zion" (Jews
imprisoned in the Soviet Union because they wanted to go to Israel), with
the names provided by Lishka.

In both the United States and Israel the activists were increasingly reinforced by Jews coming out of the Soviet Union who had been activists in
their homeland. The Soviet endeavor to get rid of the "unruly ones"
unwittingly contributed to the strengthening of the activities in behalf of
Soviet Jewry in the West. These former Soviet Jews helped in particular to
solve one of the most difficult problems—the lack of communications.

Communications Established

Before 1970 there was almost no communication between the Jews in
Israel or in Western countries and the Soviet Jews. The reason was
twofold. Most people in the West thought that it would be impossible to
contact the Jews in the Soviet Union, and Western Jewish leaders feared
that contacts might endanger the Soviet Jews. It was the Jewish activists
from the Soviet Union who, after reaching Israel, began to communicate
with the families and friends they had left behind. By 1971 an elaborate
communications network had been created through letters and even
phone calls. The Lishka representatives, on the one hand, and on the
other, the Union of Councils for Soviet Jews and later other organizations
in the United States, the United Kingdom, Canada, the Netherlands, and
elsewhere, organized regular phone connections and a virtual courier service. "Tourists" would take turns visiting the Soviet Union, so that a mes-

senger would arrive every month or even every week. Foreign newsmen, businessmen, seamen, and even foreign diplomats opened up additional channels. They all delivered letters and everything from *vysovs* (invitations; see Chapter 2), Hebrew grammars, and literary works to radios, tape recorders, typewriters, and medicines, and they generally lent encouragement to Jews and especially to the Refuseniks.[48]

Soviet authorities were aware of most of these activities, listening in on phone conversations, reading letters, and searching the luggage of travelers. Often they would cut off the calls, harass and even body-search the travelers, and confiscate the letters, the books, and the other materials. It was their custom to cut the telephone lines to the homes of Refuseniks who had foreign contacts and to prevent mail from being delivered to them. But the authorities never quite succeeded in breaking the links, as activists found ways to overcome the countermeasures. "Helping hands" would deliver letters safely; calls would be made to and from public phone boxes or exchanges. In this way news would reach the West not only from Moscow, where the foreign embassies and journalists were reporting on the local developments anyway, but also from other regions in the vast Soviet Union. A great many unnamed heroes, men but especially women, took risks and spent a lot of their time and money to keep these contacts going.[49]

Why Did the Soviets Let the Jews Go?

The question of why the Soviets let the Jews go has given rise to a lively academic debate, especially in the United States (see Introduction). One school of thought holds that

> Western efforts have had an indirect bearing upon the emigration movement, and the tenor of Soviet-American relations probably accounts for some of the variation in the rate of emigration; but the decision to allow emigration in the first place was made independent of external forces by a resolute and strong Soviet ruling class due to considerations internal to the USSR.

In other words, "The domestic context surrounding emigration was the most significant influence on emigration policy."[50] This school of thought may be called the internal theory.

In this form, the internal theory has not much support. It is clear that neither in the time of Leonid Brezhnev nor in that of Mikhail Gorbachev did there exist a "resolute and strong Soviet ruling class." It would be more accurate to describe the internal situation in the Soviet Union in both periods as one of continuous struggle between the secretary general of the Communist Party and his partisans who proposed changes in Soviet foreign (and under Gorbachev also domestic) policy and other members of its Politburo and Central Committee who tried to hold them back.

A more sophisticated version of the internal theory claims that "constant pressure by Soviet Jewish leaders and their supporters succeeded in forcing the Kremlin to look more closely at the Jewish question. . . . Soviet Jews posed [a] successful challenge to the Kremlin . . . winning some concessions and steadily weakening the edifice of totalitarism." In other words, it was the Soviet Jews themselves who succeeded in obtaining emigration concessions. But it is recognized that foreign help was required: "They turned their relationship with Western governments and advocacy-groups into an exceptionally powerful lobbying effort that made its mark on the Kremlin."[51] It is undoubtedly correct that the urgent desire of many Jews to emigrate was the origin of their exodus. It should also be noted that Soviet authorities time and again tried to "decapitate" what had become a Jewish dissident movement by allowing some of its leaders (the "unruly ones") to leave. Yet the conclusion must be that internal Jewish pressure alone would never have succeeded in forcing the authorities to allow the large-scale emigration that ensued.

A second school says that permission for the Jews to emigrate from the Soviet Union was granted largely as a result of foreign policy considerations; it was a function of the Soviet relations with the West in general and the United States in particular.[52] This argument would lead to the conclusion that it was mainly, if not exclusively, foreign pressure that induced Soviet authorities to allow the Jews to go. Referred to as the external theory here, it is elsewhere called the "barometer thesis" because it tries to correlate the yearly variations in the numbers of exit permits to specific factors in East-West political relations.[53]

The external theory has the overwhelming backing not only of the academic community but also of most observers in the field—the former leaders of the Jewish emigration themselves as well as former government officials, leaders of Western Jewish organizations, and others who were involved.[54] It does identify external reasons for many upward and downward trends. Yet it, too, has its flaws and cannot completely explain the decisions of the Soviet leadership regarding the Jewish emigration. External pressure did play a large role in urging or even forcing Soviet leaders to allow Jews to emigrate. But that foreign pressure did not spring up by itself; it had to be generated first, as claimed by the internal theory, by pressure inside the Soviet Union. The constant refusal to allow large-scale emigration, the harassment of applicants, and the maltreatment and persecution of those who were refused (the Refuseniks) in turn generated Western pressures. It stirred into action, first, Jewish activists in the United States and other countries, then the established Western Jewish organizations, then public opinion in general, and finally Western governments dealing directly or indirectly with the Soviet state.

All that pressure, however, would not have succeeded, as it sometimes did, had not the Soviet leaders had reasons of their own to give in to it. Brezhnev, as did later Gorbachev, felt that he needed a détente with the West that would enable him to reverse a deteriorating economic situation in his country. Both received clear signals, mainly from the United States, that a prerequisite for such a détente would be an increase in Jewish emigration. Emigration became for the Soviets an element in their power considerations; it was never a goal in itself. Edward Drachman, who starts out from the internal theory, finally, also concludes that

> Moscow based its policies mostly on cold calculations of gains and losses in both domestic and foreign policy. Internal considerations such as economics and control over the population and external considerations such as relations with the United States and countries in the Middle East surely were important factors in Soviet decision making. Ultimately the Kremlin developed whatever strategy seemed most advantageous at the time.[55]

The reasons for the Soviet behavior regarding Jewish emigration must, in other words, be found in the interaction of both internal and external factors.[56] The domestic context did play a role, but not so directly and decisively as postulated in the internal theory. Rather, the Jewish suffering and the stand of the Jewish leaders inside the Soviet Union focused Western attention on the problem and engendered Western pressure. That external pressure—or the lack of it—was in turn, as the external theory says, the immediate cause of the ups and downs in the flow of that emigration. But then again it was the domestic situation, now mostly in the economic sense, which at certain times made good relations with the West so desirable that emigration concessions became a necessity.

Brezhnev's Considerations

In 1971, when considerable numbers of Jews began to be allowed to leave the Soviet Union, Brezhnev's policy of détente toward the West had just begun. The Soviets urgently required Western technology and credits. The leadership knew then what has become generally known now— that their economy was in much worse shape than was assumed in the West at the time. Stagnation had already set in although it was masked by constant falsification of economic data. The Soviet Union had overextended its economy in order to play a world role while it should have diminished its defense expenditures to put its economy in order. On the proposal of Brezhnev, the Politburo decided to strive for disarmament and for a European security conference that would assure the Soviet Union the political stability on its borders needed to permit a reduction in spending on weapons. Western reactions must have shown Brezhnev that allowing Jews to emigrate would favorably dispose Western public opinion toward such a détente. The Americans also tried to push him in that direction. Henry Kissinger writes in his memoirs: "Starting in 1969 we had begun to make overtures to Moscow to ease Jewish emigration, emphasizing that such a policy would improve the atmosphere of U.S.-Soviet relations."[57] So in his "back channel" Kissinger began to discuss the matter with the Soviet ambassador in Washington, Anatoly Dobrynin. How forcefully he put it is unclear: "I mentioned it to him now and then and later [after the numbers of Jewish emigrants had increased] said that I appreciated it."[58] Dobrynin says that the subject was "cautiously" discussed,[59] and Kissinger later called the process "tacit bargaining" because there were neither formal requests nor formal answers.[60] Kissinger "was not out for confrontation," but according to him "to increase the emigration of Jews was something the Soviets could do without making too many political concessions."[61]

But that is a moot point. Soviet society was so closed at the time that it would not allow any but a very few privileged citizens to even travel abroad, let alone emigrate. It could not have been easy to make the decision to let thousands of Jews go. Would that exodus not encourage people of other nationalities or religions to ask for exit permits as well—the Baltic peoples, Armenians, Germans, Ukrainian Catholics, Pentecostals, and so on? Would not an escape hatch from the "happy land of socialism" destabilize the domestic situation? And what would be the reaction in the Arab world?[62]

Yet Kissinger's words do seem to have convinced the Soviet leaders that a more permissive policy on Jewish emigration was the best way to persuade the people and the leaders of the United States to support improved relations with the Soviet Union. "Quietly though reluctantly," according to Dobrynin, Moscow began to change its emigration policy.[63] The pain of this concession was mitigated by permitting particular groups of Jews to emigrate, namely those from the areas annexed during the Second World War, including the Baltic states and the former Polish and Rumanian parts of the Ukraine; those from outerlying areas like Georgia and Central Asia; and, in general, the "unruly ones." "Heartlanders" constituted only 10.6 percent of the emigrants in 1971, 14.6 percent in 1972, and 19.6 percent in 1973.[64] So it was to be a strictly controlled emigration—enough to take some steam out of the internal Jewish pressure and to influence Western public opinion, yet not enough to violate the Soviet notion of a closed society or pose a serious difficulty for Soviet-Arab relations.[65]

Conclusion

The large-scale Jewish emigration from the Soviet Union that began in the early 1970s was the outcome, first of all, of the urgent desire of the Jews themselves to leave that country. Their desire was caused as much by hopelessness as by discrimination, by a feeling that decent people could not live under such a regime as much as by antisemitism. And it was tremendously stimulated by the Israeli victory in the Six-Day War, which proved that the Jewish state could survive.

Then, in the late 1960s, this Jewish desire and the consistent Soviet refusal to grant exit permits stirred into action both private and public Jewish organizations, with Lishka in Tel Aviv playing a stimulating and coordinating role in the background. By the early 1970s Western governments, especially Israel and the United States, started to exert pressure on the Soviet government, first discreetly in quiet diplomacy, then more openly. Golda Meir began to mobilize world opinion in the United Nations, President Richard Nixon held his summits with Brezhnev, and Kissinger played his leverage politics. Non-Jewish organizations and national parliaments, again in particular in the United States, began to take part. Shortly afterward the U.S. Congress commenced its discussions on an amendment to the Trade Reform Act that intended to condition most-favored-nation status on free emigration.

But in the final analysis, all that pressure brought results only because the Soviet government had at the same time decided that in view of its economic circumstances it needed a détente with the West. Soviet leaders came to realize that emigration of Jews would be a necessary means of influencing Western public and parliamentary opinion. On the other hand, they may also have believed that by removing the "unruly ones"— those Jews that could not be reformed into the communist mode—it could nip in the bud the growing Jewish emigration movement. But to the contrary, in a snowball effect, the first permissions were to cause even greater pressure among the Jews to leave their country. Thus both internal and external pressures in favor of emigration were strong in the years 1972–73 and mutually reinforced each other.

2

The Ten Circles of Hell

"The ten circles of hell": this is how one Russian Jew described the difficulties encountered by all Jews who wanted to emigrate from the Soviet Union.[1] Others have called the process "the Labyrinth."[2] One could hardly imagine a worse confrontation with a harsher bureaucracy, an obstacle course with more pitfalls on every stretch and more dangers around every corner.

It should be remembered that emigration was practically impossible for Soviet citizens. The communists believed that anyone wanting to leave their "workers' and peasants' paradise" was committing treason.[3] Emigration could be allowed, grudgingly and as a gift, not as a right, for only one reason—family reunion. Thus women who married foreigners were usually allowed to join their husbands, albeit often after long waiting periods. Permission for a Soviet husband to join a foreign wife was much more rare. Four other categories of people were at times allowed to leave—Jews, Armenians, and ethnic Germans and Greeks. It sometimes looked as if these groups were not really considered a part of the Soviet community and therefore it was easier to allow them to go.

The emigration of Armenians, Germans, and Greeks, all concentrated in specific regions, as they were, never raised as much controversy as did the Jewish emigration. Soviet citizens regarded the Jews who were allowed to emigrate both with contempt and with envy: contempt because those Jews were "committing treason" by leaving; envy because they themselves were hardly ever allowed to travel to the West, let alone to emigrate.[4] No wonder that the Soviet bureaucracy, even when official policy authorized the granting of exit permits, did its utmost to make the departure of the Jews as difficult as possible.

The Invitation (*Vysov*)

The first document required was an invitation from Israel.[5] There was, in fact, no reason why such an invitation should be necessary. The United Nations Universal Declaration on Human Rights states clearly that anyone has the right to leave his or her country and to return to it.[6] But that was not the way the Soviet authorities looked at the issue. In their minds, since no one could have any reason to leave their "paradise," exceptions could be made only for a compassionate reason—family reunion. Therefore, whenever Moscow deemed it advantageous to allow some Jews to leave the country, the justification—often a fiction—had to be that it was to bring about a family reunion. And when Soviet authorities decided to restrict the emigration again, the reason given was the converse: that the reunion of families following the Second World War "had been basically completed."[7]

A *vysov* (literally, "summons") was thus the first requirement for anyone who wanted to emigrate. It had to be a notarized invitation from a close relative in Israel, translated into Russian, with a stamp from the Israeli government confirming that it was willing to receive the invited person or persons. In this way the *vysov* not only confirmed that there would be a family reunion but also provided assurance that the emigrant would be allowed to settle in another country, an unremitting Soviet demand. Of course not every Soviet Jew had—or knew of—a relative in the direct line in Israel. In Stalin's days it was extremely dangerous to maintain contacts with relatives in foreign countries. Moreover, a great many parents or other close relatives had died in the Holocaust. But as an Israeli official explained:

> The Jews are one big family, and often a distant cousin could be found. The only criterion really was, What kind of relationship was acceptable to the Soviets? In general the people of Israel were asked to sign for relatives or nonrelatives; the degree of relationship was uncertain and the office in charge did not check that out. Both we and the Soviets understood that.[8]

And it really did not matter. When the Soviet authorities wanted Jews to emigrate, they accepted any *vysov* as long as the fiction of family reunion could be maintained, and they did not care whether those *vysovs* were 100 percent correct. Nor did it matter how they were obtained. But as soon as authorities wanted to reduce the number of Jewish emigrants, strict rules were suddenly applied, relationships checked, and changes in the *vysovs* rejected.

The Jews who, in whatever way, had succeeded in obtaining a *vysov* now had to decide when to use it. Most used their *vysovs* immediately, but others waited before taking the next fateful step: apply for an exit permit at OVIR.[9]

OVIR

OVIR, the Visa Office of the Soviet Ministry of Internal Affairs, was headed by KGB officers. It had branches in all major cities and issued exit permits and passports.[10] During his first visit to OVIR, an applicant had only to obtain the questionnaires needed to request an exit permit. In an office in a Western nation that task might be accomplished in a few minutes, but in the Soviet Union one had to wait for the better part of a day. The Soviet bureaucracy traced its roots directly to the czarist bureaucracy, which in turn had incorporated the worst characteristics of the officialdom of Byzantium. The bureaucracy was not there to serve the people; to the contrary, citizens had to come and beg for its services. To show a kindness, or even civility, to its customers would lower the exalted position of the bureaucracy in the eyes of its officials. To do so to a Jew who wanted to emigrate was unthinkable. And so Jews had to stand in line in front of the OVIR office for hours. When finally allowed in, they were roughly treated.

Then, when at last an applicant obtained the necessary questionnaires, he had to provide not only all the data about his immediate family but also the names, addresses, and occupations of his close relatives. Numerous other documents had to be added. The greatest difficulties were created by the so-called production and social character references and the permission from relatives.

Character References

A prospective emigrant had to obtain a character reference from the place of his work. In itself such a reference is not unusual; most people leaving a job obtain references that can be used in future job applications. In fact, in the Soviet Union such references were an absolute requirement

for anyone changing jobs. But for emigrants the situation was more difficult. The references had to be given by the collective, which of course
included fellow workers who simply could not afford to let a colleague
go without their disapproval and a condemnation for his "treason." The
Communist Party was watching them closely, and the higher their position the more these fellow workers had to fear if their condemnation was
not strong enough. A Jew who wanted to emigrate was a traitor in the
view of the Communist Party, and a traitor he had to be called, even by
those who only a few weeks ago might have been considered friends.
Some did their "duty" with almost palpable distaste. Others, however,
would spit venom on him as communists through the years have done on
comrades who in reality or in their imagination had "defected." This
charade was abolished in January 1976 following application of the provisions of the Helsinki Final Act.[11] Thereafter the director and the head
of the finance department of the place of work could issue the necessary
document. In any case, the decision whether or not an exit permit would
be granted was not made in the place of work but by the security services.

But once a Jew's desire to emigrate became known at his place of
work, he was routinely demoted or fired or forced to resign "of his own
free will." His children had to obtain certificates from the educational
institute they attended. In an elementary or high school the child would
frequently be harassed after such a certificate was requested; university
students were often expelled.

Poor Relatives

The applicant for an exit permit had not only to list the names of his relatives but also to obtain affidavits from them stating that they had no
objections to his emigration. The International Covenant on Civil and
Political Rights limits the right to leave one's country by "restrictions
which are provided by law, are necessary to protect national security,
public order, public health or morals or the rights and freedoms of others." Thus the requirement of an affidavit from relatives could be legitimate in cases where rights of others might be harmed, as when financial
support might be due or alimony payments had been decreed by a court.
But in practice OVIR would, whenever so inclined, take into account
what it called "the moral aspects," including the attitude of parents
toward their children's emigration.[12] Often old family squabbles were
refought over this question. Estranged relatives would try to get even, and

long divorced husbands or wives would block the emigration of their former spouses or their children. Frequent also were the cases in which relatives refused to give their consent for fear that it would hurt or even endanger their own social positions. That is why the requirement of consent from relatives often kept Jews from even applying for an exit permit and why it became the second largest cause for refusal.[13] This requirement was soon named the "poor relatives clause," a pejorative reference to relatives who lodged financial claims against Jewish applicants for emigration, sometimes for no other purpose than to be paid a ransom. No appeal to a court of justice or any other authority was possible until a new emigration law came into force on January 1, 1993 (see Chapter 14).

Secrecy

No permission to emigrate was granted to anyone who had been in contact with military or state secrets. "National security" is stipulated in the International Covenant on Civil and Political Rights as a valid reason for restricting the right to leave one's country. During the cold war many Western countries restricted the foreign travel of military or civilian personnel involved in secret arms production or military planning, and they may do so even now. But in Western countries such restrictions are announced beforehand to the personnel involved and usually limited to a three- to five-year period after the employment in question has been terminated. In the Soviet Union, no such announcements were ever made. Texts specifying the travel restrictions based on involvement with secret work were never published. Thus the Covenant requirement that restrictions be "provided by law" was never met.[14] Consequently the duration of such restrictions was in practice unlimited.

Even worse, no one knew what was to be considered secret and what not. In a country without private enterprise practically everyone works for the state. The authorities therefore could—and often did—declare work secret although it had nothing to do with defense or matters of state. Moreover, while these decisions were sometimes taken by the heads of the institutions or firms involved, more often they were made by the security services of the state (the KGB) or of the armed forces. The decisions were never explained, and against them no appeal was possible. These conditions made "secrecy" such a dreaded word. Thousands of Jewish applicants were refused permission to emigrate on these arbitrary grounds; three-quarters of all refusals were nominally based on "security."[15]

The Documentation

The dossier of every prospective emigrant finally had to contain the following documents, all of which had to mention that they were issued in connection with a request for emigration to Israel:

— *vysov*, the personal notarized invitation from his relatives in Israel, on which the Israeli authorities had stamped a declaration stating that the applicant was welcome in Israel;

— questionnaires completed with all necessary data on all family members;

— production and social character references from the workplace; after 1976, references from director and head of the finance department;

— for children, references from the institution of learning attended;

— character references from the Communist Party (if a member) and, for children, from the Komsomol, the Communist Youth Organization;

— consent from relatives;

— statement from the housing authority with the applicant's address, the size of the apartment, and the number of people living in it, plus either proof that the apartment had been handed over or that—and why—it was not going to be vacated.

— internal passport containing notices of the cancellation of registration and of dismissal;

— birth certificates for children;

— certificate stating that the labor book had been returned to the last place of employment;

— certificate proving that no court order against the applicant had been issued, for example, for alimony;

— statement from the district military committee that the military identity card had been returned;

— statements from the hire-purchase office and from the phone company that there were no outstanding debts;

— receipt for payment of 40 rubles for each applicant.

Only an all-powerful and all-pervading bureaucracy could have devised and enforced such demands on people who wanted only to exercise one of their basic human rights—to leave their country.

Back to OVIR

Having gathered all the documentation, the applicant could finally return to OVIR to introduce the request for exit permits for the whole family. Again he might have to wait a long time, but now the waiting period might prove useful because it gave him a chance to make contact with other applicants. In this way information was exchanged, and addresses were noted. One applicant might have a sketch of the center of Moscow showing the Kalashny Pereulok, where the Netherlands embassy is located. Another might know the location of the Starokonyushenny Pereulok, where application for a transit visa would have to be made at the Austrian embassy. Others might relate that it was possible to present university diplomas and other certificates at the Netherlands embassy for transmission to Israel but that it would be wise to have them legalized beforehand.

After presenting the dossier to OVIR, the applicant could do nothing but wait and wait, and inquire regularly. Sometimes a small printed card would arrive in the mail asking him to come to OVIR again to receive his permit. Sometimes he would hear nothing for months or years. And sometimes he would be told that he had been refused (see Chapter 4).

The Exit Permit

Those whose applications were accepted received a simple three-page document with their picture. It no longer mentioned any citizenship or nationality. The price for this document was the same as for a passport—360 rubles. This fee had been increased from 40 rubles by a ukase, or edict, issued on September 29, 1970,[16] just before the first wave of Jewish emigration began.

Loss of Soviet Citizenship

Those who received permission still had another duty to perform at the OVIR office: they had to pay for the loss of their Soviet citizenship. A ukase from the Supreme Soviet on February 17, 1967, stipulated that all Soviet citizens emigrating to Israel would be considered to have lost their Soviet citizenship. This measure applied only to emigrants with exit permits for Israel, not to emigrants with other official destinations. It meant that from then on they were stateless during their travels until their arrival in Israel, when Israeli citizenship was automatically conferred, or their naturalization in another country such as the United States.

As usual, the ukase gave no reasons for the regulation. At first Soviet authorities told Western journalists that the decree was intended to ensure that no Soviet citizens would be fighting in the Israeli army against Arabs. Not until 1989 was it acknowledged by a high official of the Soviet Ministry of Foreign Affairs that the real reason had been the wish to "punish" the Jewish emigrants.[17]

Some Jews did not mind the loss of their Soviet citizenship. Since they had decided to emigrate to Israel, they wanted to have nothing more to do with the Soviet Union and considered themselves already citizens of their new country. But for many others the thought of traveling without a passport, as stateless persons, was most unpleasant. For those not going to Israel, moreover, it meant years of living with only a refugee document and, when traveling, the need to request a visa from every country to be entered. Nothing made the prejudice of the Soviet authorities against their Jewish citizens more obvious than this.

On top of that another ukase issued in 1970 prescribed that the Jews had to pay for "rejecting their citizenship." The charge was 500 rubles.[18] In fact no rejection took place; the loss of citizenship remained automatic on the basis of the 1967 ukase, but it had to be paid for anyway. Thus a Jewish emigrant had to pay OVIR 900 rubles for himself and 900 rubles for each member of his family, including his wife and his children over sixteen years of age (500 rubles for the rejection of citizenship, 360 rubles for the exit permit,[19] and 40 rubles for the application). Children under sixteen years of age were entered on the exit permits of their parents. This was an enormous sum (at the rate of exchange then current, it totaled about U.S. $1,455), given that the average monthly salary in the Soviet Union even in the 1980s was no more than 185 rubles.[20] Jewish emigrants could usually finance their emigration only by selling their possessions or by obtaining a loan from the Netherlands embassy or financial aid from abroad.

After their rejection of citizenship, Jewish emigrants had only one identity document left—the three-page exit permit valid for travel only to Israel.

The Visas

The exit permits usually were valid only for thirty days and sometimes for one week or less. Thus the applicant had to hurry to Moscow to obtain visas for Israel at the Netherlands embassy. He also needed to obtain transit visas at the Austrian embassy, since there were no direct connections from the Soviet Union to Israel and all Jewish emigrants therefore had to travel via Vienna. There might be long lines in front of the Netherlands embassy, but the Consular Section took pride in always helping everyone the same day. "When you enter this building," said a letter circulating among the Jews, "you are in another country and it is no longer the Soviet bureaucracy!" But to get in, the applicant first had to show his papers to the Soviet militia guarding the building. These policemen checked the applicant's exit permit and looked at the certificates or diplomas he wanted to send to Israel through the diplomatic pouch. Sometimes they would confiscate documents or papers, but normally there was no body search, so letters and requests for *vysovs* from other would-be emigrants could be brought along.

The interior of the Netherlands embassy was unimpressive. The quarters of the Consular Section were extremely small and rather dilapidated. The waiting room could barely accommodate a dozen people—one reason for the long lines outside. Moreover, applicants were received by a Russian and not by a Dutch employee. The embassy had only two or three consular employees, and they could not possibly receive, in person, each of the sometimes hundreds of applicants appearing at the embassy in one day. Anyone who requested it, however, would be received by a Dutch official during the *priyom*, a receiving hour in the afternoon. In the Consular Section the Russian employees would hand out the visa application form, check the exit permit, and accept a limited number of personal documents for shipment to Israel. Only a Dutch official, however, could stamp and sign the Israeli visa on the exit permit. In principle every applicant showing an exit permit valid for Israel would automatically be granted a visa for that country (see Chapter 5). Normally the same day the Austrian embassy would also issue a transit visa.

This speed was important not only because of the time limit on the exit permit but also in view of the lack of hotel space in Moscow. Many emigrants coming from other parts of the country left directly from Moscow for Vienna by air or train. Usually they were allowed to send some luggage ahead by train to Vienna or Trieste for shipment to Israel. Books could be sent in small parcels thanks to the rules the United Nations Educational, Scientific, and Cultural Organization (UNESCO) had adopted years before. Anything remotely "antique," however, including any book printed before 1900, could not leave the country. Personal jewelry was limited to a low maximum. Many emigrants left their country with just the two suitcases allowed by customs regulations. Even those were meticulously searched. It was not unusual for emigrants to spend the whole night before departure at the customs—the last circle of hell.

Conclusion

The treatment meted out by the Soviet bureaucracy to applicants for exit permits made clear that it did not recognize any innate rights of its citizens to leave their country. This right was granted only when the leadership had decided it was opportune, for external and internal reasons, to allow it. Even then applicants were routinely harassed and maltreated. On top of that, emigrants whose official destination was Israel had to pay a large sum for the "privilege" of automatically losing their Soviet citizenship upon crossing the border. This treatment was pure anti-Jewish discrimination.

3

Migration to the United States on Israeli Visas

In 1971 a Jewish family that had been allowed to leave the Soviet Union on an Israeli visa addressed itself after its arrival in Vienna not to the Israeli Jewish Agency but to the office of the American Hebrew Immigrant Aid Society. This was the first instance of Jewish emigrants opting to go to the United States rather than to Israel; this trickle would become a flood later.

Why Did They Request Israeli Visas?

Why had these Jewish migrants applied for Israeli visas at the Netherlands embassy rather than ask for an American visa at the U.S. embassy in Moscow? The answer is that they could not—for three different reasons: the U.S. preference system, the definition of a refugee, and the Soviet requirements for an exit permit.

The 1965 Amendments to the U.S. Immigration and Nationality Act of 1952 replaced the national origins quota system with a preference system based primarily on reunification of families and needed skills. Immigration to the United States from the Soviet Union was henceforward possible within an Eastern Hemisphere ceiling of 120,000.[1] The 1976 Immigration and Nationality Act Amendments then extended a 20,000 per-country limit, already in force for the Western Hemisphere, to the Eastern Hemisphere and thus to immigrants from the Soviet Union.[2] This limit for the Soviet Union applied, of course, to anyone born there, not just to Jews. These amendments meant that from 1965 on only applicants qualifying for a first or second preference had any chance, in practice, of being admitted—those with needed skills or with relatives in the direct line in the United States willing to send them an invitation. This invitation had to be stamped by the U.S. embassy to confirm that the applicant would really be accepted; only then could the Soviet authorities be approached for an exit permit. Unlike, for instance, the Armenians, Soviet Jews at that time did not often have close relatives in the United States. It was therefore difficult for them either to find a job to which the requirement of needed skills would apply or to obtain an invitation. The result was that only a few hundred Soviet Jews were admitted as legal immigrants to the United States each year.

But there was another route: one could enter the United States as a conditional immigrant, that is as a refugee or as a parolee. Over the years there were different legal bases for this status. Until 1978 Jews from the Soviet Union were accepted as refugees under the definition of the Immigration Act of 1952 and the Migration and Refugee Assistance Act of 1962.[3] From 1978 until 1980, they came mostly as parolees under the Immigration Act. This status was less advantageous that that of a refugee: the immigrant received less financial assistance and had to wait longer before he could obtain the status of permanent resident. The Refugee Act of 1980 eliminated refugees as a category of the preference system, a change that made it possible again for larger numbers of Soviet Jews to enter the United States as refugees.[4]

However, the Geneva Convention relating to the Status of Refugees defines "refugee" as "a person who . . . owing to well-founded fear of being persecuted for reasons of race, religion, nationality, membership of a particular social group or political opinion *is outside the country of his nationality . . . and who is unable or, owing to such fear, is unwilling to return to it.*"[5] This definition is repeated in almost identical terms in the Immigration and Nationality Act. This act does give the president authority to accept as refugees persons still in their own country, but only after specific consultations with Congress. The president never availed himself of this authorization with regard to Soviet Jews, probably because it was realized that the Soviets would not have granted exit permits to persons claiming to be refugees while still in the Soviet Union.[6]

To be eligible for entry into the United States as a refugee, therefore, Soviet Jews had to be "outside the country of their nationality." But to leave their country they needed an exit permit, which was issued, if at all, only to those with an invitation from another country and a guarantee that they would be accepted by it. Except for the very limited number who received immigration visas for the United States, and a handful granted visas for Canada, Australia, and elsewhere, all Jews hoping to emigrate from the Soviet Union therefore had to begin with an invitation from Israel that guaranteed entry into that country. On the basis of that *vysov* they were then given, if they were lucky, an exit permit valid only for Israel.

Thus it was American immigration law that severely limited the issuance of ordinary U.S. immigration visas to Soviet Jews. It was the international definition of a refugee that made it necessary for all hoping to go to the United States with that status to leave their country first. And finally it was Soviet regulations that forced them to the detour of a visa for Israel, even if they had no intention of going there.

Procedure for Traveling to the United States as a Refugee

There were no direct flights from the Soviet Union to Israel. Practically all emigrants who had received an exit permit from OVIR and an Israeli entry visa from the Netherlands embassy therefore had to travel to Vienna, after first obtaining a transit visa for Austria from the Austrian embassy. Upon arrival in Vienna, Jews would normally be received by the Israeli Jewish Agency. Those who after three or four days persisted that they did not want to go to Israel would be transferred to the office of the Hebrew Immigrant Aid Society. This office had been established to help Jewish emigrants from Czechoslovakia and, later, after the 1956 uprising in Hungary, also from that country. It was about to close when the first Soviet Jews began to arrive.[7] The Hebrew Immigrant Aid Society would arrange for transportation to Rome, where an office of the U.S. Immigration and Naturalization Service (INS) was located. For different reasons, but mostly because they were not Jewish, a number of migrants did not accept the help of the Jewish organizations and were assisted by the Tolstoy Foundation, the World Council of Churches, or others.

When the number of migrants increased enormously in the early 1970s, it became difficult to provide them in Vienna with individual transit visas for Italy. An elaborate scheme was then devised by the U.S. embassy in Vienna to arrange a collective document valid for transit through Rome. The problem was that the U.S. consular officer could not state officially that persons on the Hebrew Immigrant Aid Society's lists were in transit to Israel because, "although they had Israeli visas, they clearly had the intention of going to the United States (or in rare cases elsewhere)." On the other hand, neither could the officer state that they were in transit to the United States, because in Rome some might be found ineligible to go there, whereas "such a statement could also be construed as a commitment for acceptance by the United States."

Moreover consular officers could have no way of knowing whether individuals on a list were actually in a particular transit group without personally checking as they boarded the train. To overcome this difficulty, the embassy proposed that the Hebrew Immigrant Aid Society prepare lists of Soviet emigrés on plain white paper with a covering sheet on society letterhead stating: "The persons listed in the accompanying documents are transiting Italy for the purpose of pursuing applications for entry into the United States or third countries." A U.S. consular officer would prepare a "certificate of acknowledgement of execution of an instrument," fasten it to the documents, and sign and seal it. Austria and Italy accepted this procedure.[8] In Rome the U.S. Immigration and Naturalization Service would process the Soviet emigrés as refugees. The International Organization for Migration would then organize their transport to New York, financed largely by the U.S. government.

The Israeli Position

The problems and frictions caused by what was in Israeli eyes a misuse of their visas are discussed in Chapter 11. One more question needs to be addressed here, namely whether the Netherlands embassy knew that many of those applying for a visa for Israel did not really want to go there and, if so, why it still issued visas to them.

The application form for an Israeli visa in use at the Netherlands embassy contained a question about the desired destination of the applicant. Many filled in truthfully—the United States. During the period of the interest representation the embassy repeatedly asked for instructions on this point. In the beginning of 1974 the embassy cabled to The Hague:

> Recently Jewish emigrants have openly told embassy personnel that they did not have the intention to go to Israel but wished to go elsewhere, usually the United States. I presume that Israel wants the interest representation to be interpreted in a broad sense: Israel assumes a certain responsibility for all Jews, not only for those who are or will become Israelis.

For that reason the embassy believed there would be no objections to granting immigration visas to those who made it known that they did not really want to go to Israel or might not be Jews according to the Israelis. To grant financial aid in such cases, on the other hand, was going a bit further. Was emigration of Jews from the Soviet Union so important for Israel that financial support should be given whenever necessary—even when the emigrant went elsewhere? On the other hand, it would be difficult for Israel to object formally, both because in that case every emigrant would state he *was* going to Israel and because the funds for support were partly coming from American Jewish sources.[9]

Several weeks later the Israeli embassy in The Hague, having consulted Jerusalem, answered:

1. If a Jewish emigrant "unobtrusively" mentions that he may not intend to go to Israel, do not go into the matter further and eventually grant financial aid.
2. If it is abundantly clear that the destination is not Israel, refer the emigrant to the appropriate embassy [clearly impossible if, as usual, the exit permit was valid only for Israel].
3. Avoid provocations; use your best judgment.

The cable added that the Israeli embassy in Washington, D.C., would ask the U.S. State Department to ensure that exit permits were not already stamped by the U.S. consul in Moscow, as had apparently been done, "since that might endanger the representation of [Israeli] interests by you."[10]

The question came up again in 1987. Noting that the Israelis had repeatedly objected in principle to the improper use of Israeli visas when applicants had clearly indicated the United States as their destination, the Ministry of Foreign Affairs in The Hague instructed the embassy in Moscow to submit applications from those who did not intend to go to Israel for previous authorization to Jerusalem.[11] The embassy pointed out that this instruction could not possibly be implemented, for the same reasons as had been given in 1974. In the end the decision was also the same: visas could be issued without prior approval of the Israeli government to any applicant who had received an exit permit from OVIR on the basis of a family invitation from Israel, whether or not Israel was mentioned in the application as country of destination.[12]

Conclusion

The Israeli authorities could, it is clear, have instructed the Netherlands embassy at any time not to issue visas for Israel to applicants who were known not to have the intention to go there. Such an instruction would not have stopped, but might have slowed, the misuse of the Israeli visas. But the Israeli government, however much it regretted that misuse, apparently always decided in the end that it had an obligation to help all Jews in need. The instruction never came.

4

Refuseniks

Almost as soon as Soviet authorities resumed issuing exit permits on a limited scale in September 1968, the first cases of refusal began to be mentioned in the reports from the Netherlands ambassador in Moscow.[1] The agony of the Refuseniks (as they would later be called) had begun.

The decision to leave the Soviet Union for good was for the great majority of Jewish emigrants a wrenching one. Once it had been taken there was no way back: jobs had usually been lost, university studies of children interrupted, contacts broken off by friends and even relatives, possessions sold or given away. All had been bearable in the expectation that soon they could leave everything behind and begin a new life in a free country. Many emigrants had mentally already taken leave of the Soviet Union. Then came the terrible blow: refused!

While the political and legal aspects of refusal are the focus here, it should never be forgotten that behind them there always was the human aspect: a heartrending tragedy for thousands of Jews who had to readjust to living in the country they wanted to leave and to doing so in circumstances usually much worse than before their application. Yet most succeeded by their courage, stamina, and determination not only in maintaining themselves but in becoming the vanguard of the Jewish emigration movement. Through their contacts with each other, with foreign journalists and diplomats in Moscow, and directly with the outside world by any means available, they succeeded in waking up the West to the plight of the Jews who wanted to leave the Soviet Union. The West was never allowed to forget it again. Ultimately "Refusenik" became a badge of honor.[2]

As we have seen, "secrecy" was, from the beginning, the most common reason given for refusal. The absence of permission from relatives (the poor relatives clause) was the second. There was a third category—"unknown." In a number of cases OVIR mentioned "reasons of state" or simply refused to give any reason at all.

Until 1991 no legal basis for refusal was published and consequently no appeals against OVIR decisions could be initiated except with OVIR itself. People sometimes tried to show that their work had not been secret or that its results had been published—to no avail. On the other hand, when it suited the authorities to grant an exit permit to an applicant, the demands of secrecy or parental permission often seemed to have lost their importance. It was not unusual that of two people working on the same subjects at the same institute one was allowed to go and the other not—a strange way of guarding secrets.

The first problem Refuseniks faced after hearing that they had been refused an exit permit was how to maintain a tolerable life. Some had lost their apartments, almost all had lost their jobs. As far as a job was concerned, surprisingly, the Soviet system came to their aid. Since no unemployment was supposed to exist, everyone had to be assigned a job even if he had committed such a "treasonable act" as wanting to leave the country. The lucky ones were given a lower job in their former workplace, but many scientific workers were forced to accept menial work as watchmen or plumbers. Refusal of such employment could lead to prosecution on the charge of "parasitism"; accepting it meant at least a regular, if lower, income. True friends were more important than ever. Some broke off their friendship, but fortunately there were always others, Jews and non-Jews, who tried to help. Many a scientific article, many a translation has appeared in the Soviet Union over the years under a false name, providing additional income to a Refusenik. Contributions would be brought in by Jewish and non-Jewish "tourists" from the United States and European countries. In later years direct financial support was provided by Jewish organizations in the West.[3]

To Make Noise or Not?

After the initial adjustment came another and often very difficult choice for Refuseniks: Should they "go public"? As a first step, should they consent to having their names placed on one of the lists that would be presented to foreign diplomats and journalists and transmitted to the West? Should they sign collective letters to the leadership of the Communist Party, to foreign politicians, to Western Jewish organizations? Should they take part in actions such as hunger strikes and public demonstrations, like the yearly demonstrations by Jewish women on "Women's Day," and perhaps risk arrest?

The main consideration was, of course, whether such actions would speed up or delay their chances to obtain exit permits, would increase or decrease the danger for themselves and the members of their family. But other considerations such as their duty to their conscience and to their fellow Refuseniks played a role for many. Some did not hesitate and began "making as much noise as possible" immediately. Others kept silent in the hope of being rewarded with a speedy permission to go, but they, too, usually came to the conclusion that making their plight known through contacts with representatives of foreign embassies and foreign media was the better policy. In general, the judgment must be that making noise was more effective than silence. Some Refuseniks who joined protests, it is true, had to wait for exit permits a very long time; some were arrested and condemned to long prison terms. But their trials caused a furor that proved detrimental to Soviet relations with the West and thereafter seemed to deter Soviet authorities. To have your name on a list did, moreover, seem to provide a certain measure of protection against surreptitious arrest and harassment. Western governments and organizations were, after all, able to protest and plead on the basis of data that only the victims themselves could furnish. Those protests and pleas, although often seemingly ignored, in the end did have their influence on the decisions taken by the Soviet leadership. The Soviet authorities several times tried to "decapitate" the Jewish dissident movement by giving exit permits to the "unruly" ones, those who had made the most noise. But new leaders always came forward to join the perennial Refuseniks of yore. The KGB tried to exploit the plight of the Refuseniks, approaching many with a simple proposal: inform on your friends and acquaintances, and in due time you will get your exit permit. Some gave in, but the great majority refused.[4]

One may wonder whether the Refuseniks should not have expected their applications to be rejected. Some obviously realized that they had been involved in work considered classified by the authorities. But even those applicants imagined that the time of denial would be limited, as in other countries, to three or five years. After all, scientific work in the present age does not remain new very long and is soon superseded by later discoveries and inventions.[5] Others knew only that somewhere in their scientific institute there was a secret department, but they had had nothing to do with it. Others again, looking back, call themselves naive: "It never occurred to me that I could be refused." There was no way of checking eligibility beforehand because no law on secrecy was published until 1991, no rules or regulations were ever shown or quoted to applicants. The proceedings of OVIR remained shrouded in secrecy.

What is clear, however, is that Soviet authorities had completely misread the reactions of the victims of refusal and the chain reactions they would create in the West. As one of the victims said:

> Theirs was a short-term policy of complete intimidation. But they should have expected it would not be so easy to intimidate the Jewish intelligentsia. Those Jews who had "made it" in Soviet society against all antisemitism and discrimination had already shown that they possessed character and stamina. Pushed against the wall, they would show their full capabilities. But this was beyond the comprehension of the KGB.[6]

How many Refuseniks there have been is difficult to estimate. Only OVIR knew how many applicants were turned down. The Israeli author Z. Alexander estimated in the 1970s that there were then between 2,000 and 2,500. He states that 20–25 percent of them were allowed to go every year (the figures include the members of the family); their places on the list were then taken by others.[7] The willingness to be listed increased in the late 1980s, when lengthy, accurate lists were compiled. In 1985, reportedly 7,358 Jews had been refused an exit permit;[8] in 1986 the number was about 11,000.[9] Alexander states that 20–25 percent of the Refuseniks were from Moscow, 10 percent from Leningrad; 5–7 percent from Kiev, Riga, Vilnius, and Kishinev, and 2–3 percent from Odessa. The waiting period varied from several years to ten, twelve, and up to twenty.

It would not be possible to name here all the leaders of the Refusenik movement or even the most important ones; there have been too many, and to make a choice would leave out others who were equally worthy. Two of the earliest Refuseniks have already been mentioned in Chapter 1—Boris Kochubyevski and Yasha Kazakov. The Refusenik of longest duration was probably Benjamin Bogomolni, who waited for an exit permit for twenty years (see Chapter 14). Others will appear in the text for specific reasons. Two others are named here because they personified the

high moral standard, the strong convictions, and the stamina of
the Refuseniks as a group. Professor Alexander Lerner was the first
Refusenik from the highest ranks of the scientific community and
thereby became a natural leader of the movement. Anatoly (later, Natan)
Sharansky, because of his incredible courage and steadfastness during his
trial and imprisonment and through the ceaseless activities of his wife
Natasha (later, Avital) in the West, became the international symbol of
resistance to Soviet repression of human rights in general and Jewish
rights in particular.

Alexander Lerner

Professor Alexander Lerner applied for an exit permit to go to Israel in
1971 and was destined to remain a Refusenik for sixteen and one-half
years.[10] He had, as he describes it himself, reached a very high position
in the Soviet scientific community as an expert in cybernetics. He had a
comfortable life with a large apartment, a country house with a large
piece of land, and two cars. Moreover, every year he received permission
to go abroad to participate in international scientific congresses—the
greatest privilege for any Soviet citizen. Why would a man in such a position want to emigrate?

Lerner explains that he "had strong feelings as a Jew" and "many
contacts with Zionists." At the same time he became more and more
appalled by the system in which he had to live and for which he had to
work. He decided that if there appeared to be a chance to get out of this
system and to go to his historic homeland Israel, he should try, for his
sake and for the sake of his family. He fully realized that it would not be
easy to get permission since he had taken part in important secret
research in the late 1950s and the beginning of the 1960s as one of the
leading experts in the automatic control of submarines with nuclear
engines. But he had stopped doing that research in 1962 or 1963, and so
when he applied for emigration in 1971 his secret work was already
almost ten years behind him. He thought that even if he was initially
refused, the authorities would surely let him go after a certain time. He
was therefore not overly surprised when he received his refusal in 1971
within a month, but he hardly suspected that it would be repeated time
and again until 1988. It seems likely that, as he thinks himself, he was
punished for being one of the first scientists to seek emigration.

Lerner was also one of the first to realize that it would not help him
to keep silent. On the contrary, he was convinced that only publicity and

constant action might bring him some protection and, he hoped, in the end permission to leave. He expected that the international community, and in particular the scientific community, would act on behalf of himself and his Refusenik colleagues—and in this he was not disappointed. So he made himself available to the representatives in Moscow of the international press, gave press conferences in his home and elsewhere, talked to foreign diplomats, and generally "was as noisy as possible." He and his colleagues regularly drafted declarations that were sent to official organs of the Soviet Union and to international organizations. A yearly confidential report on the situation of the Refuseniks was presented to foreign embassies.

Taking part in demonstrations in front of the buildings of the Central Committee of the Communist Party and of the Supreme Soviet and at many other places, Lerner was arrested more than once and taken to a local station of the militia. Once he was locked up for ten days to keep him away during the visit of President Richard Nixon in May 1972. But no criminal charges were ever leveled against him, and he was never tried. The KGB must have realized that, as was the case with Andrei Sakharov, a trial of such a high-ranking scientist would cause a flood of negative publicity in the West and strong reactions from Western governments. Those consequences would have canceled out any advantage his conviction might have had in deterring others. Perhaps the high regard in which top-ranking scientists were held in the Soviet Union also had something to do with the relative restraint the authorities showed as far as Sakharov and Lerner were concerned. A show-trial was reserved for a younger and at that time less well known scientist—Anatoly Sharansky.

Next to his decision to "go public," Lerner took another initiative that would have a lasting influence on the Refusenik movement: he began to organize scientific seminars in his home. Early on he and other Refusenik scientists realized that their enforced idleness and inability to keep up with the latest developments in their scientific field would inevitably cause them to fall behind in their specialties and diminish their chance to resume their work elsewhere. So they began to hold seminars, in the beginning weekly, during which Refusenik scientists would meet under Lerner's chairmanship and discuss scientific problems as well as Jewish history and culture. Later non-Refuseniks who had the courage to come, such as Professor Andrei Sakharov and Professor Leonid Korochkin, would give lectures. Foreign experts, sometimes sent to Moscow especially for that purpose by Western scientific organizations, would take part and speak about the latest developments in their field. The KGB was, of course, well aware of what was going on and interfered for the first time in 1974. Phones of participants were disconnected, and foreign mail was intercepted. Some organizers were arrested, but they were not charged and were soon released. The seminars went on with more or less harassment by the KGB.[11] Similar seminars were organized in Leningrad after 1978. There was even an "Independent Moscow University" organized for children of Refuseniks.[12]

In 1981 all participants were suddenly prevented from entering the apartments of Lerner and others where seminars were planned, and foreign participants were refused visas. The same measures were taken in Leningrad.[13] These actions deterred the Refusenik activities only temporarily. The seminars became "wandering," the venue being determined only shortly before they were to begin. Since arrangements were mainly made by telephone, the KGB was undoubtedly as aware of this new system as it had been of the old, but it did not further interfere. Seminars were held until the late 1980s, and they not only contributed to the scientific knowledge of the participants but—perhaps equally important—raised their spirits.

Does Professor Lerner regret his decision to ask for an exit permit in 1971 and the almost sixteen years of his life that he lost? On the contrary. Because of his Refusenik activities and contacts, his existence became more purposeful. He is sure that his "years of refusal" were the most important years of his life, that is, until he arrived in Israel. His only deep regret is that his wife did not live to be there with him.

Anatoly Sharansky

Anatoly Sharansky was much younger than Alexander Lerner when he decided to apply for an exit permit in the spring of 1973.[14] But he was already privileged in that he had been admitted at the Moscow Institute of Physics and Technology (Jewish applicants had to score especially high to be admitted) and then found a good job as a computer specialist at the Institute for Oil and Gas. Like Lerner, however, he became more and more appalled by the life the regime forced him to live, the constant "double-think."

At first, like many Jews, Sharansky thought the way to escape this double-thinking and antisemitism was "to go into silence and to build a castle of silence around me in which to hide." Two big events changed the situation for him. First, in 1967 the Six-Day War on the one hand exacerbated antisemitism in the Soviet Union but on the other generated new respect for Israel and self-respect among the Jews. Second, the Soviet invasion of Czechoslovakia in 1968 provoked the response: "Then I was really ashamed to be part of this system, this constant lie which we were living." The famous article Sakharov wrote in *samizdat* in 1968, entitled "Thoughts about Progress, Peaceful Co-Existence, and Intellectual Freedom," had also a great influence on Sharansky.[15] "I was thinking," recalls Sharansky, "Why does this man who has already reached the top of his scientific profession have the courage and you don't?"

And so by the time of his graduation, Sharansky had decided to go on *aliyah* (literally, "ascent" to Israel) and ask for an exit permit. This, he says, was

> a very bold step, not only physical at that point. You're finishing your life of a loyal Soviet slave saying only what is permitted. You feel so free when you have broken with this double-think, it's such a great change. Then you feel strong enough to speak for your rights or the rights of other Jews and also for the rights of non-Jews.

In this way Sharansky became an activist in 1973, taking part in demonstrations, helping to collect data for lists of Refuseniks, and drafting petitions to the authorities. His knowledge of English soon brought him into contact with foreign correspondents. He began to help with translations at the press conferences organized by Lerner and after 1975 also by Sakharov and then to organize press conferences himself. Soon he was meeting with a steady stream of correspondents, diplomats, politicians, and Jewish activists from the West. "In order to translate," he explains,

> you must understand not just the two languages but also the two mentalities, not only translate words, but also ideas and understanding. We were regarding the [foreign] correspondents as our allies who were glad—and whose duty it was— to inform the world about our views. Of course there always was a difference of opinion about this in the foreign press. I think on the whole we succeeded and we became very friendly with some of the correspondents.

Sharansky was watched by the KGB, detained, brought in, warned, threatened, and tailed day and night. "But," he says, "their harassment was merely an annoyance that inspired me to become even more active." In 1975, a few months after the Helsinki Accords were signed (see Chapter 7), he proposed to Yuri Orlov and Andrei Amalrik that they ought to make it as difficult as possible for the Soviet Union to ignore those accords. After months of discussions Orlov proposed a public group to monitor compliance with the human rights agreements and Sharansky became one of the founding members. This was a momentous decision, by no means self-evident. Many Jews did not want to have much to do with the non-Jewish dissidents and kept aloof. "We only want to go to Israel," they reasoned "and we have nothing to do with—indeed could be harmed by—the activities regarding human rights inside the Soviet Union." Sharansky saw correctly that, on the contrary, focusing on human rights, and especially monitoring the application of the Helsinki Final Act with its provisions concerning freer movement, would help Jewish dissidents and provide a legal and internationally supportable basis for their actions. The Helsinki Watch Group, as it was soon called, was also active on behalf of people from many other national and religious groups whose rights were brutally violated by the Soviet regime, including Pentecostals, Ukrainian Catholics, and Crimean Tatars. The group also provided the West with documents about human rights violations in Soviet prisons, labor camps, and psychiatric hospitals.

Looking back now, it seems amazing that the KGB allowed the Helsinki Watch Group to continue its activities for almost two years. Then, in early 1977, it was clearly decided that stronger measures were required (see also Chapter 8). Orlov was arrested on February 10. On March 4, 1977, *Izvestia* carried a full-page article accusing Sharansky and several others of working for the U.S. Central Intelligence Agency and carrying out espionage against the Soviet Union. He was arrested on March 15 and charged under Article 64A of the criminal code with "treason" and not under Article 70, with "anti-Soviet activities," the charge against Orlov and others.

Why had Sharansky been singled out? He himself believes it was because the Jewish movement presented a much greater danger than other dissident movements and therefore had to be crushed more forcefully. It seems more likely, however, that he was chosen for other reasons. He was the conduit with the West for news about dissidents and Refuseniks. Notwithstanding the warnings the KGB had issued, he continued to give information to Western diplomatic and press representatives. And last but not least he was, as he acknowledged himself, the bridge between the Jewish movement and the other dissidents. When, in view of President Jimmy Carter's new emphasis on human rights, the KGB started looking for an appropriate scapegoat to present as a warning to all the others, it could hardly fail to think of Sharansky first. His foreign contacts, moreover, made it especially easy to accuse him of working for a foreign intelligence service.

The KGB may well have regretted its choice. Sharansky remained steadfast during his trial—which ended with his condemnation to thirteen years of imprisonment—and in the jails and camps in which he spent the next nine years. His book *Fear No Evil* is testimony to his extraordinary willpower and endurance. Not until February 1986, after Mikhail Gorbachev had become secretary general of the Communist Party and had his first meeting with President Ronald Reagan, was Sharansky released and reunited with his wife Avital.

Does he regret what he did—the loss of some of the best years of his life? Sharansky's answer resembles that of Lerner. In his book he wrote, "These five years [of dissident action before the arrest] have been the best of my life. I am happy that I have been able to live them honestly and at peace with my conscience."[16] In his interview he said:

> The Soviet system could be stable only if it had full control over the brains of the people. In fact it was a very insecure system. And that is why even the existence of one person, whose public sayings were his own and his right, was a danger for them. That is why they made such an effort not only to put you in prison but to make you say publicly that you were wrong and they are right.

Sharansky never did.

5

The Dutch Role in the Seventies

The Netherlands embassy in Moscow was given the task of representing Israeli interests in the Soviet Union on June 10, 1967. Its chancery was then—and still is—located on the ground floor of a two-story building along the Kalashny Pereulok (Pastry Bakers' Lane), a small side street in the center of Moscow. The ambassador's residence is on the first floor. The structure was built as a private mansion in 1812 and given a new facade in 1888. In February 1944, during the Second World War, it was rented by the Soviet Government Administration for Service to the Diplomatic Corps (Upravlenye Po Obsluzhivaniyu Diplomaticheskgo Korpusa, UPDK) to the newly arrived Netherlands ambassador who took up residence there in September.[1] The building is not large, but in 1967 it was sufficient for the staff of the embassy, which at that time consisted of only four diplomats, two administrative officers, and two secretaries (see Tables 4 and 5, page 225, for the names of key officials). The Consular Section grew very cramped, however, when the Jewish emigration became a flood in the 1970s. There were no waiting facilities to speak of, and the Russian assistants were crowded into one room.

When diplomatic relations are broken off, it is not unusual for a small number of staff officers, often below diplomatic rank, to be allowed to stay behind and work under the aegis of the "protecting power." But not in this case: no Israeli officer was permitted to remain, and until 1988 none was allowed to return. The Dutch officials had to do the additional work themselves, with the help of Russian assistants hired especially for this purpose. Those assistants were, like all the personnel hired through UPDK, obliged to report regularly to the authorities about their work and experiences in the embassy.

The embassy never had a separate section for the Israeli interests. The consul signed the Israeli visas next to the Dutch visas, and the administrative officer kept the Israeli accounts next to the Dutch ones. In the beginning that did not matter, since the embassy did not have much to do. The Consular Section in particular had little work: only a few Soviet officials needed visas to travel to the Netherlands, and there were only a handful of Dutch citizens living in the Soviet Union who might require consular assistance. In fact the consular work was done by a diplomat who also handled trade relations. But when the flood of Jewish emigration started in 1970, he soon had to neglect his other work. There were even periods when almost the entire embassy staff had to help out issuing visas for Israel. Complaints were rare. Practically all Dutch officers considered it an honor and a challenge to help as many Jews as they could to leave the Soviet Union. Some went beyond their instructions or even beyond the call of duty to give as much assistance as possible.

The Task of the Embassy

From the beginning the question of what should or should not be considered to fall within the limits of the representation of Israeli interests led to a lively exchange between the embassy and the policy makers at the Ministry of Foreign Affairs in The Hague. Should the embassy, for instance, maintain special contacts with the Jews in the Soviet Union? The Israelis, as well as many Soviet Jews, hoped that the Netherlands embassy in Moscow would keep contact with the Jewish community there and perhaps assist them as part of their work for Israel. But The Hague made it clear to its ambassador that the representation of Israeli interests should remain strictly separate from specific Jewish questions. The ambassador should not maintain special relations with the Jewish community and not, for instance, accept an invitation to attend the birthday celebration of the chief rabbi unless other ambassadors were also going.[2]

Did this instruction mean that Dutch diplomats could have no contacts with Soviet Jews? The answer was no, as anyone who wanted to see a Dutch official would be received in the consulate. But those who would do so had first to be allowed to pass by the Soviet militia guarding the embassy. In general, that restricted entrants to those who had exit permits for Israel. It was therefore natural that Dutch officials would get requests for meetings with Soviet Jews in the street or in private homes.

In the beginning the official Dutch attitude in this matter was very restrictive. In 1971 the ambassador instructed his staff to "politely, but clearly refuse all contacts outside the embassy. We must all realize that the task of the embassy is to represent the interests of Israel. For Soviet citizens we can—and must—do nothing."[3] This policy was in accordance with the feelings in The Hague. Time and again the foreign ministry would point out that the embassy was carrying out a humanitarian mission in behalf of Jewish emigrants that might be jeopardized if Soviet authorities would be irritated by actions of the Dutch officials. Soviet authorities might, it was felt, prevent the Netherlands embassy at any time from continuing that mission.

This attitude must be understood in the context of the cold war then raging full blast and of the situation of the diplomatic community in Moscow at that time. Foreign diplomats were closely watched and spied upon by the KGB. Soviet citizens could be—and were—severely punished for having contacts with foreigners. Soviet police had tried to prevent American diplomats from talking with Jewish activists in the street, and their actions led to scuffles. The Netherlands embassy was convinced that "in the interest of the many hundreds of Soviet Jews who are helped out of the country by the Netherlands embassy every week," such incidents should be avoided.[4]

Only in hindsight can one conjecture that a Soviet measure to prevent the Netherlands embassy from representing Israel was not very likely. In fact Soviet authorities had an interest in the efficient handling of the issuance of Israeli visas to Jews once they had received exit permits. It should be remembered that the permits were granted not to please the emigrants but to impress Western public opinion and governments or to remove "unruly elements."[5] The Netherlands embassy was able to ensure quick delivery. If that task were taken away from the Dutch, another embassy would have to take it on, most likely the American embassy. That arrangement might have further aggravated the almost continuously tense relations between that embassy and the Soviet authorities. All in all, it was probably in the Soviet interest that Israel be represented by a small but efficient embassy[6] that could also, if the need arose, be bullied a bit easier than the American one.

That bullying was tried at an early date. In 1971 the Dutch diplomat charged with consular affairs was told by his maid that "he should not mix too much with the Jews."[7] This maid had, of course, been engaged through UPDK. A simple Russian woman, she had no way of finding out whether her boss was or was not "mixing" with Jews. UPDK, however, was under the control of the KGB, and that is where the warning must have originated.

A more explicit warning was given when the embassy in Soviet eyes went too far in supplying information to future emigrants. From the beginning Israeli authorities had stressed that they considered the emigration issue of paramount importance in the context of the interest representation. They would have liked the Netherlands embassy to act more or less as an Israeli embassy would have done in handing out information about their country and the desirability of migrating there. A brochure with color pictures was printed for that purpose in Israel and the first copies were handed out in Moscow in 1972. But this activity was not to the liking of the Soviets. The Dutch chargé d'affaires was called in by MID and told that the second secretary for consular affairs was "actively distributing a propagandistic brochure," a "manual for emigrants." He was accused of having "encouraged further distribution to other Soviet citizens." The brochure was called "propagandistic," especially since it had been printed in Israel. The Soviet official ended with what in diplomatic language had to be considered a rather strong warning: These actions "went outside the framework of normal diplomatic practice," and "it could hardly be the intention to disturb the relations between the Netherlands and the Soviet Union by distributing a publication that did not serve a Dutch interest."[8] The distribution of the brochure was stopped, and the incident had a restraining influence on similar activities of the embassy for many years.

Nevertheless, contacts between Dutch diplomats and Jewish activists never quite ceased. The world of foreign diplomats, journalists, and businessmen in Moscow was a small one during most of the 1970s and 1980s, and contacts among them frequent. Dutch officers would be invited to parties in the apartments of colleagues or Western journalists and meet with Jews who took the risk of coming there.[9] The Dutch may have felt more constrained than other diplomats, but not all of them followed their instructions to the letter and street meetings did also take place. Official policy remained, however, that contacts with Refuseniks and dissidents were not desirable. In 1975 the Netherlands foreign minister, on a visit to Israel, was asked why his embassy in Moscow did not maintain contact with prominent Refuseniks like Professors Alexander Lerner and Levitch. He answered that such contacts would not be in the interest of smoothly running emigration.[10] A fundamental change in embassy policy regarding contacts with dissidents and Refuseniks had to wait until the late 1980s.

Visas

The main task of the embassy in connection with interest representation was in a sense also the easiest one—to deliver the visas. The Israelis had given the Dutch permission to grant a visa for Israel, without preliminary authorization, to anyone presenting an exit permit valid for that country. Dutch officials simply had to check the validity of the exit permit (the only identity document left in the possession of the applicant), stamp and sign the Israeli visa, and register it (even the register was in the end abolished). It was largely an "automatic and technical act"[11] that became a burden only when the number of applications started to rise enormously.

The embassy also handled visitors' visas. In the 1970s there were few requests. Occasionally a Soviet citizen—usually an elderly person—would receive permission to visit relatives in Israel. In these cases the embassy was required to stamp a tourist visa for Israel in the Soviet passport of the applicant. During certain periods this action was allowed without preliminary authorization; at other times Jerusalem had to give its permission beforehand. In both cases the Israeli Ministry of Foreign Affairs would be informed by telex via The Hague that a visa had been issued. In the late 1980s the number of visitors' visas increased so rapidly that they became an additional burden for the Dutch Consular Section.

Nationality Certificates

A question that led to long discussions between the Dutch and Israeli authorities was whether the embassy should deliver certificates of Israeli citizenship to Refuseniks. Early in 1970 a Jewish Soviet citizen wrote to the Netherlands embassy explaining that his request for an exit permit had been denied and that he now wanted to become an Israeli citizen in the hopes that this step might improve his position.[12] Shortly afterward a second similar request was received, from a Jew who wanted to reject his Soviet citizenship and become an Israeli citizen. This time the embassy in its report added that the applicant had been warned of the dangers such a step might entail but had said he would take the consequences. This particular applicant received permission to leave a month later, but others made similar requests.[13]

There was no answer from Israel for almost a year. On March 17, 1971, the Israeli government announced that it intended to create a legal possibility for Jews to become Israeli citizens before actually emigrating to Israel. If the Israeli parliament—the Knesset—would approve this proposal, Soviet Jews could, it was thought, obtain Israeli nationality by proxy in the Netherlands embassy in Moscow.[14] On July 1, the embassy was informed that the Knesset had approved the proposal as an amendment to the Israeli nationality law and that Israeli instructions could be expected. The ambassador answered in a cable to The Hague that he saw serious objections. Not mincing his words, he called the exercise "futile," since Soviet authorities were not going to change their attitude one bit. Any initiative by the embassy to approach Jews and hand them certificates would be regarded by those authorities as an interference in Soviet internal affairs and as a provocation. Such an initiative would be outside the strict interpretation of interest representation and could have unfavorable repercussions on what the Netherlands embassy was attempting to do for Israel. The Jews in question would not be allowed to enter the embassy, and they might be in danger of arrest. Last but not least, an embassy officer handing out certificates could be declared *persona non grata* and expelled from the Soviet Union.[15] The Hague answered that the only intention on the Israeli side had been to extend moral support to Jews who were prevented from migrating to Israel. The ambassador's objections would, however, be studied and taken up with the Israelis. In the meantime the embassy should not take any action.[16]

A triangular discussion involving Moscow, The Hague, and Jerusalem went on for several months. On November 30, 1971, the Netherlands ambassador once more summed up all his objections, emphasizing that an Israeli ambassador, had there been one in Moscow, would also have warned of the consequences of handing out Israeli citizenship certificates to Soviet citizens. Now it was his duty to do so. The exercise would endanger both the recipients and the Dutch officers and was therefore, in view of the Soviet mentality, "unwise." Should the ministry nevertheless decide to accommodate the Israelis, then the document should at the very minimum make clear that it would not absolve recipients from their duties as citizens of the Soviet Union.[17] Thereupon the ministry finally informed the Israeli ambassador that the question had been studied *a fond* but that to grant Israeli citizenship through the intermediary of the Netherlands embassy would not be in conformity with generally recognized international practice. Such intermediary could therefore not be given. Israeli authorities answered that they understood the reason for the Dutch decision and would now send citizenship papers directly to carefully selected Soviet Jews. The certificates would make clear that the granting of Israeli citizenship did not infringe on Soviet citizenship. They would not, in other words, entitle bearers to expect assistance from the Netherlands embassy.[18]

One would expect the matter to have ended at that point, but there was a sequel a year later. In October 1972 the legal adviser to the Israeli foreign ministry went to The Hague and pleaded once more for the embassy in Moscow to be allowed to deliver the certificates.[19] On November 16, 1972, the embassy was indeed instructed by the new foreign minister to deliver Israeli citizenship certificates to recipients in the Soviet Union. The ambassador, in return, addressed a personal letter to the secretary general of the ministry asking whether it was really the minister's intention to reverse the policy formerly agreed on in this matter. Twice within one month he had himself been warned that his embassy should not exceed the limits. To execute the new instructions now would play into the hands of the KGB.[20] The ambassador received a personal answer a week later: the minister had carefully considered the matter but he had declared himself "willing to take an accommodating attitude" to the Israeli request.[21] Negotiations went on regarding the text of the certificate. At the instigation of the ambassador, the Dutch side demanded that a sentence be added reading: "Persons granted Israeli nationality are not released automatically from the citizenship of their country of residence."[22]

Nevertheless the files in the Ministry of Foreign Affairs in The Hague do not show that any certificates were ever actually transmitted to the embassy during the 1970s. A later report mentions "a few dozen certificates sent," and one or two instances can be identified in which the embassy was involved in the 1980s. Undoubtedly most certificates were sent by mail directly from Israel. The recipients seem to have kept these documents for moral support only. There is no evidence that anyone ever tried to use one to enter the embassy or to obtain Dutch assistance.

Vysovs

It could be dangerous to ask for the required legalized invitation or *vysov* from Israel by ordinary mail. A letter to a foreign country would be spotted at the post office and passed on to the KGB, which would thus learn of the sender's intention to emigrate. Thereafter anything might happen, from harassment at one's home or workplace to dismissal from one's job. For that reason requests were usually transmitted by others—by migrants who had already reached Israel or through the Netherlands embassy, which could send them to Jerusalem by diplomatic pouch. Ordinary Soviet citizens could not get past the militia guarding every embassy in Moscow, and in particular the one representing the interests of Israel. Only those with valid exit permits were allowed through the gate. But once inside they could hand to the Netherlands representatives requests from other Jews who also wanted to emigrate.

Vysovs were normally sent directly from Israel to their recipients in the Soviet Union by ordinary mail. This procedure was risky not only in view of the notoriously inefficient Soviet mail system but also because the KGB routinely intercepted all incoming foreign mail as it did the outgoing. In accordance with the policy of the moment, KGB officials could then either send the *vysov* on to its destination or confiscate it. They could also call in and question the recipient about his intentions or his real relationship with his "relative" in Israel.

The safest way to transmit *vysovs* might have been to send them all by diplomatic pouch to the Netherlands embassy, which could then have mailed them locally. Domestic mail might, of course, also be checked, but the chances of safe arrival were better. Israeli and Netherlands authorities decided, however, that there were other objections to this procedure. First of all, the demand for *vysovs* from Israel became a flood during the early 1970s. Tens of thousands of these documents were dispatched by Israeli authorities. The small staff of the Netherlands embassy in Moscow was not equipped to handle such a flood. The second and decisive objection against sending all *vysovs* through the embassy was that wide-scale use of that procedure would again enable the Soviet authorities to accuse embassy staff of actively promoting emigration to Israel. The Netherlands authorities felt that distributing invitations from Israel did not fall within the normal exercise of consular interest protection.

For a short time in the 1970s the embassy did issue so-called official *vyzovs* to Jewish citizens who could not find relatives in Israel. These were direct invitations to come to Israel without relation to, or mention of, any relatives.[23] As these invitations went straight against the principle of family reunion, they should have been more objectionable to the Soviets than handing out brochures about Israel. Curiously, they were accepted by OVIR, but not for long. More than four years later the

Dutch official who had been head of the Consular Section at the time was accused by name in a televised report of "issuing *vysovs* without checking whether the inviters had any relation with the invited." It was, explained the head of OVIR, "all part of a dishonest campaign mounted by the rulers in Tel Aviv."[24] The embassy again concluded that it should not lend its intermediary in publicly distributing *vysovs*.

All the same, *vysovs* constituted a large part of the work in the embassy. Requests for invitations were received from visitors and passed on to Jerusalem by diplomatic pouch. Some—and sometimes many— *vysovs* were also returned along that route. The embassy would not mail them to recipients but handle them in the same way as the requests had come in: they were given to visitors who had already received their exit permits[25] and who would then pass them on to relatives or neighbors. Sometimes foreigners living in Moscow would act as go-betweens.[26] In a few cases the domestic mail service was used, but only if the recipient expressly requested it and could not be reached in any other way.

Vysovs were valid for one year. Usually Soviet authorities accepted the embassy's extending or correcting them or adding new spouses or children.

Loans

Just before leaving Moscow in June 1968, the Israeli ambassador had authorized his Netherlands colleague to advance money to emigrants for their travel expenses. A loan was allowed up to the cost of one-way transportation by air to Vienna.[27] Since very few exit permits were granted at the time, there was as yet no great demand for loans either. But when the Soviet authorities began issuing exit permits on a larger scale in 1971, they decided to make the recipients pay heavily for the privilege. According to a ukase of September 29, 1970, as of October 7 a fee of 400 rubles was to be charged for an exit permit, including the application fee, and another 500 rubles for the rejection of citizenship (see Chapter 2). Every adult emigrant thus had to pay 900 rubles. Some were able to scrape these enormous sums together by selling valuables, but almost immediately one would-be emigrant asked for help at the embassy.[28] Israeli authorities then authorized a loan covering these new expenses.[29] The embassy at first thought that no general authorization to grant such loans would be necessary.[30] But with the "first wave" of emigrants in the spring of 1971, Israeli authorities allowed financial support for payment of exit documents without preliminary authorization.[31]

This procedure clearly put an additional burden on the consular officers: they now had to decide who did and who did not need a loan. "You could not—and should not—honor every request in full," remembers one of them. "But which one deserved money and how much?"[32] There was no mechanism in Israel for the recovery of the loans, and when this fact became known in the Soviet Union the requests naturally multiplied.[33] In 1972 the Netherlands ambassador in Moscow complained that it was becoming increasingly difficult to administer the loans properly. He had decided to restrict them to exceptional cases.[34] In their reply the Israelis asked that he continue giving loans as before, pending further decisions. The ambassador then discussed this question in The Hague with Dutch and Israeli officials and stuck to his guns: the volume of the loans could be slightly increased but they would remain limited. Meanwhile the announced restrictions had had their effect, and demand tapered off to a "manageable" level. [35] Shortly thereafter the introduction of the diploma fee in August 1972 caused huge new problems (see Chapter 6). In 1974 the embassy found it necessary to emphasize to applicants that no loans could be given for the payment of alimony, for new clothes, for transport of household goods, or for the purchase of foreign currency.[36]

Transmission of Documents

Another task for the Netherlands embassy was caused by the restrictive policy of Soviet customs regarding personal documents emigrants wanted to take with them. It was routine for the custom officials to confiscate all such documents, not only private letters but even birth and death certificates and school and university diplomas. Soon after undertaking the interest representation, the Netherlands embassy was asked to transmit documents by diplomatic pouch to Israel. It agreed and continued to do so up to the end. The Hague did stipulate that this service had to be restricted to official documents and could not extend to personal letters, mementos, or scientific texts. Accepted documents would be sent in sealed diplomatic pouches to The Hague, where they were handed unopened to the Israeli embassy there for transmission to Israel. If the owner had gone to the United States or elsewhere, the Israelis would send the documents on to the Israeli consulates in the country of destination. Delays were unavoidable, and Dutch consular representatives in several countries received inquiries and complaints. Those had to be referred to the Israelis.

If Soviet citizens were allowed to enter the Netherlands embassy in Moscow, they were, of course, checked by the militia guarding it. Their bags were opened, and anything the militia did not like was confiscated. But there was no body search, and often the same documents that the customs would have confiscated were allowed to be brought to the embassy for safe transmission to a foreign country. Soviet authorities were well aware of this practice, as local assistants made regular reports to them, but they never stopped it; this was one of the anomalous situations typical for the Soviet state. On their side, Dutch officials tried to carry out their instructions but did not always have the time to check the precise contents of the great volume of documents presented to them. Moreover, their tendency was toward lenience, since they recognized how important it was for an emigrant to dispose of the doctoral thesis or a scientific work he had written in the Soviet Union. So Dutch officials sometimes let important writings or manuscripts slip through.

In 1976 this practice led to a curious incident. An emigrant succeeded in handing over some writings, belonging, not to him, but to the Roman Catholic Cardinal Slipiy, who had been arrested by the Soviet authorities but later released and allowed to leave the country. The Ministry of Foreign Affairs in The Hague was troubled when the Vatican asked for information about the cardinal's papers and asked the Moscow embassy for an explanation. The embassy replied that documents applicants would need for the exercise of their profession in Israel were generally accepted and that strict control was not always possible.[37] A letter personally signed by the secretary general of the ministry followed, expressing surprise. The applicant, said The Hague, was not Jewish, and in any case use of the diplomatic pouch for nonofficial documents could be allowed only within the context of official duties, that is, the representation of Israel. Only indispensable documents could be transmitted and no other papers, except with special permission from the ministry. A later cable repeated that using the pouch for writings presented as scientific treatises but actually of a different nature was not allowed. The papers of the cardinal were retrieved in Israel and returned to The Hague, where it became clear that all the ado had been made about two completely innocent scrapbooks.[38] They were finally delivered to the Vatican.[39]

Out of fear of jeopardizing the task of the embassy, the official attitude remained very restrictive. Even letters addressed to the Israeli government by Soviet citizens were not sent on. It was painful to discover that as late as December 1986 a letter from the well-known Refusenik and activist Josef Begun, addressed to the Israeli prime minister, Yitzhak Shamir, and transmitted by the ambassador in Moscow to the Ministry of Foreign Affairs in The Hague, had not been delivered but remained in the file in The Hague. The diplomatic courier service is not meant for private correspondence, but transmission of letters and petitions from private citizens to a government that the embassy represents would seem to fall well within the normal framework of interest representation. The Hague was overly cautious here. On the other hand, even its strong injunctions do not seem to have altered the lenient attitude of many Dutch officials in Moscow regarding the transmission of documents. Several of them also took personal letters and manuscripts of Jewish authors along with them when they went on leave.[40]

Priyom

People wanting to transmit papers would naturally try to hand them personally to the Dutch consul or a Dutch assistant. Despite the fact that the consul held a *priyom*, or receiving hour, every afternoon and saw as many applicants as he could, there were sometimes complaints that applicants were not received personally by a Dutch official. "Once inside the embassy, the 'gate of freedom,'" reported the embassy in 1973, "emigrants are disappointed when they are still faced by Russians."[41] But with several hundred applicants appearing every week it was obviously impossible to allow all of them to meet with a Dutch official. The ambassador assured the Ministry of Foreign Affairs that anyone who really should see a Dutch official was given the opportunity.

Other complaints were made regarding the attitude of the local assistants, and in fact they sometimes did treat applicants in the Russian rather than the Dutch manner. But their workload and the cramped quarters in the Consular Section should not be forgotten. Many Dutch consular officials afterward expressed satisfaction with the efficiency and industry of their Soviet assistants.[42]

Those who were received by the consul often wanted just some attention. Others needed help finding a hotel room in Moscow, for which the consul could issue standard forms, or wanted information about relatives in Israel. There were also more tragic stories and instances in which assistance was desperately needed. Sometimes mistakes made by the Soviet officials in exit papers caused one or more family members to have to stay behind.[43] Exit permits might, for example, have been refused to sons who were almost of military draft age. The consul might be asked to support requests for an exit permit to travel to Israel for a visit to a seriously ill relative or to attend a funeral, or for an entry permit for relatives in Israel to come to the Soviet Union for the same reasons. OVIR would routinely deny such requests, and the Dutch consul might take up such cases with the lower echelons of the Consular Department of MID. The subject of the conversation had to be mentioned beforehand, and the Soviet official would then be completely informed about it from his side before the conversation started. Bringing up another case during the same meeting would lead to the cold statement that "the conversation was finished."[44] Former emigrants living in Israel would practically never be allowed, until the late 1980s, to return for compassionate reasons, and others only rarely. The basic cruelty of the Soviet system showed very clearly in these cases.

Depending on the policy of the moment, smaller difficulties such as the legalization of documents or the shipping of luggage could sometimes be quietly solved at this low level.[45] But all demarches having to do with Refuseniks and prisoners had to be made at a higher level.

Demarches

Diplomatic actions could be taken only at MID: no other Soviet authority would accept contact with a foreign diplomat. Steps by the ambassador or his deputy in behalf of Jewish prisoners or Jews who had been refused exit permits, or whose exit permit had been canceled, were invariably met with indignation. These actions, it was always claimed, concerned Soviet citizens and therefore constituted interference in the internal affairs of the Soviet Union. The Dutch diplomat would then answer that he was speaking out of "humanitarian concern" only.[46]

During the 1970s such diplomatic demarches were undertaken exclusively at the request of the Israeli authorities within the framework of the interest representation. (The Dutch demarche carried out during the Leningrad Trial was the single exception; see Chapter 1). The Dutch diplomat made this situation clear at the outset. Although requests were received in The Hague for representations to be made with Soviet authorities in behalf of Jewish victims of the regime in the name of the Netherlands itself, the Ministry of Foreign Affairs always refused. It was thought best not to irritate the Soviet authorities[47] and to avoid endangering the embassy's work on behalf of Jewish emigrants.[48] Another consideration was that the Dutch government was concerned with those who were persecuted or refused as a whole, so that individual cases should not be mentioned.

A typical instance occurred in 1972 when the Netherlands minister of foreign affairs, then W. K. N. Schmelzer, visited Israel and heard of two sad cases there. In one a husband, in the other a wife, was unable to join a spouse in Israel. The minister intended to take these cases up with the Soviet foreign minister, Andrei Gromyko, who was about to visit the Netherlands.[49] He also considered whether to speak about a letter he received from a Dutch professor in physical chemistry who had pleaded for an exit permit for a Jewish colleague in the Soviet Union.[50] But ministry officials dissuaded him, maintaining that these cases "fell outside the representation of Israeli interests." The two cases in Israel "were particularly delicate" since "in Soviet eyes objectionable acts" had been committed.[51] One of these concerned the failure of a violon- cellist to return from a trip to the West—a legitimate exercise of his right to freedom of movement. Had this case occurred after the signing of the Helsinki Final Act in 1975, the minister might have decided dif- ferently. But as Schmelzer remembers, he took into consideration in 1972 that the preparations for the Helsinki agreements had begun and that the intention was to bring human rights into that process. He concluded that the framework for Helsinki would not be advanced by discussion of individual cases in which the Netherlands was itself not involved and about which the background was insufficiently known. He still believes that it was wise for him to have followed the departmental advice at the time.[52]

Schmelzer's successor as foreign minister, Max van der Stoel, paid a visit to Moscow in 1974 but did not discuss any individual humanitar- ian cases. Yet Van der Stoel showed a lively interest in human rights questions, and a year later he asked the ambassador in Moscow whether anything could be done for a Soviet Jew who had been condemned to eight years of imprisonment on charges of corruption. Would this case fall exclusively under the interest representation, or could general humanitarian concerns serve as a basis for the Netherlands authorities to approach Soviet authorities?[53] The ambassador answered:

> I see no humanitarian motive for the Netherlands to approach
> the Soviets other than a very general one that would apply
> equally to others who are in jail and have relatives abroad.

I cannot answer the question whether he can be blamed for
the corruption of which he is accused. We have to be particularly careful because of the interest representation. The man
in question is a Soviet citizen.[54]

The conclusion reached in The Hague was that, since the case concerned
a Soviet citizen, a demarche would be interference in the internal affairs
of the Soviet Union and might harm both the victim himself and the
interest representation.

Demarches in favor of Refuseniks, except at the request of the Israeli
government, also remained excluded. An internal ministry memorandum
of August 15, 1977, made this very clear: "For over ten years it has been
standing practice that no initiatives are taken by the Netherlands in
order to obtain exit permits for Soviet citizens. There is no reason nor
latitude to deviate from this line of conduct."[55] In the name of the
Israelis, however, demarches were made regularly, for example for Sharansky.[56] Purely Dutch demarches on humanitarian grounds did not start
until the early 1980s.

Other Paperwork

Besides the work already mentioned, the embassy handled a great many
requests from former Soviet citizens now in Israel. Copies of legal documents or certificates from the Soviet civil registry were required, and
some hoped that Soviet pensions could be paid to them in Israel. Even
licenses for the transport of mortal remains were sometimes requested
when the last wish of a Jew had been to be buried in Israel (they could
be provided only after permission had been obtained from the Israeli
authorities). Other requests concerned original certificates of labor, marriage, birth, education, and invalidity, Soviet driver's licenses, and copies
of university diplomas.[57] For this purpose the embassy would engage
the services of a collective of lawyers, *Injurkollegia*, in Moscow, which
had been formed to represent foreigners and former Soviet citizens in
legal matters, undoubtedly with the permission of the authorities.[58] Its
work was slow but not without success; sometimes very old certificates
were unearthed in distant corners of the Soviet Union. Pensions for
disabilities, however, could be transferred to Israel only in exceptional
cases. Soviet pension law did not provide for such pensions to be paid
to persons who had moved abroad after October 1, 1958, except where

the disability was due to accidents at work caused by the applicant's occupation.[59]

Confidentiality of the Work for Israel

The Ministry of Foreign Affairs in The Hague maintained and demanded the highest confidentiality for the work done on behalf of Israel. It was an axiom that it was up to the Israeli authorities to decide which activities undertaken in the framework of the representation should or should not be published. No information about these activities should therefore be provided from the Dutch side. Dutch officials went to great lengths, for instance, to keep secret the number of visas issued within a given period. Such information was often sought by the press and by other embassies. When foreign journalists discovered that they could deduce how many Israeli visas had been issued by checking the serial numbers, the embassy immediately started a new series.[60] When it was—much later—discovered that the German Ministry of Foreign Affairs disposed of data on the number of visas issued, the Netherlands embassy in Moscow had to apologize to the ministry: numbers had indeed been given "on a confidential basis" to the German and American embassies. "The practice would be stopped immediately."[61]

One wonders whether such secrecy was really necessary. There are no requests for secrecy from the Israeli authorities in any of the files. The number of emigrants was registered by the Jewish Agency in Vienna and monitored by the International Committee on Migration in Geneva. It has been supposed that Dutch officials were trying to head off Arab reactions whenever the numbers of visas for Israel were high,[62] but the Arabs were certainly well aware of what was going on and could obtain figures from the International Committee on Migration. The secrecy of the numbers made it difficult, on the other hand, for Dutch officials in Moscow to explain what they were doing and to maintain good relations with their Western colleagues and the foreign press. All in all, the need for secrecy on numbers seems to have been exaggerated.

Still, the standing instructions that information about the work done for Israel in general should come from the Israelis and not from the Dutch had a reasonable foundation: they were given out of courtesy for the Israeli authorities and because questions of internal Israeli policy might be involved. Doubt is possible on the question of whether this secrecy was not sometimes used too quickly and too easily to head off questions from parliamentarians, press representatives, or ordinary citizens about what actions the Netherlands authorities themselves could undertake in behalf of Jewish dissidents and Refuseniks.[63]

Conclusion

All in all, during the 1970s Israeli interests in Moscow were efficiently represented by the Netherlands embassy there. Although it then was the Dutch policy to restrict any contacts between the embassy and the Soviet Jews and not to extend the work beyond a strict interpretation of the task, private contacts with the Jewish community did exist at a lower level outside the embassy. And while the fear of harming the interest representation generally precluded any action in favor of Refuseniks or prisoners on behalf of the Netherlands itself, demarches in the name of Israel regarding Refuseniks and prisoners were frequently carried out. The embassy further extended help by transmitting requests for invitations from Israel, transporting documents by diplomatic pouch, and providing loans to indigent applicants.

Early on, Soviet authorities issued a stern warning to the embassy not to "make propaganda" for emigration to Israel. This warning had a restraining influence on the activities of the embassy well into the 1980s. It is nevertheless likely that Soviet authorities preferred to see a small embassy executing the task of issuing Israeli visas efficiently whenever they decided it was in their interest to allow Jews to emigrate.

Some disputes took place between the Israeli and Dutch authorities, especially over the handing out of Israeli citizenship certificates. They did not, however, threaten the excellent relations between the two governments at any time.

6

An Amazing Spectacle:
The Jackson-Vanik Amendment

In 1972 a new player suddenly intervened in the relationship between the United States (the White House and the Department of State) and the Soviet Union—the United States Congress. A Democratic senator from the state of Washington, Henry "Scoop" Jackson, introduced an amendment that he later attached to a Trade Reform Act the president had sent to Congress for approval. This act would have authorized the president to grant most-favored-nation status to, among other countries, the Soviet Union. The senator tagged on an amendment prohibiting such a grant to "non-market-economy countries" unless they gave assurances on a liberal emigration policy.

Thus the legislative branch of the American government exercised its constitutional power in foreign affairs. After the amendment had been ignored for a time by the administration, Congress subsequently forced the secretary of state to negotiate on its behalf with the Soviet government. When this negotiation yielded a result that seemed satisfactory to the administration, Senator Jackson declared it insufficient. Another amendment introduced by Senator Adlai E. Stevenson III of Illinois then restricted the authorization of the U.S. Export-Import Bank to provide large credits to the Soviets, thereby throwing a second wrench into the bilateral relations between the two countries.

The whole proceeding was hard to understand for anyone not familiar with the constitutional framework and legislative practices in the United States—let alone for the Kremlin. The Soviets first reacted angrily and finally rejected the whole deal: they refused to provide the explicit assurances regarding emigration demanded by the amendment and lost the promised trade agreement, including most-favored-nation status from the United States. Jewish emigration from the Soviet Union went down.

This amazing spectacle needs to be analyzed here, since it exercised a large influence on the whole process of the Jewish emigration from the Soviet Union (and from other countries) over a long period of time.

The Diploma Fee

The difficulties began with an incredible blunder by the Kremlin: the introduction of a tax on the exit of Soviet Jews.

The summit between Presidents Richard Nixon and Leonid Brezhnev in Moscow in May 1972 was probably the peak of détente.[1] Henry Kissinger called it "the culmination of our four years of insistence on linkage."[2] Both sides had found it in their interest to relax tension and sign two major accords: the Strategic Arms Limitation Treaty (SALT I), and the Principles of International Conduct. The question of Jewish emigration did not figure prominently on the agenda of the summit, although Nelson Rockefeller (who himself had not been present) is said to have reported that an "understanding" was reached according to which emigration of Jews would reach 35,000 per year.[3] The emigration had increased to more than 14,000 in 1971 and was to exceed 30,000 in 1972.

The Soviets showed themselves very interested in a commercial treaty that would give the Soviet Union most-favored-nation status (MFN). The term is loftier than its content: it means not much more than that the country in question receives the same rates of import duties in the other country as most other trading partners already have. Yet the Soviets hoped to be able to export more to the United States and especially to qualify for export loans from the Export-Import Bank. In Moscow in July 1972, U.S. Secretary of Commerce Peter G. Peterson reached virtual agreement with the Soviets on the text of a trade pact in which MFN and credits were promised in return for a partial repayment by the Soviets of the Lend-Lease debt from World War II.[4] It would be implemented on the basis of the Trade Reform Bill pending before Congress.

But the agreement was put into jeopardy when on August 3, 1972, the Soviet government decided to levy a heavy tax on any would-be emigrant who had a higher education. The wording of the decree was kept secret for several months, but a Jewish emigrant in Kiev succeeded in copying it, and soon Lishka director Nehamiah Levanon supplied the text to Israeli and American officials.[5] The decree applied to all emigrants, not just

Jews, but as a group, Jews had by far the highest percentage of university graduates. This diploma fee[6] began at 4,500 rubles (for a graduate in the humanities) and went up to 19,400 rubles (for a doctor of sciences).[7] These fees—enormous for a Soviet citizen—came on top of the already high fees charged for exit permits and for the renunciation of citizenship.

How could the Soviet leaders have made such a mistake? To introduce a measure like this just after the success of the summit and at the moment when the U.S. Congress was taking up the Trade Reform Bill and the ratification of the SALT agreement, both urgently desired by the Soviet Union, looked like sheer madness. President Nixon and his national security adviser, Henry Kissinger, were "dumbfounded." The Soviet ambassador in Washington, Anatoly Dobrynin, who now says that he was "both surprised and disturbed," and "never received an explanation,"[8] went to Kissinger to tell him that the decision was made not in the Politburo but by the relevant ministry on its own. Supposedly a midlevel functionary had made a routine decision mechanically ratified by the relevant technical minister. Brezhnev would later call it "a bureaucratic bungle."[9] In the first book of his memoirs Kissinger calls this explanation "unlikely but not totally impossible." "Foreign governments, particularly totalitarian ones," he claims, "always appear more homogeneous than one's own but may not be."[10] But later on in his second book, Kissinger rejects that possibility: "The Soviet system does not work that way."[11]

Ambassador Dobrynin has now revealed what had really happened in Moscow. According to him the Soviet Ministry of Education had proposed to seek a "refund" for the cost of the free education the emigrants had received. Apparently this idea had been under discussion for quite some time: the Netherlands embassy in Moscow had reported rumors about it more than a year before, in July 1971.[12] When the proposal reached the Kremlin in the summer of 1972, Brezhnev and Gromyko were vacationing at the Black Sea and the chief ideologist of the Politburo, Mikhail Suslov, saw his chance. He had always been reluctant to accept the new, more liberal, emigration policy, and he now made sure that the new tax was accepted.[13] It was finally confirmed by the government, then led by Kosygin, on August 14, 1972.[14]

Kissinger supposes that the decision was a panicky reaction to Anwar Sadat's expulsion of Soviet troops from Egypt[15] or an attempt to generate foreign exchange.[16] But those were not considerations for Suslov or the Ministry of Education. More likely it was an attempt to control the size of the emigration, especially to stem the departure of increasing numbers of highly educated specialists.[17] The claim that departing Jews constituted a brain drain was repeatedly made by Soviet leaders, even by Mikhail Gorbachev. At face value this claim was absurd, since Jews constituted not much more than 1 percent of the total population of the Soviet Union. But several surveys have shown that about one-third of the Jewish emigrants had a higher education. Moreover, these well-educated Jews were concentrated in the cities and then in a few specialties such as medicine, mathematics, biology, and music—for the simple reason that numerous other occupations were not open to them. So their loss may have been keenly felt in certain institutes of research and higher education. Most Jewish leaders remained convinced, however, that the purpose of the new fee was to stop not a brain drain but Jewish emigration altogether. One thing is certain: if fear of a brain drain was behind the diploma fee (certainly a compliment for the Jewish intellectuals!), the proponents totally misjudged its impact in the West.

The diploma fee, in fact, created an uproar in the Western world, especially among the Jews. On August 23, 1972, Prime Minister Golda Meir made a statement to the Knesset. She pulled no punches:

> Like a bolt out of the blue the news came upon us of the new and heavy oppression inflicted on the Jews in Soviet Russia. The Soviet authorities resolved that every Jewish intellectual who wishes to come to Israel be compelled to make an exorbitant payment—a head-tax—as a personal ransom in exchange for the right to leave for Israel and a penalty for their educational achievements. . . . A cruel and shameful decree.

The Knesset adopted a resolution urging the government of the Soviet Union to repeal "this shameful decree." It also appealed "to all governments, parliaments and international institutions and organizations as well as to the enlightened public opinion in all countries, to work towards the abolition of the head-tax imposed on the Jews in the Soviet Union who wish to return to their historic homeland."[18] This second appeal was to find an enormous response. It was the beginning of actions by numerous Jewish as well as non-Jewish organizations, committees of academicians, scientists, doctors, and others in almost all countries of the Western world. Official bodies like the Council of Europe later joined in, and eventually legislatures in many countries prodded into action the governments that had until then preferred quiet diplomacy. The Jackson-Vanik Amendment was to be the sharpest parliamentary response of all.

In Washington, Jewish leaders went to see Secretary of State William Rogers soon after the new tax was announced. He gave them another example of the old school of thought. "In difficult cases in the past," the secretary pointed out, "it had turned out that the best course and the most effective course had been to refrain from making strong public statements on behalf of the government but rather to work quietly with a definite aim in mind." In past cases he had resisted making strong public statements and had been proven correct. He added that if the Soviets felt that the United States was trying to take advantage of their situation in a political way, their reaction was never helpful and a cold war "incident" might result. In view of the generally good U.S.-Soviet relations, Rogers thought it was important not to eliminate the possibility of negotiation by permitting an open confrontation to develop.[19]

The Jewish leaders themselves were hesitant. A large part of the established leadership objected to the notion of manipulating Soviet-American trade relations for the sake of Soviet Jews, fearing that Jews in the Soviet Union might suffer additional harm as a result. As always, they were also looking toward the American-Israeli relationship, for support of the American administration was vital for Israel. Jacob Stein, chairman of the Conference of Presidents of Major American Jewish Organizations, and Richard Maass, chairman of the National Conference on Soviet Jewry, asserted that the Jewish organizations were under considerable pressure. They had tried to calm their members and to reassure them that the administration would take up the question. Under the circumstances, they thought it was essential that a strong statement of official U.S. concern should be made.[20]

In September 1972, President Nixon ordered the State Department to call in the Soviet ambassador. Dobrynin was on leave, but Assistant Secretary Walt Stoessel called in the chargé d'affaires Yuli Vorontsov and told him that the diploma fee had begun to have an effect on U.S.-Soviet relations and might make it more difficult, especially in Congress, to move ahead on matters "we both feel are beneficial and important to our relations."[21] Quiet diplomacy was at work with fairly strong language, but in public there was prudence and no statement.

Israel's ambassador in Washington, Yitzhak Rabin, was equally reticent in public. As late as March 1973, he still insisted that "U.S.

interference in Soviet internal affairs—no matter how warranted by the injustice of the exorbitant emigration-tax—would be counter-productive."[22] Rabin was clearly trying not to antagonize the American administration, but the head of Lishka, Nehamiah Levanon, was already at work behind the scenes with the Jewish organizations to support the amendment.[23] The more militant of the Jewish organizations working for the Jews in the Soviet Union—the Union of Councils for Soviet Jews and the Student Struggle for Soviet Jews—had no hesitations at all and "went all-out."[24] Jackson himself spoke to the National Conference on Soviet Jewry on September 26, 1972. The conference endorsed his approach, but the American Jewish Congress did not.[25]

Meanwhile in Moscow the Netherlands embassy faced a barrage of questions about the new tax; Soviet Jews wanted to know if they could get loans for the amounts now needed. Jewish organizations and the Israeli government agonized over their ability to provide the necessary funds, as well as the desirability of doing so. Within the U.S. Department of State there was a similar discussion on whether the United States could and should "help pay" for the tax. Funds might have been available under the Migration and Refugee Assistance Act of 1962 but could not, it was thought, be used to cover the costs within the Soviet Union. Money could be provided, however, to the Israeli Jewish Agency for other expenses, which would free other funds for the diploma fee.[26] But in the end both the private agencies and the U.S. as well as the Israeli governments decided against providing the enormous sums of money that would have been needed.

Levanon went to The Hague on August 25, 1972, and explained that the Israeli government had made this decision for moral and financial reasons. The amount estimated would exceed $1 million per month, while there was no guarantee that the Soviet authorities would not increase their demands later. He asked that the Netherlands embassy be told to inform applicants—but only orally—that it had received no instructions from the Israeli authorities and could therefore not grant loans for payment of the diploma fee. There should be no public announcement.[27] The embassy was not happy with that instruction, for, as a cable explained, the resentment among the applicants would then be directed against the embassy. Would it not be better to say that the Israeli government had decided not to allow payments? The answer was ambiguous: "Please state that the embassy has only received instructions to grant loans in conformity with the existing practice." But now the chargé d'affaires knew what to do. "You can leave out the word 'only,'" he wrote on the incoming cable, "and if anyone asks who has given that instruction you can answer truthfully."[28]

The Amendment Takes Shape

Shortly after the news about the diploma fee had reached the West, some U.S. Senate staff members met to discuss it. As one of them recalled, "There was a lot of handwringing."[29] It was assumed that Soviet authorities wanted to reduce or even abolish Jewish emigration because it was running out of control. What could be done?

Richard Perle, assistant to Senator Jackson, came up with the idea of linking the emigration flow to the granting of MFN. Someone else proposed to link emigration flow with credits as well. These proposals changed the tone of the meeting: here was something the Senate could do. Perle quickly drew up a first draft of an amendment.[30] He was fairly certain that Senator Jackson would be prepared to introduce it, because Jackson was already working on his own response to the May summit. One writer has explained, "He thought that SALT was bad and that the plans for trade were moving at an unguardedly rapid pace."[31] On September 27, 1972, Jackson announced in the Senate that he would propose an amendment. It would, he said,

> establish a direct legislative link between that status [MFN] and other trade and credit concessions, on the one hand, and the freedom to emigrate without the payment of prohibitive taxes amounting to ransom, on the other. . . . No country would be eligible for MFN or to participate in U.S. credit and credit-and-investment guarantee programs unless that country permits its citizens the opportunity to emigrate to the country of their choice. . . . The President would be required to judge and report in detail upon the compliance with this condition. [32]

Jackson introduced his amendment on October 4, 1972. The operative paragraph read:

> To assure the continued dedication of the United States to fundamental human rights . . . no non-market economy

country shall be eligible to receive most-favored-nation treatment or to participate in any program of the Government of
the United States which extends credits or credit guarantees,
directly or indirectly, during the period beginning with the
date on which the President of the United States determines
that such country

1. denies its citizens the right or opportunity to emigrate
   to the country of their choice;
2. imposes more than a nominal tax on emigration or on
   the visas or other documents required for emigration,
   for any purpose whatsoever; or
3. imposes more than nominal tax, levy, fine, fee, or other
   charge on any citizen as a consequence of the desire of
   such citizen to emigrate to the country of his choice,
   and ending on the date on which the President determines that such country is no longer in violation of
   paragraph (1), (2) or (3).[33]

The amendment had no less than seventy-two cosponsors, although
President Nixon had indicated through his spokesman that he was
opposed to it.

In the House, Representative Charles Vanik of Ohio introduced a
similar amendment on October 10, with an interesting additional feature—a limit of $50 on the fee the Soviets could charge for an exit per-
mit without losing MFN. The amendment was adopted by a voice vote,
but in the conference committee, where differences between the House
and Senate versions were negotiated, this stipulation was eliminated.

The growing congressional action worried the administration enough
to cause it to discuss the problem with the Soviets at a high level.
Kissinger had gone to Moscow in September and had finalized the agreement on repayment of the Lend-Lease debt ($722 million over thirty
years) and the text of the trade agreement in which MFN and credit
facilities were promised in return. On October 2 and 3, 1972, Nixon and
Kissinger discussed the emigration question with Soviet Foreign Minister
Andrei Gromyko at the presidential retreat Camp David. Later that
afternoon, Secretary of State Rogers met again with the Jewish leaders to
tell them of a "favorable response" by the Soviet Union. According to
published reports, Gromyko had indicated that the education tax would
"fade away."[34]

The president had meanwhile decided no longer to oppose Jackson's amendment in the Senate. After all, the elections were coming up in November, and Nixon wanted no more confrontation. Besides, he reasoned, the amendment would surely die when the Senate adjourned. And so it did. But Jackson did not give up. He reintroduced the amendment in March 1973, and Vanik then proposed the same text in the House.

The Amendment Becomes a Political Issue by Itself

Kissinger wrote in his memoirs: "Up to a point Jackson's efforts and ours complemented each other. But gradually his amendment became for him an end in itself. . . . Once it was passed, it was no longer useful as leverage." This remark is vintage Kissinger. His whole foreign policy was built on leverage, on keeping as many carrots and sticks in the air as possible that could be pulled down by the great magician at will. In that he was frustrated by the perseverance of Senator Jackson. "He wanted an issue," says Kissinger, "not a solution."[35] That judgment may be unfair, but it is true that the senator went doggedly on even after it became clear in the spring of 1973 that the diploma fee was in fact no longer collected and when, later, Kissinger obtained substantial Soviet concessions. On the other hand, many Jewish activists were—and are—convinced that the most important thing accomplished by the amendment was that it "put the Jewish emigration from the Soviet Union on the map" and focused both Congress and the administration, and in turn other Western governments, on the issue of freedom of movement.[36] For them that was the issue.

Toward the end of 1972 the diploma fee did indeed begin to fade away. On December 27, the Soviet minister of the interior gave an interview to the press agency Novosti in which he reconfirmed the need for a diploma fee: "The Soviet Union does not intend to act as a philanthropist." But at the same time he announced important changes: men over age sixty and women over age fifty-five were exempt, and for the others the number of years during which they had already worked would be taken into account. It is interesting that Assistant Secretary of State Stoessel, in his conversation with chargé Vorontsov, had mentioned that no allowance seemed to be made for work performed following education and that the fees seemed to be applied even to persons in retirement. The first Soviet concessions were made on exactly those points, although the Soviets pretended they had been in the law all along.[37]

When the ukase of August 3, 1972, was finally published on January 23, 1973, it did contain the exemption the minister had mentioned. The Netherlands ambassador in Moscow correctly observed that if these reductions had been part of the diploma fees from the first, too much tax had been levied for five months. It therefore seemed more likely that the reduction had been decided upon later, but antedated to avoid the impression that a concession had been made to pressure from the West. The ambassador added that the reductions had been applied everywhere since January 15.[38]

On March 11, 1973, George Shultz, U.S. secretary of the treasury, arrived in Moscow to discuss "problems" with the trade agreement. He had a personal meeting with Brezhnev and conveyed a clear message: progress in trade and credit depended on the liberalization of emigration. At the same time Shultz extended a loan from the Export-Import Bank for $101 million. This time the strategy worked. Within a week after his departure, as from March 19, the diploma fee was no longer levied. This was Schulz's first success with regard to the Jewish emigration. Many more would follow when he became secretary of state in the 1980s.[39]

American embassy officials informed their Dutch counterparts of the Brezhnev-Shultz meeting and commented that Brezhnev had personally intervened both because he had staked his political future on détente and in view of the Soviet conflict with China. He depended on the West for economic, technical, and financial progress and had to weigh these potential benefits against a loss of prestige and criticism by hard-liners. The financial gain that would come through the trade agreements, said the U.S. embassy, was worth many times the diploma fee.[40] It was understood that the tax was suspended indefinitely, although the law would remain on the books.[41]

Senator Jackson had not waited for the result of Shultz's trip. On March 15, 1973, he formally reintroduced his amendment, now with seventy-three senators cosponsoring. At that time Jackson stated he would not be satisfied with the canceling of the diploma fee only. "The fact is," he said, "that the so-called education tax was only one small part of an elaborate system of threats, obstacles, reprisals and intimidation designed to prevent Soviet citizens from exercising the right to free emigration."[42] Jewish leaders visiting the Department of State on March 28 now stressed that it was absolutely essential to get the Jackson-Vanik Amendment on the books as the only guarantee against Soviet backsliding. American Jews had not pushed Jackson on the issue; the initiative was his. But the Jewish community had been impressed by the effectiveness of the proposed Jackson amendment, as it had already caused the Soviets to react.[43]

On April 10, President Nixon submitted to Congress the Trade Reform Bill, which would authorize him to negotiate with the nations of the world for a mutual lowering of trade barriers. Senator Jackson immediately attached his amendment to this bill. A week later Nixon and Kissinger met with Jackson and other senators and tried to convince them not to insist further on the amendment, reading to them an "Official communication of the Soviet Union." Kissinger relates that it contained the contents of a private message to Nixon from Brezhnev of March 30 that Kissinger had put in the form of an "official statement" of the Soviet government. It confirmed that the diploma fee had been suspended. Kissinger had added a sentence according to which "any interpretation implying the existence of a time limit [attached to the exemption of the fee] would not correspond to the position of the Soviet Government."[44] In other words, the fee would not be reintroduced. This statement had been cleared with Soviet Ambassador Dobrynin, who had, of course, asked for guidance from Moscow. Dobrynin emphasizes how much importance his authorities apparently attached to U.S.-Soviet relations on the eve of the second Brezhnev-Nixon summit, because he was authorized to approve the statement and to allow it to be sent to Congress as an official Soviet declaration.[45] Kissinger drew the same conclusion.[46] This episode in a sense marked the beginning of tripartite negotiations among Jackson, with other senators and their staffs, and the Soviet authorities through Kissinger's intermediary. But it was the beginning only, for Jackson was not satisfied: "Mr. President, if you believe that, you are being hoodwinked."[47] Jackson demanded that the Soviets give assurances not only on the diploma fee; they also had to guarantee a minimum number of exit permits, and they had to ease emigration not only for Jews but for all nationalities.

For Jackson, these demands were in character; from the beginning he had insisted that his amendment was meant not only for Jews but that it had to have universal effect.[48] But Kissinger correctly remarks that "anyone even vaguely familiar with the Soviet system" knew that there was no chance whatever that such terms would be met.[49] Dobrynin also emphasizes that for the Soviet Union to commit itself publicly to a fixed number would imply that there was an unlimited mass of Soviet citizens eager to emigrate.[50] And, as Kissinger adds, there was literally no telling what would happen to the Soviet system if that kind of concession were made.[51] However, the Watergate scandal had exploded by that time, and the senators were not about to let up on a weakened administration. What should have been a fight over tactics—after all, both the senators and the administration wanted to increase Jewish emigration—instead became a ferocious battle of principles that would put the Jackson-Vanik Amendment, and thus the whole question of Jewish emigration from the Soviet Union, on the books—but fail to increase the flow of that emigration itself.

Tripartite Negotiations

After this meeting with Jackson, Kissinger clearly began to focus more intently on the amendment. In Moscow in May 1973, he obtained an informal promise from Brezhnev that Jews would continue to be permitted to emigrate at the current rate of 36,000 to 40,000 a year and the tax would remain suspended. Brezhnev also accepted a list of hardship cases.[52] In June the Soviet leader visited the United States for a summit. He faced many questions about Jewish emigration. Providing some obviously incorrect figures on the number of refusals, he generally failed to convince the proponents of the Jackson-Vanik Amendment.[53]

On September 14, 1973, the Soviet dissident Professor Andrei Sakharov sent an open letter to the U.S. Congress, urging passage of the amendment "to protect the right of emigration . . . and as a stimulus in the general efforts for human rights." Much later he would write that the amendment had to do with the observance by the Soviet Union of its international obligations and was therefore primarily a question of international and not just internal significance. It concerned, he said, the openness of society and international confidence and would give détente a healthier basis.[54] Kissinger, who had meanwhile become secretary of state, did not agree. "For a Secretary of State," he writes, "moral issues become transmuted into operational ones: in this case to what extent these conditions could be changed by overt American pressure."[55] Here is the same conviction that quiet diplomacy was more efficient than public pressure, especially where a prickly superpower was concerned. The difference between him and the "activists" was that he believed he had to keep all the contentious issues in play (he still needed the Soviets' help to end the war in Vietnam), while the activists in the United States as well as in Moscow could afford to focus on just the one issue that concerned them. Yet Kissinger himself went on to prove that at that moment the Soviet Union was susceptible to public pressure such as the Jackson-Vanik Amendment generated.

Although President Nixon put his prestige—or what was left of it—on the line in a letter to the House Speaker urging rejection of the amendment, the House passed it on December 11, 1973, by a huge majority: 319 to 80. Kissinger was at a disadvantage because of his frequent absences from Washington: he had to deal with many other questions relating to Vietnam, the Middle East, and other areas. He finally had a meeting with Jackson—the first in a series—on March 6, 1974. A week later Senators Abe Ribicoff of Connecticut and Jacob Javits of New York began to join in. Jackson suggested a written guarantee of 100,000 emigrants per year. Kissinger rightly called that figure out of the question. He then began to formulate a compromise solution which he first discussed with Gromyko in Moscow shortly afterward. To get around the reluctance of the Soviets to submit their internal practices to another country's review, Kissinger proposed that the United States would itself formulate its "understanding" of those practices in a letter, which was originally to be sent to the Soviet leadership but was later directly addressed to Senator Jackson. To Kissinger's own surprise, Gromyko did not reject this proposal, and during discussion in Geneva in April he grudgingly admitted that Kissinger could transmit to the senators the Soviet "criteria for emigration" and a figure of up to 45,000 emigrants per year "approximately as a trend."[56]

This amazing concession on the Soviet side must have been authorized by Brezhnev personally, since Gromyko would never have taken a decision in such a matter on his own. For the first time the Soviet leaders let it be known that they would try to reach a certain number of exit permits per year and that "harassment was contrary to Soviet law." This grudging admission by Gromyko meant that emigration would increase by 50 percent. Even if it would not fully eliminate harassment, it would henceforward make it much harder for the Soviets to refuse any discussion of this issue with the usual excuse that such discussion would constitute interference in their internal affairs. Kissinger is gallant enough to give some of the credit to Jackson.[57]

Although Kissinger showed a draft to Dobrynin in June, the letter to the senators would not be written until October. This time not only Kissinger's travels intervened, but Watergate came to a final head, ending with the resignation of President Nixon on August 9, 1974. The new

president, Gerald Ford, faced the question of the Jackson-Vanik Amend- ·
ment shortly after he took office. He told Dobrynin already on August
14 that there would never be a trade bill unless the Soviet Union accepted
some compromise on the amendment. Dobrynin answered in confidence
that the Soviet Union was willing to promise a Jewish emigration of
50,000 each year but would not sign any official document to that effect,
"lest it be used by Senator Jackson for his own political ends." The president received the three most involved senators the next day and relayed
to them Dobrynin's unofficial promise. They requested a letter from the
administration to "clarify matters."[58]

The Stevenson Amendment

In the meantime another issue had arisen that would become entangled
with the Jackson-Vanik Amendment and would eventually diminish the
Soviet interest in the trade bill. On June 30 the president's authority to
use the facilities of the Export-Import Bank came up for renewal in
Congress. This would ordinarily have been a routine action, but now,
during the height of the Watergate drama, it was not. Several senators
had become worried about what they thought was too much magna-
nimity on Nixon's part in granting credits to the Soviet Union. In particular, Senator Adlai Stevenson III, a democrat from Illinois and the
chairman of the subcommittee on International Finance, wanted to
"combat Nixon's way of pursuing détente." He felt that "paying for
détente in cash was not sound." He also regarded an amendment he had
proposed as an alternative to what he calls the "hard-handed approach"
of Jackson.[59]

The Stevenson Amendment set a ceiling of $300 million on total
Export-Import Bank loans to the Soviet Union over four years. Congress
would have to approve by concurrent resolution any higher limit, which
the president could set if he determined that an increase was in the
national interest. In other words, if the Soviet Union wanted an Export-
Import Bank loan of, for instance, thousands of millions of dollars for
grain imports—not an unusual amount—the request would lead to a
full-blown debate in Congress in which compliance with the Jackson-
Vanik Amendment, or even Soviet foreign policy decisions unrelated to
emigration, would undoubtedly play an important role.[60]

It is interesting that the two senators cosponsored each other's amendments although each side now says it had its doubts about the other's

proposal. Stevenson says he had reservations about Jackson's amendment and calls Jackson's assistant Richard Perle "the mastermind who wanted to undermine the Soviet Union by any means." Perle, in turn, says that Jackson supported Stevenson's amendment only because Stevenson claimed that he "had cleared it with Kissinger." Stevenson denies he made that claim and doubts that Kissinger's "clearance" would have carried much weight with Jackson. Kissinger says that he did not like the amendment but does not recall "with what vehemence" he told Stevenson so.[61] As he says when discussing the Stevenson amendment in his memoirs: "In a big government it is impossible to give equal attention to all issues simultaneously."[62]

The Senate now held hearings on both amendments, and finally in October the draft of the letters to be exchanged between Kissinger and Jackson was readied by Perle and Kissinger's assistant Helmut Sonnenfeldt. There were long negotiations over the number of emigrants that could be regarded as a "benchmark." Perle had started out from Jackson's 100,000, went down to 75,000, and says that the final compromise was 60,000, with which Kissinger agreed. The letters do not bear that out. Yet the figure of 60,000 appeared in the press as probably acceptable to the Soviets, and the Netherlands ambassador in Moscow was already worried whether his embassy could handle that many.[63] (It could and did in 1979.)

The Exchange of Letters

The letters were signed on October 18, 1974.[64] Kissinger was precise about what would be considered "harassment":

— Punitive actions against individuals seeking to emigrate from the USSR would be violations of Soviet laws and regulations and will therefore not be permitted by the government of the USSR. This applies to various kinds of intimidation or reprisal, such as, for example, the firing of a person from his job.

— No unreasonable or unlawful impediments will be placed in the way of persons desiring to make applications . . . such as interference with travel, communications, documentation, or other obstacles.

— Applications . . . will be processed in order of receipt . . . and without discrimination as regards place of residence, race, religion, national origin and professional status of the applicant. . . . [Those who are refused on security grounds] will be informed of the date on which they may expect to become eligible for emigration.

Kissinger added that the so-called hardship cases would be processed "sympathetically and expeditiously" and that the "emigration tax" (diploma fee) would remain suspended. Finally there was the very important assurance that the administration "will be in a position to bring to the attention of the Soviet leadership indications . . . that these criteria and practices are not being applied" and that those representations "will receive sympathetic consideration and response."

In his answer, Jackson remained true to form. He sought to further nail down the administration and the Soviets and added as his "understanding" the following about what would constitute unlawful harassment:

— the use of punitive conscription against persons seeking to emigrate or against members of their families;

— the bringing of criminal actions against persons in circumstances that suggest a relationship between their desire to emigrate and the criminal action against them;

— the requirement that adult applicants receive permission of their parents or other relatives [the so-called poor relatives clause].

Jackson added as his further "understanding" that refusal for considerations of security would be valid for three years only (instead of indefinitely as was so often the case). Finally he stated that he "would consider a benchmark—a minimum standard of initial compliance—to be the issuance of visas at the rate of 60,000 per annum," adding for good measure that "persons whose emigration has been the subject of discussion between Soviet officials and other European governments will not be included in that benchmark" [presumably meaning in particular Germans and Greeks].

Kissinger had Gromyko's grudging admission that a yearly number of Jewish emigrants up to 45,000 was possible. Dobrynin had orally confirmed the figure of 50,000 but had warned the secretary that the Soviet Union would not accept any reference in the letter to any official Soviet guarantees on the number of emigrants.[65] The secretary of state was convinced that that was the end of the line. But in his dire need to find a solution, he apparently decided not to oppose the 60,000 as a "benchmark of good faith" in Jackson's letter, regarding it only as a threat of future congressional action if the Soviet Union did not behave according to appropriate guidelines.[66] His own letter combined his assurances about Soviet emigration practices with an answer in advance to Jackson's letter. It did not fully confirm acceptance either of the benchmark figure or of the other understandings added by Jackson but said only: "I wish to advise you on behalf of the president that the understandings in your letter will be *among the considerations* [emphasis added] to be applied by the President in exercising the authority [to waive the restrictions of the trade bill]." (This authority to effectively grant MFN status for eighteen months, provided the provisions of the amendment were fulfilled, was later inserted into the trade bill by Jackson as part of the deal.) No number of emigrants was cited at all; Kissinger stated only that it "would begin to rise promptly from the 1973 levels."

The letters make clear that both sides, or more precisely the authors Perle and Sonnenfeldt, were very well informed about the practices of the Soviet authorities regarding Jewish emigration. All the habitual harassments and punishments were meticulously spelled out. The Soviets, however, certainly never intended—and were shocked by—such precision. Senator Jackson cannot have improved their mood—to say the least—by remarks he made in a press conference in the White House, of all places, after the signing ceremony. Jackson had earlier indicated his understanding that it was essential not to embarrass the Soviet Union and to find a face-saving device for the Soviet leaders lest publicity push them to repudiate. But "basking in the light of TV cameras," he stated that the Soviet government had capitulated, made a "complete turnaround."[67]

The Final Phase

When Kissinger met with Brezhnev a week later in Moscow, the Soviet leader was "livid." On October 28 Foreign Minister Gromyko handed his American counterpart a letter in which he attacked the exchange between Kissinger and Jackson in violent terms:

> I believe it necessary to draw your attention to the question concerning the publication in the United States of materials of which you are aware and which touch upon the departure of a certain category of Soviet citizens. I must say, straightforwardly, that the above-mentioned materials including the correspondence between you and Senator Jackson create a

distorted picture of our position as well as what we told the
American side about the matter.

Gromyko emphasized once more that the question as such was
entirely within the internal competence of his state—but that point, he
said, had been passed over in silence in the exchange of letters. On the
other hand, the "elucidations" he had given were now described as
"assurances," and "even some figures were being quoted with regard to
an anticipated increase of emigration as compared with previous years."
Gromyko "resolutely declined such an interpretation." What he had said
concerned only the real situation, and in fact there was "a tendency
toward a decrease in the number of persons wishing to leave the USSR
and seek permanent residence in another country." There should be no
ambiguities, he said, as regards the position of the Soviet Union.[68]

The letter seemed to end all chances for an agreement with the Soviet
Union if the Jackson-Vanik Amendment was attached to the Trade
Reform Act. But Gromyko did not spell out a definite rejection.
Kissinger decided to bet on one last chance: he kept the letter secret and
did not even mention it to Jackson.[69] That approach seemed vindicated
when Brezhnev, during the Vladivostok summit with Ford on November
23 and 24, 1974, reportedly said that while the Soviets did not like the
exchange of letters between Kissinger and Jackson, emigration would go
forward on the basis explained earlier in that year.[70] Kissinger once more
failed to mention Gromyko's letter when he testified before the Senate on
December 3.

The Senate passed the Jackson Amendment by 88 to 0, and the entire
Trade Reform Act with both the Jackson and the Stevenson Amendments
by 77 to 4 on December 13. After House-Senate conference committee
negotiations, it received final approval in both houses on December 20.
But by then the Kremlin had made its final decision. On the morning of
December 18, the Soviet news agency TASS came out with a scathing
statement: "TASS is authorized to state that leading circles in the Soviet
Union flatly reject as unacceptable any attempts . . . to interfere in the
internal affairs that are entirely the concern of the Soviet State and no
one else."[71] Worse, it released Gromyko's letter of October 28.

Still the State Department reacted coolly, stating that the letter did not
change the understandings referred to in Kissinger's letter by which the
secretary stood. Nor did the senators get very excited. Said Senator Russell Long, a Democrat from Louisiana, "I don't pay attention to what the
Russians are saying anyway."[72]

President Ford signed the Trade Reform Act into law on January 3, 1975. On that occasion he stated: "I must express my reservations about the wisdom of legislative language that can only be seen as objectionable and discriminatory by other sovereign states." Kissinger then began talks with Dobrynin. If the president wanted to grant MFN to the Soviet Union, he had to certify that waiving the restrictions of the Jackson-Vanik Amendment would "substantially promote the objective freedom of emigration and that he had received assurances from the Soviet Union" to that effect. That he could not do without explicit assurances from the Soviets which they could not repudiate. Dobrynin soon made clear that this was a forlorn hope. On January 13, 1975, Kissinger announced "that the 1972 Trade Agreement [with the Soviet Union] cannot be brought into force at this time and the president will therefore not take the steps required for this purpose in the Trade Act. The president does not plan at this time to exercise the waiver authority."[73]

The end had been reached.

Conclusion

A great deal of attention has been paid here to the Jackson-Vanik and Stevenson Amendments, not just because they present such an amazing spectacle but because they had a lasting influence on Jewish emigration from the Soviet Union and some other countries. In 1996 the Jackson-Vanik Amendment was still law, although President Bill Clinton had issued a waiver and granted MFN to Russia. The Stevenson Amendment was repealed in April 1992 with the full consent of the former senator.[74]

From the beginning and up to the present, there have been heated discussions about these amendments: Were they wise, and could they have served their purpose? Were they in the end a failure? And if so, who is to blame?

Jackson was undoubtedly sincerely interested in human rights in general and Jewish emigration in particular. In a speech before the Pacem in Terris Conference on October 11, 1973, he said:

> A true peace, an enduring peace, can only be built on a moral consensus. What better place to begin building this consensus than on the principle embodied in the "Universal Declaration of [sic] Human Rights," among which the right to choose the country one lives in—the right to emigrate freely—is perhaps

the most basic. . . . It must be a purpose of the détente to
bring the Soviet Union into the community of civilized
nations, to hasten the end of what Sakharov has called "an
intolerable isolation, bringing with it the ugliest consequences.". . . The argument is not between the proponents
and detractors of détente, but between those who wish a
genuine era of international accommodation based on
progress toward individual liberty and those who, in the final
analysis, are indifferent to such progress.[75]

The Jackson-Vanik Amendment did focus American—and indeed
world—attention on the plight of the Soviet Jews. The Jewish activists in
the Soviet Union were themselves given heart: Sharansky, who courageously signed an open petition with sixty other Soviet Jews in favor of
it, relates that they were all "intoxicated" with optimism by the amendment. He calls it a humane act of the U.S. Congress and the first real link
between human rights and American-Soviet relations.[76] The amendment
certainly helped to bring about the suspension of the diploma fee, and
the link it made with human rights remained a warning for the Soviet
Union (and other countries) in later years: The Soviet Union had to make
concessions regarding freedom of movement if it wanted to obtain concessions from the United States in other fields. In this way the amendment was undoubtedly one of the factors that induced the Soviets to
increase Jewish emigration in 1978–79 and again in 1987—albeit, as we
shall see, only one factor among others. The claim that "hundreds of
thousands have gained freedom under its general aegis"[77] seems exaggerated. It did play a useful role in U.S. relations with other nonmarket
countries like China and Rumania.

It should be stressed, furthermore, that the introduction of Jackson's
amendment was in itself legitimate. The Senate has its own constitutional
role in foreign affairs, and anyway a democratic parliament has the right
to force its government to make choices, in particular when large parts
of public opinion are responsive. If Kissinger wanted to treat the emigration issue as just one element in his "carrots-and-sticks" policy, Congress could demand greater emphasis on that particular point. Other parliaments can do the same and have done so. The Netherlands parliament
later forced its government to abandon its policy of not making representations to the Soviets in behalf of dissidents and Refuseniks out of
fear it would harm its task as the representative of Israeli interests (see

Chapter 9). Governments, in turn, have the right and duty to point out the risks of such a change of emphasis. Of course, this kind of parliamentary action does interfere with the free hand of a government to run its foreign policy. A former official of the U.S. Department of State voices his objections as follows: "If Congress is dissatisfied with what the president is doing, all it has to do is come out against him and recommend to the people that he not be elected again. But attaching these amendments to specific pieces of legislation, I think, is a mistake."[78] In the strict constitutional sense, that evaluation is correct for the United States, but U.S. presidential elections give the people a chance to express their opinions only once every four years, and then, at best, in connection with only a few of the main issues. Tying human rights considerations to foreign policy will always remain difficult and controversial, since so many political, commercial, and other interests are involved. Yet a foreign policy without regard for human rights is unworthy of a democratic nation. A thorough evaluation of the manner in which that link should be made and of the publicity it should be given is, however, essential.

That said, for the short run the amendment failed in what was, after all, its purpose: to increase the flow of emigration of Jews from the Soviet Union. The number of visas issued by the Netherlands embassy had already declined in 1974 by about 42 percent and went down by about 35 percent in 1975 compared to the previous year (see Table 1, page 221). Thus thousands of Jews had to wait longer. The Soviet rejection of the trade agreement was also detrimental for U.S.-Soviet relations and cost the United States a large amount of money, for the Lend-Lease debt was never paid. Could that failure have been prevented, and if so, where lies the blame?

Everyone who has written about this question seems to point to a different culprit: to Jackson, who is accused of overreaching; to Stevenson, who supposedly gave the *coup de grace*, perhaps unwittingly; to Kissinger, who did not always have time to focus on the problem and is accused of not warning the proponents sufficiently of the consequences; and to the Soviets, who are said to have had a change of heart. Who was it? The answer has to be "all of the above," and perhaps "presumptuousness" should be added as one of the culprits.

Jackson and his forces must share part of the blame. The thorough evaluation of the manner in which the linkage between human rights and foreign policy should be made and the publicity it should be given seems to have been missing on Jackson's side. The Soviet concessions, which the threat of the amendment had brought about, were tremendous—suspension of the diploma fee, a tentative figure of 45,000 or even 50,000 emigrants yearly (an increase of 30–40 percent over 1973), plus a promise to reduce harassment. Jackson's staff, well aware of the touchiness of the Soviet regime, should have realized that more—and especially more binding and more precise—commitments and higher figures could not be demanded of the sort of power that the Soviet Union was. At that stage quiet acceptance with subdued publicity might—just might—have worked. The text of the exchange of letters seemed, to the contrary, designed to vex the Soviet authorities, for whom it was difficult enough to make any concessions at all. Gromyko, whatever one thinks of his bluster, was not incorrect when he claimed that the texts of Kissinger and Jackson did not faithfully reflect his (more or less tacit) agreement with the secretary of state in Geneva. And while it was, of course, necessary to publish the letters, a press conference at the White House and expressions like "capitulation" certainly made matters worse. Considerations of internal politics should, at that moment, have taken a back seat. Senator Jackson's presidential ambitions may well have been a factor. Dmitri Simes, an immigrant from the Soviet Union and now a senior associate at the Carnegie Endowment for International Peace, makes the following assessment: "Frankly I thought that this was very unfair to Soviet Jews because I felt they were being used as a political pawn once again, but this time by some of their best friends in the United States. At that point I stopped being supportive of the Jackson-Vanik Amendment."[79]

Stevenson's amendment was certainly very detrimental to the American relationship with the Soviet Union. It lowered the credit ceiling of the Export-Import Bank to what Kissinger later called "peanuts."[80] That ceiling could be increased upon special request from the president, but only after what was likely to be a bruising debate in Congress. Senator Stevenson was certainly pushed by the Jackson forces and is now clearly unhappy with the initiative he took. He did not see it at the time as having anything to do with the emigration issue but only with restraining Nixon and refusing to subsidize exports to the Soviet Union.[81] In 1989 he wrote: "Tying MFN and access to U.S. export-facilities to another nation's emigration rules never made sense. Such selective linkage implies that if Moscow releases enough Jews, its actions elsewhere are relatively unimportant as far as trade is concerned. This is an untenable stand in international politics."[82] But this afterthought does not, of course, diminish his responsibility for his amendment and its results, although by itself it was probably not the clinching factor for the eventual rejection of the whole deal by the Soviets, as has been claimed.[83] The Stevenson Amendment would, after all, have come into play only after the Soviet Union had complied with the terms of the Jackson-Vanik Amendment, which prohibited *any* credits or credit facilities to a non-market-economy country that denied its citizens the right to emigrate.

Kissinger was in a very difficult position, first with Nixon under the cloud of Watergate and then with the new and untried Ford, a president who did not have a mandate from the voters. Kissinger was also, as he recognizes, too busy with other pressing issues, including Vietnam and the Middle East. Having too quickly rejected the Jackson approach in the beginning, to his credit he himself went on to prove that it could be successful up to a point. Where he went wrong is when he approved the text of the exchange of letters with Jackson and, together with Ford, allowed Jackson's press conference in the White House.[84] Kissinger has also been blamed for not sufficiently warning the proponents of the amendments of the risks involved.[85] While he did sound general warnings in several speeches and in Senate testimony, he may not have sufficiently emphasized the menace that the Soviet Union might in the end reject the whole deal. In particular, he did not publish Gromyko's letter of October 28. That, however, was a calculated tactical gamble that might have turned out to be worth the taking. There remains the reproach to Kissinger that even in his memoirs he treats the question as only an element of his "carrots-and-sticks" foreign policy. He regrets the interference with that policy and its consequent failure but does not even mention the Jews in the Soviet Union who had hoped that the amendment would enable them to leave and now had to wait for many years.[86]

Soviet policies were, let us not forget, at the basis of all the trouble. Soviet authorities were refusing their citizens the right to leave the country as guaranteed in their own constitution and in international agreements. They also undoubtedly had a change of heart. Contemplating the deal as it was presented to them in the meeting of the Central Committee on December 16 and the Politburo on December 18, 1974, they must have felt that its political costs outweighed its economic advantages.[87] They would have had to accept what they thought of as serious interference in their internal affairs and pay more than $700 million on their Lend-Lease debt (albeit over a period of thirty years) in exchange for the rather doubtful benefits of MFN and by now very limited credit facilities. It should not be forgotten that the economic situation of the Soviet Union had dramatically improved in the meantime by the tripling of the price of oil, something the Jackson forces seem to have ignored.[88] And so the Soviets did renege on the promises they had explicitly or implicitly made—not only regarding the number of emigrants but also declaring that harassment was against Soviet law. The harassment never stopped.

There is one more culprit: presumptuousness, or the assumption, so often prevalent among lawmakers in the United States, that the internal reasons for their own policies always have preference over all other considerations. This notion is not unknown in other parliaments, but it sometimes seems that Americans, perhaps because of the sheer size of their country and its distance from Europe and Asia, are more prone than others to forget about the sensitivities of countries in other parts of the world ("I never listen to what the Russians say anyway"). Coddling the Soviet Union would have been the worst thing to do, but forgetting about the other party's sensitivity, and publicly spelling out—and then rubbing in—its concessions, are something else.

7

Helsinki: The Conference on Security and Cooperation in Europe

Almost from the beginning, the question of Jewish emigration from the Soviet Union played a role in the Western preparations for a Conference on Security and Cooperation in Europe. The results of that conference and what has become known as the Helsinki Process influenced, in turn, the position of Jews in the Soviet Union and the conditions under which they could emigrate.

The Preliminaries

A conference on European security had been proposed by the Soviets soon after World War II. In February 1954, V. M. Molotov, the Soviet foreign minister, suggested an "all-European treaty of collective security."[1] The following November the Kremlin formally proposed convening a European security conference. The reasons for this Soviet proposal were obvious. Like any conqueror who has obtained territory by force of arms, the Soviet Union did not feel secure within its new borders. It wanted those borders, as well as those of its client states in Eastern Europe, especially Poland and later the German Democratic Republic, legally confirmed by a treaty.[2] The reasons for the opposition of the North Atlantic Treaty Organization (NATO) were equally obvious: in those days it would have been politically impossible to confirm those borders, in particular the division of Germany, in a binding instrument.

Leonid Brezhnev repeated the proposal for a European security conference at the Twenty-third Party Congress, at which he outlined more specific points for an agenda: settling the German question, recognizing postwar borders, developing cooperation, achieving arms reduction, and removing the presence of foreign (i.e., non-European) troops from Europe. In 1966 the communiqué of a meeting in Bucharest of the Warsaw Pact, the Soviet-dominated defense alliance in Eastern Europe, endorsed Brezhnev's proposal and spoke for the first time of a need to foster greater cooperation between East and West in science, technology, art, and culture.[3]

At first, Western reactions were negative, especially in the United States. Washington saw Brezhnev's proposals in the light of the perceived Soviet wish to exclude the United States (and also Canada) from Europe and to dominate European cooperation on Soviet terms. Henry Kissinger later regarded a security conference as no more than "one of those alternative structures to NATO that the Russians used to come up with."[4] Indeed, any possible advantage of such a conference for the West could only be long-term, while many Western politicians feared that it could give an adroit Soviet diplomacy a chance to wean the Germans away from the West. Fortunately adroitness (until Mikhail Gorbachev) was not the predominant quality of Soviet diplomacy, while pro-Western sentiments in the Federal Republic of Germany proved more than strong enough to counter any Soviet "weaning."

The invasion of Czechoslovakia by members of the Warsaw Pact in August 1968 strengthened the negative reactions of the West and was a moral defeat for the Soviet Union. At the Warsaw Pact meeting in Budapest on March 17, 1969, a new peace offensive was therefore launched with a renewed appeal for a European security conference as its centerpiece. As it happened, new leaders came to power in the West that year: Richard Nixon was inaugurated president of the United States in January; Georges Pompidou succeeded Charles de Gaulle as president in France in April; and Willy Brandt became chancellor of the Federal Republic of Germany in October. In his election campaign Brandt had proposed a new policy toward Eastern Europe—the *Ostpolitik*. It accepted that Germany could not be unified by force and that it would therefore be best to recognize the existing situation and borders. Following such recognition, a peaceful penetration of Eastern Europe through economic and cultural cooperation might be undertaken in the hope that in a distant future the two parts of Germany could unite through the free will of their populations. But dialogue and rapprochement had to be undertaken first.[5]

Western public opinion in general now began to see merit in the idea of trying to find accommodations with the Warsaw Pact and defuse the tensions in Europe. It is to the credit of the U.S. Department of State that a constructive answer to the Warsaw Pact proposals was found within NATO. If the West were to accept a conference on European security, the department reasoned, the Western position would have to be carefully prepared within the alliance. Furthermore a *quid pro quo* would have to be demanded for any concession regarding the European borders. The State Department consistently followed this line, at times even circumventing Kissinger's wishes after he had become secretary of state.[6] At first the department was severely criticized by powerful forces in the United States for even being involved in the process.[7] Not until much later did Kissinger and others perceive the advantages the West could reap from a European conference.[8]

In December 1969 the West's response to the Budapest proposals of the Warsaw Pact was presented in a NATO communiqué. The idea of a conference on European security was no longer rejected, but NATO stated its conditions: first of all the United States and Canada should participate; second, the conference must address the subject of free movement of people, information, and ideas.

Where did the notion of "free movement of people" come from? The Universal Declaration on Human Rights, adopted by the United Nations on December 10, 1948, states in Article 13.2: "Everyone has the right to leave any country, including his own, and to return to his country." In 1963 the United Nations published a study on the right to "leave a country," by José Ingles in which this right was singled out for the first time.[9] Did the Department of State propose the subject with the Soviet Jews in mind? Not at first, for the notion of family reunification appeared only later in NATO consultations. Did the authorities in the Federal Republic of Germany, observing how East German border guards were shooting their citizens if they tried to scale the Berlin Wall, want the subject included? Did it come from Paris, where Pompidou was interested in fostering contacts and exchanges between East and West? (But he aimed especially at the cultural field.)

It seems likely that ideas and experiences from various Western capitals converged during the meetings at NATO headquarters in Brussels in the demand that free movement of people be on the conference agenda. It was a master stroke. The West would answer the Soviet insistence on the communist ideology with a demand for respect of its own ideas on human rights in general and free movement for people, information, and ideas in particular. Thus a perceived Soviet victory on the question of the borders could be offset by Soviet concessions in favor of the people living behind those borders.[10] The name eventually chosen—"*freer* movement"—expressed this policy position clearly: simple reconfirmation of existing treaties and declarations would not do, but a real improvement would be demanded. The NATO communiqué of December 1970 stated decisively: "Freer movement of people, ideas and information is an essential element for the development of such [international] cooperation."[11]

There was a third condition: NATO demanded separate negotiations on arms reductions in Europe in order to try to reduce the preponderance of Warsaw Pact armed forces over those of NATO. Negotiations on "mutual and balanced force reductions" (MBFR) between the members of NATO and the Warsaw Pact would have to run parallel with the proposed conference on European security, which at NATO's insistence was renamed the Conference on Security and Cooperation in Europe (CSCE). It was still another two years before CSCE preparatory talks opened in Helsinki at the end of 1972 and MBFR talks in Vienna early in 1973. Those two years were used by NATO to prepare intensively for both conferences.

During that period the role of the United States remained crucial. Cables exchanged between the Department of State and the U.S. Permanent Mission to NATO in Brussels make clear that the mission made important contributions toward strengthening the U.S. position and toward the formulation of concrete proposals.[12] Many of those contributions came back as instructions from Washington to Brussels. When the German delegation suggested in 1972 that "winning concrete gains is more likely if a separate agenda item bears a more neutral heading than 'freer movement'" the answer from Washington was clear:

> Soviet interest in a "successful" conference provides potential bargaining leverage which should be used by the West to obtain some concrete improvement in the freer movement area. We do not expect a radical transformation of practices in the Warsaw Pact states, but many specific liberalizing measures probably could be accepted by the USSR and other East European countries without risk.[13]

Among the NATO allies strongly supporting this American view was the Netherlands.

It is remarkable that the Jewish organizations in the United States did not at that time perceive the interest that the outcome of a CSCE might have for the Jews who wanted to emigrate from the Soviet Union.[14] On the contrary, most seem to have feared that a confirmation of the borders would make it even more difficult for the Jews to get out.[15] Yet they were active during the preparation period in bringing the plight of the Soviet Jews to the fore in general. Resolutions on the subject were introduced in both houses of Congress, and hearings held. There can be no doubt that, when the instructions for Brussels were drafted, these activities influenced the thinking at the U.S. Department of State as well as in other Western foreign ministries.

The Final Act

After the preparatory talks in Helsinki were concluded, the real negotiations began in Geneva in 1973. There the Americans took a backseat while for the first time the political cooperation among the members of the European Common Market became active. It took two more years until the Final Act could be signed by all the heads of state, back again in Helsinki, on August 1, 1975. It was a long and complicated document that met with much skepticism, especially among the American public. In fact, President Gerald Ford was urged by many not to go to Helsinki and sign this bad document; and during the next presidential election campaign the Democratic candidate Jimmy Carter accused Ford of having made too many concessions. The State Department played down the importance of the Final Act and the potential significance of its human rights provisions.

Yet the Final Act was a victory for the West. The Western nations, and also the members of the Neutral and Nonaligned Group, recognized the inviolability of the existing borders in Europe and thereby legitimized them, but nobody in his right mind had any thoughts of changing those borders by force anyway, and the UN Charter had already stated the same inviolability. Much more important was that the Final Act also recognized that frontiers could be changed by peaceful means and by agreement.[16] People, it said, "had the right, in full freedom, to determine when and as they wished their internal and external political status without external interference"—exactly as happened fifteen years later in Germany.

On top of that, human rights were incorporated on an equal basis in the Declaration of Principles,[17] and important provisions regarding freer movement were accepted in a separate chapter (Basket III), although expressed in terms of family reunion.[18] Those provisions made clear that the fate of the Soviet Jews had undoubtedly been in the negotiators' mind. The participants pledged

— to deal in a positive and humanitarian spirit with the applications of persons who wish to be reunited with members of their family;
— to deal with applications in this field as expeditiously as possible;
— to lower where necessary the fees charged in connection with these applications to ensure that they are at a moderate level;
— that an application concerning family-unification [would] not modify the rights or obligations of the applicant or of members of his family.

The most common complaints of harassment of the Jews by the Soviet authorities were thus spelled out.[19] When the human rights clauses were for the first time submitted *in toto* to the members of the Politburo in Moscow, they were stunned and Gromyko had great trouble in making them accept the text.[20]

The Soviets did try to protect themselves by general clauses. Among those, the principle of nonintervention in the internal affairs of participating states became the most frequently used Soviet counter to any Western human rights complaint. At Western insistence, however, the language of the sixth principle makes clear that the term "intervention" here means activities like armed intervention, coercion, or assistance to terrorist acts. Diplomatic representations or other forms of governmental complaints about violations of Basket III could hardly be described as "coercion" and therefore remained legitimate.

A second "protection-clause" was seen by the Soviets in the first principle, in which participating states promised to respect each other's right to determine their own laws and regulations. This clause had also been qualified by a Western insertion: "All the principles [were] of primary significance and . . . [would] be equally and unreservedly applied." Thus the human rights principle was held to be equally important as the rights of nonintervention and self-determination. The grounds for Western complaints were clearly spelled out, as were Soviet counterarguments; but the point remained that for the first time human rights were formally recognized in an international agreement as a fundamental principle regulating relations between states.[21] The West would make good use of that point in the following years, although it took some time before the full potential of the Final Act was brought to bear.

William Korey claims that the final impact of the Final Act was a surprise even to Western negotiators. "History offers instances of international agreements producing consequences totally unanticipated and reversing the role of major parties to the agreement," he has written. "The Helsinki Accord would constitute an archetype."[22] There were indeed unexpected consequences, and no one could have foreseen that the Final Act would come to play a role in the eventual demise of the Soviet Union. But those who drafted the original NATO proposals and those who negotiated with the Warsaw Pact representatives and the neutral delegations in Helsinki and Geneva did intend to create an issue that could in the long run help erode Soviet power in Eastern Europe.[23]

One clause in the Final Act did give an advantage to the West, especially where Jewish emigration was concerned, which was indeed "totally unanticipated" by negotiators—the agreement on follow-up meetings. In fact, this clause was inserted as a concession to the East. The Soviets had proposed setting up a permanent European security organization in which they would naturally have played a leading role. The West perceived this proposal as the danger to NATO it was meant to be, but Western negotiators did accept, indeed proposed, a compromise: a follow-up meeting would be held every three years to review progress. These meetings developed into a valuable mechanism for checking compliance by the participating states with the provisions of the Final Act regarding human rights in general and Jewish emigration in particular.

The Helsinki Watch Groups

Another provision the West inserted in the Final Act fulfilled its role in a way that, although not totally unanticipated, certainly surpassed the Western expectations. It was agreed that the full text of the Final Act would be published in all participating states. The Soviet Union did so even before most Western states. (Although later the text was no longer for sale and distributed only through *samizdat*.) The Soviet authorities scored some short-lived diplomatic points with that publication, but neither they nor the West foresaw that the published text would almost immediately induce courageous dissidents inside the Soviet Union to set up groups to support compliance with the Helsinki Accords in their country.[24] Later these became known as Helsinki Watch Groups.[25] Professor Andrei Sakharov called a press conference to announce the formation of the first group in Moscow on May 12, 1975. Sakharov himself did not become a member, not wanting to "misuse his authority" as an academician, but his wife Jelena Bonner did, along with Ludmilla Alexeyeva, Alexander Ginzburg, Pyotr Grigorenko, Anatoly Marchenko, Vitaly Rubin, and Anatoly Sharansky.[26] Larissa Bogaraz was in internal exile at the time, but she signed the appeal.[27] Similar groups were formed in other Soviet cities and in some of the Warsaw Pact member states.

In the book she later published in the United States, Ludmilla Alexeyeva writes that the Helsinki Accords noticeably promoted cooperation between the Jewish and the human rights movements in Moscow because Jews such as Vitaly Rubin and Anatoly Sharansky, and later Vladimir Slepak and Naum Meiman, joined the Helsinki Watch Group. This cooperation was important, because until then Jews had often kept apart from the beginning of a democratic movement. Alexeyeva notes that a majority of Refuseniks reasoned: "I do not want anything to do with this country. I want to leave and to achieve this I must avoid quarrels with the authorities. After all, permission depends on them, not on the dissidents. So the further away one is from the dissidents, the better."[28] That attitude did not disappear after the Helsinki Accords, but more Jews came to understand that non-Jewish dissidents worked for goals which included the freedom to emigrate; it was therefore in the interest of both sides to cooperate.[29] Sharansky played an important role as a liaison between the two groups since he worked closely with both Andrei Sakharov and Alexander Lerner, and that was undoubtedly one of the causes for his arrest and conviction in 1977–78.[30]

Toward the end of the 1970s almost all activities of the Helsinki Watch Groups had been snuffed out by the KGB. Many members were in jail or in internal or external exile. Yet the flame never died completely. When in December 1986 Sakharov was allowed to return to Moscow from his forced internal exile in Gorki, one of his first demands to Gorbachev was for freedom of movement for all Soviet citizens.

Influence on Jewish Emigration

How much direct influence did the Conference on Security and Cooperation in Europe have on Soviet Jewish emigration? It seems likely that one of the reasons why the Soviets allowed the first wave of emigration in the early 1970s was their desire to see a European security conference begin. It formed part and parcel of the general détente that Brezhnev so much desired. By the time the Helsinki Final Act was signed, the volume of emigration was down, for reasons which probably had more to do with the Jackson-Vanik Amendment and the general state of relations with the West than with CSCE. In any event, the downward trend had begun well before the end of the conference.

Brezhnev declared in Helsinki: "We assume that all countries represented at the conference will implement the undertakings reached. As regards the Soviet Union, it will act precisely in this manner."[31] But it is now known that the Kremlin had, in fact, no intention of honoring the Helsinki Accords' basic obligations regarding human rights; they were to be "pigeon-holed."[32] Thus the Soviets completely ignored their obligation to "deal in a positive and humanitarian spirit with the applications of persons who wish to be reunited with members of their family." In typical fashion they did, however, take certain administrative measures enabling them to claim compliance with at least some of the provisions of the Final Act. The obligation to "lower where necessary the fees charged in connection with these applications to ensure that they are at a moderate level" was carried out in 1976 by lowering the price of a passport or exit permit from 360 rubles to 260 rubles. The total cost for a Jewish emigrant, who also had to pay 500 rubles for the obligatory rejection of citizenship and a 40-ruble application fee, thus decreased from 900 rubles to 800 rubles—still far above what could be considered a "moderate level" in comparison to the average income. The waiting period for resubmission of a rejected application was reduced from one year to six months.[33]

Furthermore, according to a report by the Helsinki Commission of the U.S. Congress, the requirement of a detailed character reference from the workplace was dropped at this time. In general the commission found that "post-Helsinki conditions were much more favorable than those preceding the Helsinki accord." The waiting time for an answer to one's application was reduced and "75 percent of the applicants now received permission to leave within six months of filing their applications."[34] In February 1977, however, the Netherlands embassy reported that the Soviet authorities were still applying all possible means to frighten away prospective emigrants and to impede them by administrative procedures or other means when they began, or wanted to finish, emigration procedures. According to the embassy the Soviet authorities hoped to show in this way that the number of Jews wishing to emigrate was relatively small, and thereby to diminish the pressure from the West. Intimidation, terror, blackmail, extortion, and bureaucratic arbitrariness were still being applied.[35]

CSCE Follow-Up Conferences

And so the picture remained mixed: a limited number of improvements in the treatment of the Jewish emigrants by Soviet authorities but continued negation of the primary human rights obligations and the humanitarian spirit. Any concession they made could, and often would, in time be offset by other measures and harassments. Yet the CSCE was to exert a continuing influence on Jewish emigration, primarily through the follow-up conferences.

The first follow-up conference was scheduled for October 4, 1977, in Belgrade. Apparently anticipating criticism of their treatment of human rights in general and Jewish emigration in particular, in the autumn of 1977 Soviet authorities began to increase the number of exit permits issued, while some of the more prominent democratic activists and nonconformists (although not the leaders of the Helsinki Watch Groups) were suddenly allowed to leave and encouraged to stay abroad permanently. The number of Israeli visas issued by the Netherlands embassy increased from around 1,200 per month in the first half of 1977 to more than 1,500 in the last five months of that year. There were undoubtedly other reasons for this increase (see Chapter 8), but the Helsinki Process clearly began to play a role. That did not prevent the Belgrade conference from failing; the concluding statement did no more than reconfirm all the provisions of the Final Act and set a date for the next follow-up meeting in Madrid. Yet the Belgrade conference has been called a breakthrough because the head of the U.S. delegation, Arthur Goldberg, speaking in a working group, suddenly started naming specific cases; the next day another U.S. delegate detailed crude Soviet practices aimed at preventing emigration, especially the persistent references to state security. Later he mentioned the case of the Refusenik Joseph Begun and named American journalists who were expelled from the Soviet Union. Not everyone in the Western caucus was happy with the abrasive way in which Goldberg operated, especially as he did not consult much with the allied or neutral delegations. But he did create a precedent and he "broke the silence barrier."[36]

Arthur Goldberg and his successor as head of the American delegation to the next CSCE follow-up conference, Max Kampelman, thought alike about the significance of the Final Act. For Goldberg it "permanently established the interrelationship between the 'universal significance of human rights' and 'the prospects of international peace, justice and well-being.'" Kampelman said the same thing in different words: "The unique ingredient of the Helsinki Final Act is that it reflects the integrated totality of our East-West relationships. It assumes that the commitment to the human dimension is as necessary to peace as is our commitment to respect one another's borders and to refrain from the use of force against any state."[37] Kampelman continued and intensified his predecessor's policy in naming names and presenting individual cases during the next follow-up conference, in Madrid, 1980–83. He established a good working relationship with the other allied delegations and with the neutral and nonaligned group. This time the Americans were joined by numerous other delegates in denouncing the repression of the dissidents in the Soviet Union and the refusal of Soviet authorities to implement the provisions of the Final Act regarding freer movement, especially as far as Jewish emigration was concerned. The sharp downturn in the volume of that emigration that had set in toward the end of 1979 gave ample grounds for complaints. Soviet deputy foreign minister Leonid Ilyichev, in a speech to the conference, responded that the Soviet Union was "prepared to consider, in a businesslike way, problems concerning the conditions for the reunification of families." What did that mean? A key Soviet spokesman suggested: "The more détente prospers, the more Basket III [humanitarian affairs] prospers." It has been rightly remarked that "this assertion had the ring of blackmail, signaling the West that, indeed, Soviet Jews were hostages to the Kremlin's détente purposes."[38]

In Madrid the Soviets were again demanding a disarmament conference. As the Mutual and Balanced Force Reduction Talks in Vienna between the members of NATO and the Warsaw Pact were dragging on, the Kremlin once again dusted off its old idea of "general and complete disarmament." According to the Soviets, this subject would have to be discussed in a conference involving all European states and the United States and Canada. The West saw nothing to be gained by a conference with such utopian ideas but once again decided to try to turn this Soviet wish to its advantage. What came out of the Madrid conference—the longest follow-up conference ever held—was the decision to hold a CSCE conference on Confidence and Security Building Measures and Disarmament in Europe. It was scheduled for Stockholm, beginning in 1984. On the agenda were such measures as prior notification and observation of large troop movements or exercises, a step designed to strengthen confidence and reduce the risk of military confrontation in Europe.

As a condition for this "concession" (which in fact covered many Western desiderata), the West obtained some modest improvements of the provisions in the Helsinki Accords:

— Applications for family meetings, reunification and marriage would be favorably "dealt with" and "decided upon in emergency cases as expeditiously as possible." (The Final Act asked only that signatories "consider" applications and "deal with [them] in a positive and humanitarian spirit.")

— Making or renewing applications for family reunion would "not modify the rights and obligations of the applicants . . . concerning *inter alia*: employment, housing, residence status, family support, access to social, economic or educational benefits."

— The necessary forms and information on procedures and regulations would be provided.

— Fees would be gradually reduced "to bring them to a moderate level in relation to the average monthly income."

— Applicants would be informed "as expeditiously as possible of the decision" on their cases and of their "right to renew applications after reasonably short intervals."[39]

Those points indeed covered the most serious complaints of the Jewish applicants for emigration; they were also destined to be largely ignored by the Soviets until Gorbachev's policy of *perestroika*. On the other hand, the Madrid conference did establish that a follow-up conference was the appropriate forum for discussing compliance with the Final Act and for bringing up individual dissidence and emigration cases, both publicly and "in the corridors."

The next follow-up conference was held in Vienna. It opened on November 4, 1986, just when Gorbachev's *perestroika* began to influence the Soviet attitude toward the West, and it closed on January 19, 1989. The results of this conference, which proved to be by far the most productive to that point, will be discussed within the framework of the Gorbachev era in Chapter 10.

Conclusion

The Helsinki Process provides a clear example of the interaction of internal and external factors regarding the Jewish emigration from the Soviet

Union. It influenced that emigration, although the impact was uneven and varied considerably over the years. The plight of the Jews already played a role in the preparations for the negotiations that produced the Helsinki Final Act of 1975, especially for the subjects of human rights in general and freer movement in particular. Western negotiators did intend to open up chances for the freer movement of ideas and persons in the Soviet Union and the states under Soviet control in Eastern Europe. The Final Act led directly to a slight improvement in the administrative handling of emigration requests in the Soviet Union and to an increase in the ınumber of exit permits issued in the months just before the first follow-up conference in Belgrade. These developments were not repeated in the period just before the second follow-up conference in Madrid, but that conference undeniably established follow-up conferences as the main forum for checking the human rights performance of the participating states and the right of all participants—not only from the West, but more and more also from the neutral and non-aligned states—to bring forward individual cases. Hardship cases were often resolved this way even in periods when the general emigration trend was down. Furthermore, the Final Act led to the establishment of Helsinki Watch Groups inside the Soviet Union, dissident movements that also pleaded for the Jews and in which Jews took part.

In the longer run, the Final Act provided a yardstick for the human rights treatment the Eastern European regimes meted out to their subjects and a standard of obligations that Western diplomacy time and again held up, publicly and privately, before the unwilling authorities in the Soviet Union and its satellites. Those authorities usually denied their transgressions, or their obligations, or the right of the West to even mention them, but even so they felt the pressure of what their leaders had, after all, signed in Helsinki. And depending on their need for good relations with the West, they would reject the Western representations and persecute their citizens who based their demands on the promises of the Final Act, or grudgingly make concessions.

The Soviet authorities had no intention of fully honoring their human rights obligations after the signing of the Final Act, and by and large they did not. But the Final Act did have much more influence than some pessimists thought possible at the time it was signed. And in the end, during *perestroika*, it became "a familiar feature of domestic and international life in Europe"[40] and the generally accepted yardstick for the human rights performance of all Eastern European governments. In that way, as

Anatoly Dobrynin confirmed, "It generated the fundamental changes inside the Soviet Union and the nations of Eastern Europe that helped end the Cold War."[41] Or, as the Charter of Paris for a New Europe, adopted in November 1990, stated: "The courage of men and women, the strength of the will of the peoples and the power of the ideas of the Helsinki Final Act have opened a new era of democracy, peace and unity in Europe."[42]

8

Down and Up in the Seventies

In the last quarter of 1973 there was a decline in Jewish emigration compared with the same period of 1972. At the request of U.S. Secretary of State Henry Kissinger, Soviet ambassador Anatoly Dobrynin provided statistics as well as an explanation for this downturn. He claimed that "recent events in the Middle East [the October War] had made Soviet citizens reluctant to emigrate there." Kissinger accepts that explanation in his memoirs, although the previous war, that of 1967, far from diminishing the desire for emigration among the Soviet Jews, had increased it (see Chapter 1). He further calls it remarkable that the Soviets volunteered any explanation at all "for what was, after all, legally a domestic matter."[1] But that begs the point. As Andrei Sakharov and many others emphasized, the Soviet Union was flaunting an international obligation.

The Downturn of 1974

In October 1973, the month in which another war in the Middle East, the Yom Kippur War, broke out, visas were issued for 4,266 persons—an all-time high. In November the number remained high: 3,498 (see Table 2, pages 222–23). These figures mostly reflect, of course, the number of exit permits issued by OVIR during previous months, before the war.[2] But they do show that those who had obtained exit permits did not hesitate to get visas for Israel as well, the war notwithstanding. It should also be remembered that more than 90 percent of the Jewish emigrants did go to Israel at that time. The number of visas issued did not drop substantially until early 1974, and the percentage of those not going to Israel then also rose steeply. In other words: if there was a reluctance to go to Israel, it was reflected in an increase in the percentage of what the Israelis called the dropouts among those who had been granted exit permits and Israeli visas (see Chapter 11). If there was a decrease in the number of applications for exit permits, it was clearly engineered by Soviet authorities. That assumption finds confirmation in the fact that requests for *vysovs* from Israel continued to pour in. In May 1974 Israeli authorities estimated that 135,000 *vysovs* had been sent to applicants in the Soviet Union. Many recipients may not have applied for an exit permit immediately; it was customary to keep invitations in reserve. Yet with so many of those invitations dispatched from Israel, a voluntary decrease of 50 percent in applications for exit permits, as claimed by the Soviets at the time, is unlikely. The Netherlands embassy, reporting these figures, in fact added that there were many complaints of *vysovs* not arriving, of applicants having to present themselves at a police station and sometimes being kept there, and of many other forms of harassment meant to discourage applications.[3]

The question remains as to why the Soviets decided to begin throttling emigration in late 1973. There can be no doubt that the issuance of exit permits by the local offices of OVIR was centrally and tightly controlled from Moscow. For example, when it was decided to suspend the diploma fee in March 1973, the Netherlands embassy reported that the suspension had been applied by OVIR offices everywhere within one week except for one isolated office in Central Asia.[4] Whether specific quotas were set for each OVIR office or region, as has been assumed by some observers, is difficult to prove, but the trends, up and down, were certainly determined in Moscow. It is likely that quotas then were set at least for each republic.

Possible reasons for the downturn include the Soviets' frustration over the new defeat suffered by their Arab clients in the Middle East and their desire to show them some kind of support. U.S. policies almost certainly played a role. The Jackson-Vanik Amendment tying trade to freedom of emigration (see Chapter 6) had prevented the development of the large foreign trade exchanges Leonid Brezhnev had foreseen. This development gave his opponents a chance to push for a more conservative and independent foreign policy. The December 1974 Plenum of the Central Committee of the Communist Party decided on such a policy, and détente went into decline.[5] The number of visas issued to Soviet Jews in 1975 further decreased by some 35 percent from 1974. On July 1 of that year the tax levied on the transfer of money from abroad was increased by 30 percent, bringing the total tax to 60 percent.[6] The conclusion seems unavoidable that the Soviets were signaling to the United States if you can't keep your side of the bargain, we won't keep ours.[7]

The signing of the Helsinki Final Act on August 1, 1975 (see Chapter 7) had no perceptible impact on the emigration figures. For three years, until 1977, the annual emigration level remained between 13,000 and 17,000.

The Upturn of 1977

President Jimmy Carter began his administration in 1977 with a strong emphasis on human rights: "I am consistently and completely dedicated to the enhancement of human rights, not only as it deals with the Soviet Union but with all other countries." He exchanged letters with the dissident Andrei Sakharov and published them. Carter even thought that the number of the Jews permitted to emigrate from the Soviet Union had increased in the few months preceding his inauguration, but the figures do not bear that out (see Table 2, pages 222–23). At the same time he said, "I think this [the enhancement of human rights] can legitimately be severed from our inclination to work with the Soviet Union, for instance, in reducing dependence upon atomic weapons and also seeking mutual and balanced force reductions in Europe."[8] In other words: no linkage.

Henry Kissinger's linkage policies had become so unpopular that Carter had made an election promise to do away with the concept. Carter did not, however, explain the way in which his administration would enhance human rights. At his first press conference as president he stated: "I can't go in with armed forces and try to change the internal mechanism of the Soviet government. But I don't think this [the Soviet conduct] is designed to aggravate me or to test me or to test the will of this country."[9]

Carter's approach suited the Soviets very well. Brezhnev had set great store by the SALT II negotiations. In 1974, at Vladivostok, he had agreed on a framework for these negotiations with President Ford; he had overridden his own military to achieve this agreement.[10] He wanted nothing better than to proceed with SALT II without being bothered by thorny human rights issues. If Carter thought he could "enhance" human rights in dealing with the Soviet Union without linkage, so much the better. But, as was almost predictable, the Soviets did want to test

Carter and the will of his country on this point. The combination of several factors had clearly convinced the Kremlin that it was time for strong measures. The Helsinki Accords had stimulated a growing internal dissident movement and the establishment of Helsinki Watch Groups; Carter had written a letter to Sakharov; and Jewish pressure for emigration was continuing.[11] Three of the most prominent Soviet dissidents were therefore arrested: Alexander Ginzburg on February 3, Yuri Orlov on February 10 (two days after Carter's press conference), and Anatoly Sharansky—who was a dissident, a member of the Helsinki Watch Group, and a Jewish Refusenik—on March 15, 1977. In addition, two American journalists and a businessman were arrested in Moscow on trumped-up charges.

During this period Carter and Brezhnev exchanged letters on their future relations.[12] Carter's first letter raised hopes in Moscow that SALT could indeed proceed within the Vladivostok framework. His second letter, however, dated February 14, 1977, proposed important changes: he wanted to discuss a range of new issues. The American embassy had meanwhile protested the arrest of Ginzburg and demanded his release. Brezhnev was furious on both counts and began to apply linkage from his side. The Politburo instructed Soviet ambassador Dobrynin to tell Secretary of State Cyrus Vance that raising the question of freeing Ginzburg "aroused the utmost bewilderment." In typically heavy-handed Soviet style, it was stressed that bringing questions "thoroughly under the jurisdiction of the Soviet state" into the sphere of interstate relations would "complicate" these relations. Statements of concern over human rights served "the purpose of support and even outright instigation" of some persons who "separated themselves from Soviet society." Some staff members of the U.S. embassy were directly involved, it was asserted, even "secretly" meeting with Sakharov. Dobrynin was told to call this "a direct act of the American intelligence services against the USSR," an ominous prelude to the Sharansky trial (see Chapter 4).

Brezhnev's answer on SALT, sent on February 25, was, as Carter later said with some understatement, "moderately sharp" in tone. Brezhnev accused the American president of "not valuing what we had already managed to accomplish" and of "abandoning a responsible, realistic approach." For good measure he further accused him of starting a correspondence with a "renegade [Sakharov] . . . who stands against normal, good relations between the USSR and the USA." Secretary Vance's first visit to Moscow on March 28–30, 1977 ended in utter failure.

Under these circumstances it is surprising that an upswing in the Jewish emigration began to be noted in the second half of 1977. Laurie Salitan, defending the internal theory, claims that what she calls the "barometer theory" of the external school "can not explain the surge in emigration in '76 [*sic*] –'79 when American-Soviet relations were deteriorating rapidly." Salitan believes that Soviet Jewish emigration policy in the second half of the 1970s was conditioned primarily by the same issues that had influenced it during the first half: Soviet nationality policy, the uneasy position of Jews in Soviet society, and a confrontation with the demands of a significant segment of the population that could no longer be quieted by imprisoning outspoken critics. According to her, Soviet authorities thought that letting that segment emigrate would remove individuals who would not accept their lot in Soviet society and at the same time satisfy those who felt that the Soviet Union was better off without the troublemakers.[13] These considerations may be true to a certain extent, but they do not explain the upswing in emigration in 1977, 1978, and 1979, or the decline in the early 1980s.

Robert O. Freedman, as a spokesman for the external school of thought, first of all denies the "rapid deterioration" in U.S.- Soviet relations during this period. To the contrary, he says, the Soviets once again urgently wanted trade and technology from the United States. The American gross national product was double that of the Soviet Union, and the gap in computer technology was widening. Freedman also notes that the Soviets badly wanted a strategic arms agreement. And finally there was "the China card": the fear of a Sino-American alignment against the Soviet Union.[14] This view is more to the point; yet it leaves open the question why Brezhnev, having just decried American interference in questions "thoroughly under the jurisdiction of the Soviet state," would nevertheless yield to foreign pressure on the emigration question.

A look at the interaction of external factors with internal economic development provides a clue. Brezhnev was, of course, well aware of the damage his crackdown on dissidents might do to Soviet-American relations. He also wanted more grain from the United States. The 1975 harvest had been disastrous, and the Soviets had to conclude a grain agreement with the United States that became operative on October 1, 1976. Soviet grain imports from the United States jumped from 6,116 million tons in 1976 to 14,585 million in 1977 and 15,684 million in 1978.[15] Détente and SALT also remained very important to Brezhnev as a means of effecting savings in the Soviet defense budget. He therefore gambled on a two-pronged policy: the crackdown would be offset by considerably increased Jewish emigration and by a pardon to five of the Jews condemned in the Leningrad Trial in 1970.[16] In the autumn of 1977, when Andrei Gromyko arrived in New York for the UN General Assembly and was, as usual, invited to Washington, Vance noted that

> there were modest grounds for hope that the erosion in US-Soviet relations could be halted. . . . The Soviets had taken several steps that suggested they wished to reduce the strain between us. . . . Jewish emigration levels rose to the highest number in five years; recent trials of Soviet dissidents ended in relatively light sentences and restrictions on US newsmen in Moscow were eased.[17]

The word "relatively" needs to be emphasized here, and the Sharansky trial was still to come, but nevertheless it looked as if the Soviets were once again prepaying for things they badly wanted from the Americans. They may also have been trying to stave off criticism during the CSCE follow-up meeting that opened in Belgrade on October 4, 1977.

The gamble seemed to pay off. The Carter administration did respond soon afterwards; it requested in November 1977 that Congress consider altering the Jackson-Vanik Amendment to remove the need for Soviet emigration assurances and instead allow the president to extend tariff benefits annually if emigration levels were "adequate."[18] The forces around Senator Henry Jackson did not agree, however. His amendment had specified that the Soviet Union would have to give "assurances" on future emigration, and there were no such assurances. Jewish activist organizations were opposed to a change in the amendment for a more practical reason: they were afraid that waiving this requirement and relinquishing the leverage it provided would undermine the democratic rights movements in the Soviet Union.[19] And so the requirement remained in force.

What did change was the attitude toward credits for agricultural exports to the Soviet Union. In June 1978 the American Jewish Congress announced support of a bill allowing export credits for sale of farm products to the Soviet Union in return for a continuing high level of emigration. By October, 25 million tons of grain had been sold to the Soviets with financial support from the United States.

During that autumn the emigration figures indeed continued to climb; in October 1978 the Netherlands embassy for the first time since October 1973 issued Israeli visas for more than 4,000 persons in one month. Toward the end of 1978 OVIR offices had suddenly become cooperative. Invitations corrected or extended by the Netherlands embassy, often rejected in the past, were now quite acceptable. New OVIR offices were opened in Odessa.[20] But the Soviet policy remained two-pronged. More dissidents were arrested, in particular Vladimir Slepak, who had been a member of the Helsinki Watch Group, one of the most outspoken Refuseniks, and a teacher of Hebrew. Orlov and Sharansky were taken to trial and received heavy sentences.

By April 1979 the embassy was issuing 230 visas per day, and on May 28 the 200,000th visa was handed out since the Netherlands began the representation of Israel in 1967. In 1979 visas had been issued for 50,461 persons; more Jewish emigrants left the Soviet Union that year than ever before.

Discussions on a Waiver of the Jackson-Vanik Amendment

Once more the Carter administration held discussions about the Jackson-Vanik Amendment with Jewish organizations and, among others, Representative Charles Vanik; Vanik himself supported a presidential waiver. On February 5, 1979, Senator Adlai Stevenson III had introduced legislation altering the Jackson-Vanik Amendment. No more assurances from the Soviet authorities would be required, only a presidential decision that emigration had been sufficiently liberated. The president would, moreover, be authorized to grant a waiver for five years instead of just one. The senator's professed goal was to remove any appearance of interference in the internal affairs of the Soviet Union, realizing its extreme sensitivity on this point.[21]

On April 12, 1979, an internal State Department memorandum concluded that "it would be timely now to call in [Soviet ambassador] Dobrynin to explain our intention to proceed with a waiver based upon an expectation of a continuation or improvement of the present level of emigration." A specific response would not be required because "any insistence that they give their blessing through a positive act runs the risk of being flatly rejected, which would worsen the prospects of using the waiver procedure in the future."[22] Secretary of State Vance did meet with Ambassador Dobrynin on April 29, 1979. He explained the president's intention, adding that "there was no need for USSR to confirm or deny." It was essential, however that the Soviet Union "say nothing inconsistent with the President's waiver and [his] report to Congress." Vance further asked for a private assurance from Dobrynin that "the President is correct in his understanding of prevailing Soviet policies and practice in the matter of emigration." These included an upward trend in the numbers of emigrants; improvement of the efficiency of emigration processing and of the circumstances of persons who had applied for emigration; and no intention of changing the foregoing policies.[23] Unfortunately the State Department has not released the Soviet reply.

In June, congressional hearings were held on Stevenson's proposal. Strong arguments were made against using trade as a weapon in foreign policy. But meanwhile Jewish activists in both the Soviet Union and the United States were mobilizing against any change in, or a waiver of, the Jackson-Vanik Amendment. Refusenik leader Alexander Lerner wrote a strongly worded letter from Moscow to Representative Vanik urging him not to accept changes. The National Conference on Soviet Jewry asserted that Congress should avoid making a waiver decision based solely on emigration figures, maintaining that this focus would constitute a "very narrow and technical interpretation" of the amendment. Instead Congress should consider the entire picture of Soviet Jewry.[24]

Senator Jackson himself also remained opposed to any concession in this matter that would not be based on public Soviet assurances, as demanded by his amendment. Said Jackson:

> Some argue that the recent rise in the number leaving the Soviet Union justifies bending the law to accommodate the Soviets. Others argue that we must extend benefits to the Soviets because the People's Republic of China will qualify for benefits and we must treat both the Soviets and Chinese alike. I cannot accept either view. This is no time to pretend that the Soviets have met the test of the law.[25]

Later the senator testified before the Senate Finance Subcommittee on International Trade, which was considering granting MFN to China. Jackson noted that on several occasions Chinese leaders had publicly given assurances regarding their government's future policies on emigration. But, he said, "The country that has chosen not to conform to Section 402 of the Trade Act of 1974 [the Jackson-Vanik Amendment] is the

Soviet Union. . . . China and the Soviet Union, in our national interest
. . . cannot be treated alike."[26] Jackson was convinced that the Soviets
could have produced a statement similar to the Chinese declaration that
he would also have been able to accept.[27] He and his assistants—and not
for the first time—ignored the fact that public assurance about a matter
the Soviets considered an internal affair was precisely what the Soviet
Union, aspiring as it was to equal superpower status with the United
States, felt it could and would never provide.

Facing a reelection campaign in the autumn of 1980, President Carter
could ill afford to antagonize an important senator from his own party,
as well as a significant number of Jewish organizations, by waiving the
Jackson-Vanik Amendment. He considered that the People's Republic of
China had offered sufficient assurances in the sense of the amendment.
The People's Republic obtained MFN on October 23, 1979, and Congress approved.[28] Hungary and Rumania soon followed. But the demands of the amendment, as interpreted by the Jackson forces, continued to forestall granting MFN to the Soviet Union. This must have been
a blow to the Soviet authorities, especially since they may have considered that the 60,000 benchmark demanded by Senator Jackson in 1973
had been met in 1979, if the exit permits granted to Germans and Armenians were added to the Jewish totals[29] (which Senator Jackson, however, had expressly excluded).

Conclusion

Thus the ups and downs in the emigration of Jews from the Soviet Union
during the 1970s clearly showed the interaction of internal and external
factors. In 1974 the adoption of the Jackson-Vanik Amendment and the
resulting loss of trade opportunities weakened Brezhnev's internal position and strengthened the hand of his more conservative opponents in
the party who had doubted the wisdom of his new policies from the
beginning. Then an increase in the price of oil improved the economic
strength of the Soviet Union considerably. Détente went into decline, and
the endeavor to influence American public opinion through an increased
Jewish emigration, which had failed in any case, was put on hold for the
time being. A downward trend in Jewish emigration was the result.

The election of Jimmy Carter in 1976 created a new situation to
which the Soviet authorities responded with a two-pronged policy
regarding dissidence and emigration. The KGB clamped down hard on

dissidents in the human rights movement, including Jews. But at the same time Soviet authorities allowed a perceptible increase in Jewish emigration in the hopes of influencing American opinion regarding nuclear disarmament agreements, a possible waiver of the Jackson-Vanik Amendment, and the granting of credit facilities for large grain exports. This effort culminated in the top emigration year of 1979. Toward the end of that year, when it had become clear that neither a waiver of the Jackson-Vanik Amendment nor a ratification of SALT II was forthcoming, the Soviets began to reconsider their policy once again.

Anatoly (Natan) Sharansky, Rosh Hashana, 1986. *WZPS photo by Richard Nowitz, courtesy Center for Documentation and Information Israel, The Hague*

Avital Sharansky in Jerusalem, 1983. *WZPS photo by Sam Silver, courtesy Center for Documentation and Information Israel, The Hague*

Professor Alexander Lerner

Joseph Begun, one of the most militant Refuseniks. *Photo courtesy Center for Documentation and Information Israel, The Hague*

Ida Nudel, called the mother of the Refuseniks. *Photo courtesy Center for Documentation and Information Israel, The Hague*

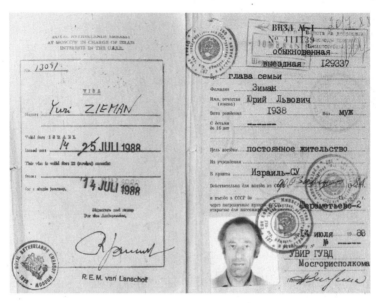

Soviet exit permit, with the visa for Israel issued by the Netherlands embassy in Moscow. *Zieman Collection, Boston*

Filling in the visa application form. Exit permits were usually valid for only thirty days. Soviet Jews who had received a permit thus hurried to the Netherlands consulate in Moscow where they could obtain visas for Israel. They also needed transit visas for Austria, since there were no direct connections from the Soviet Union to Israel. *Photo by Marc de Haan, courtesy Hollandse Hoogte, Amsterdam*

Demonstration of the Refusenik family E. O. Prilutsky in front of the Institute for Research and Patents of the Energy Industry in Moscow. The sign in the middle reads, "Your authority's collective refusal to cooperate prevents us from going to Israel." The sign on the right reads, "Stop torturing Mom and Dad." *Photo courtesy Nan Greifer, London*

Militia breaking up a demonstration of Refuseniks. The sign in the middle reads, "[I want?] to see my son and grandson." *Photo courtesy Nan Greifer, London*

Opening session of the Refusenik "Symposium on State Secrecy" in an apartment in Moscow in 1988. In the background, from left to right: Tsilya Raiburd, Pavel Abramovitch, Emil Manjeritsky, Tatyana Zieman. *Zieman Collection, Boston*

Freedom March demonstration by some 25,000 Jews in Washington, D.C., December 1987. *Jewish Federation Delegation, South Broward, Florida*

PART II

THE 1980s

9

The Bleak Years

In November 1979 the monthly number of visas for Israel issued by the
Netherlands embassy in Moscow began to drop. This meant that Soviet
authorities had begun to reduce the number of exit permits in October.[1]
What were their motivations? Hopes of obtaining a waiver of the Jackson-Vanik Amendment and the ratification of SALT II had undoubtedly
been major reasons for permitting a high level of Jewish emigration in
1978 and 1979. By the autumn of 1979, those hopes had effectively been
dashed. The amendment had not been waived,[2] and although SALT II
had been signed in June, its ratification was hopelessly stalled.[3] So the
Soviet leadership may well have felt that there was not much to be lost
anymore as far as international repercussions were concerned, because
"détente was already effectively dead."[4]

Richard Schifter, counselor at the National Security Council and former assistant secretary of state for humanitarian affairs, thinks that in
the autumn of 1979 the Soviet leadership decided in fact on an altogether
different approach in its relationship with the United States: more confrontational, more demanding of equal superpower status. Decisions to
invade Afghanistan, to join Fidel Castro in his subversion in the Ameri-
cas, and to diminish the Jewish emigration might have been part of the
new approach.[5] However, recent research in former Soviet archives by
the Cold War International History Project has uncovered a document
revealing that the decision to invade Afghanistan was taken by a sub-
group of the Politburo as late as December 12, 1979. The project has not
yet uncovered archival documents that would permit a clear reconstruction of Soviet decision making earlier that year. In fact, remarkably few
documents for the months preceding the invasion have so far become

available. The project's bulletin notes, however, that "U.S.-Soviet ties had been sinking ever since the signing of the SALT II treaty in Vienna in June 1979."[6]

Western public opinion next reacted with fury to the Soviet invasion of Afghanistan. The United States and other nations boycotted the Moscow Olympics of 1980. President Carter imposed a grain embargo. Relations between the Soviet Union and the United States (and the West in general) were now really deteriorating rapidly. External influences, in other words, were strongly negative for Jewish emigration.

It should also be remembered that there had always been a great deal of internal resistance to Jewish emigration inside the Soviet Union, from the KGB and the military security services as well as from conservatives in the party and in the population in general. No doubt that resistance was enormously strengthened by the high emigration levels of 1978 and 1979. Many felt that such a massive emigration harmed the Soviet Union's international prestige. A new crackdown on dissidents in general was clearly part of the new confrontational approach. Andrei Sakharov and his wife were sent into internal exile in Gorki in January 1980 for having criticized the invasion of Afghanistan. Almost all human rights groups were suppressed between 1980 and 1982, and their *samizdat* publications ceased to appear.[7]

The End of the First Wave

The convergence of these negative external and internal factors must have led to the decision also to curtail the Jewish emigration. The numbers went down sharply: visas were issued by the Netherlands embassy for 50,461 persons in 1979, but for only 20,342 in 1980. It was the beginning of the worst period for Jewish emigration since 1967.

At first people in Moscow could not believe the numbers. The Netherlands embassy reported at the end of February 1980: "The indications are that there will be fewer exits issued in 1980, but no decrease like that in 1975."[8] But the decrease turned out to be much worse, in comparison, than the one in 1975. It was first noted in the Ukraine, and the embassy remarked: "The deteriorated political relations with the United States have naturally played into the hands of those who are in favor of limiting emigration. It is striking that Ukrainian emigrants, who relatively more often go to the United States than to Israel, are suffering most."[9] In Moscow, on the other hand, there was a brief increase in the number of exit permits issued in May 1980. Apparently the authorities were again trying to quickly decapitate the Jewish movement, probably with an eye to the Olympic Games scheduled for their capital that summer. That increase did not last. Embassy figures tell the story: in January 1980, it had still issued visas for 3,271 persons; after September 1980 the monthly figure dipped below 1,000, and it was not to reach above 1,000 again until February 1988, with one exception: in February 1981 there was again a sudden but brief upsurge (see Table 2, pages 222–23). The embassy noted then that many highly qualified Jews received permits with great speed but with a very short period of validity. The intention was clearly again to remove some "unruly" Jews, this time before the Congress of the Communist Party in March.[10] After that the figures continued their downward slide; in 1984 and 1986 the annual totals did not even reach 1,000.

Soviet authorities took pains to explain that the reduction in Jewish emigration was not the Kremlin's doing. An anti-Zionist committee, consisting mostly of Jews, was set up on April 21, 1983. It held a press conference in June to explain that "the family reunification after the Second World War had been basically completed."[11] The world was supposed to draw the conclusion that there was now no reason anymore for Jews to emigrate. In fact, of course, it was OVIR that engineered the decrease in the number of applications by

— confiscating or delaying delivery of invitations;
— variously restricting the issuing of questionnaires needed for applications;
— regulating the number of applications accepted in a given city within a certain time;
— limiting the opening hours of OVIR offices in the main cities of Jewish emigration (such as Kiev, Kharkov, Odessa, Kishinev) to one or two days a week, causing long queues;
— checking family relationships and refusing to accept invitations from anyone except parents or children;
— refusing to accept changes inserted in *vysovs* by the embassy;
— refusing to accept application documents from persons of military draft age or close to it;
— refusing to accept application papers in cases in which part of the family did not wish to, or could not, leave;

— demanding that the questionnaire be registered at the place of
  work, which often led to the dismissal of the prospective emigrant
  even before he had actually submitted his application;
— imposing a very high tax on several items of personal property
  that could be taken out of the country.[12]

As was to be expected, the number of refusals also increased. Refusal
now was often an even worse blow than it had been earlier. In the 1960s
there had been almost no hope that an application for an exit permit
would be granted at all, but in the 1970s many came to hold expectations that an early departure would be possible. Plans and preparations
were made, and sometimes postponed "until next year," for the door was
now open anyway—and then suddenly that door was closed again.
Harassment was stepped up, applicants were arrested and condemned
for "hooliganism," the scientific seminars of Refuseniks were interfered
with, and teachers of Hebrew were severely persecuted. Several
Refuseniks were informed that they could not expect to receive an exit
permit, ever.

The reasons for the Soviet decision to end the enormous surge in the
Jewish emigration that they had allowed in the late 1970s must first of
all be sought in the failure of Soviet policy to obtain from the United
States either the ratification of SALT or the waiver of the restrictions of
the Jackson-Vanik Amendment. The more liberal emigration policy had
failed to sufficiently influence Western—and in this case especially American—public opinion. Soviet opponents of that policy now grabbed the
chance to discard it. Then the Soviet invasion of Afghanistan proved that
the Soviet foreign policy had become more confrontational; at the same
time, it precluded any Western concessions on trade or disarmament.
Détente was dead, and the Soviet Union entered an era of political and
economic stagnation. Internal factors, this time mostly of a political
nature, interacted with the external ones. Together they led to a very
negative result for Jewish emigration, which went down to its lowest
level since the early 1970s.

A Change in Dutch Policy

There was very little the Netherlands embassy could do in 1980 to stem
the continued decrease of the number of exit permits issued by Soviet
authorities and the increased harassment of applicants. A change did

occur in the official attitude of the Netherlands government regarding demarches in favor of Refuseniks. For the first time such a demarche was made independently of the representation of Israeli interests. Just as happened in the United States, when Congress took the initiative with the Jackson-Vanik Amendment, it was the Dutch parliament that forced the government to change its policy. Early in 1980 the Ministry of Foreign Affairs in The Hague instructed the embassy to carry out a demarche in behalf of the Refusenik Ida Nudel. This demarche, said The Hague, was to be made at the request of the chairman of the First Chamber of parliament (the Senate), Th. L. M. Thurlings. The ambassador should therefore "bring it to the attention of the authorities in an appropriate manner, quite separate of the interest-representation of Israel."[13]

Ida Nudel had been refused an exit permit in 1972. By 1978 she was so exasperated that one day she hung a sheet out of the window of her Moscow apartment on which she had written: "KGB, let me have my visa."[14] Promptly arrested, she was condemned to four years of interior exile for "hooliganism." Requests for her release came from all parts of the world, but she had to wait until 1987 before she received her exit permit. Before and after her trial she kept up a lively correspondence with Jewish prisoners, sending them packages as often as she could and receiving in her home those who were finally released. She fully deserved the title given her: "the guardian angel of the prisoners and Refuseniks."[15]

In Nudel's behalf the Netherlands ambassador carried out a demarche in January 1980—not, as was customary when Israeli interests were concerned, with the Middle Eastern Section of the Consular Department, but with the head of the First European Department of MID, Zaitsev, who was responsible for Netherlands affairs. The reaction was as sharp as had to be expected: "Nudel, a Soviet citizen, had contravened Soviet law and could not claim treatment different from that of others. The MID did not want to hear her name."[16]

The question must be posed—and was undoubtedly posed in the Netherlands Ministry of Foreign Affairs at the time—whether such demarches served any purpose if their outcome was so predictable. The first answer to that question is that, even if no results could be expected, a government with traditions and convictions like those of the Netherlands owed it to itself to act in behalf of victims of oppression and to demand from the Soviet government the application of human rights provisions that both governments had signed.[17] Such actions could not be left to the United States alone. Moreover, as conversations with Soviet insiders have much later made clear, humanitarian cases would be dealt with on the Soviet side in accordance with the level and the frequency of the Western demarches.[18] It was significant that this first demarche does not seem to have influenced the exercise of the representation of Israeli interests by the Netherlands embassy, although an incident did occur several months later when the militia in front of the Netherlands embassy tried to prevent a couple carrying Israeli passports from entering the building and a scuffle broke out with some Dutch officials.[19] The constant refusal to let former Soviet emigrants in Israel travel back to the Soviet Union to visit seriously ill relatives or to attend a funeral remained another nasty aspect of Soviet policy. Soviet Jews were unfailingly refused permission to go to foreign countries for medical treatment.

Demarches in the name of the Netherlands only, or jointly on behalf of Israel and the Netherlands together, became more frequent. In July 1980 the embassy asked the Consular Department of MID for information about four cases in which Jews who had already been handed their exit permits were suddenly deprived of them again under some pretext. The answers were, according to the embassy, "unsatisfactory and very short—but the fact that they were given at all [was] rather remarkable."[20] Another demarche was carried out when it became known in 1981 that the Refusenik Anatoly Sharansky was seriously ill in prison (see Chapters 4 and 14). The ambassador obtained an interview with the head of the Consular Department, Teterin. He stated that his demarche was on behalf of Sharansky's wife in Israel on the one hand but had to be understood in a wider humanitarian framework on the other, "in view of the great concern of the Dutch public and public opinion." The Soviet official answered first that Sharansky was not married; there was no Mrs. Sharansky and therefore Israel had no standing in the matter, it was an internal affair. (The Sharanskys had been married in a religious ceremony and not before a civil magistrate, as was legally required.) He added that the Netherlands was also interfering with the internal affairs of the Soviet Union. No, said the ambassador, that was applying a legalistic norm; humanitarian concerns had a wider meaning. Teterin then unbent just enough to declare that he did not know anything disquieting about Sharansky's health.[21] Several more interventions for Sharansky were to follow. A year later the new head of the Consular Department of MID, Aganin, finally refused to discuss Sharansky's health anymore, saying that "Israel should pay more attention to victims in Lebanon than to one Soviet citizen undergoing his punishment."[22]

Further demarches were carried out by the embassy in behalf of other well-known Refusenik prisoners such as Vladimir Slepak.[23] The Ministry of Foreign Affairs sent a list of "poignant" cases to the embassy in August 1982 with the instruction that it be presented to the Soviet authorities during a "chance meeting."[24] Complying might be difficult, was the answer: "We did present some poignant cases to Aganin some weeks ago, but he said MID could not intervene in decisions of autonomous authorities and could not even receive some written particulars." The chargé d'affaires wondered therefore whether it would not be counterproductive to present another list at that moment.[25] The Israeli embassy in The Hague, expressing concern at the lack of results, requested the embassy to continue its efforts nevertheless, although Israel fully realized the problems.[26] When the Dutch deputy chief-of-mission then paid another visit to the deputy head of the Consular Department, this official did begin by refusing to accept the list. Emigration, he said, was an internal affair. But after a lengthy discussion he did accept a note regarding nondelivery of *vysovs*, made notes himself on one humanitarian case, and finally accepted written particulars about another.[27] These demarches were to remain an uphill struggle for many years to come.

In the summer of 1983, when a new anti-Zionism campaign was started in the Soviet Union, there was a renewed discussion between the ministry in The Hague and the ambassador in Moscow about the caution with which the Netherlands embassy had to operate. A member of the Dutch parliament questioned whether so much restraint had to be maintained when bringing cases to the attention of the Soviet authorities. The ambassador of Israel also indicated, in very diplomatic language, that the embassy was perhaps too cautious: "The situation was hopeless anyway." But his Dutch colleague in Moscow did not agree: "In view of the global East-West framework in which the Soviet Union has placed its Jewish emigration policy, steps by the Netherlands could have little or no positive effect. But such steps could further limit the room for useful humanitarian steps by the embassy." He therefore advised that caution should be maintained.[28]

Shortly afterward it was proposed that the Netherlands foreign minister write a personal letter to his Soviet counterpart Andrei Gromyko regarding the Jewish dissident Josef Begun. The head of the European Section in the Ministry of Foreign Affairs advised against such an action. "Only if parliament would urge you to act could you contemplate steps," he wrote. But the director general for political affairs added:

"Whatever Gromyko's attitude, letters from our foreign minister and many other ministers might perhaps have an influence. Why should we act only at the urging of parliament?" The minister decided to wait for the advice from the ambassador in Moscow.[29] This advice has not been preserved; it most likely was given orally. In any case, no letter was sent.

An important step toward closer relations between the Netherlands embassy and the Refusenik community was taken in the summer of 1984. The ambassador allowed the head of his Consular Section to attend one of the scientific seminars held in the apartment of Alexander Lerner (see Chapter 4)—a great change from the standard line followed in the 1970s.[30] During the seminar the expected arrival in Moscow of a large Israeli delegation for a biochemistry congress was discussed. The delegation duly arrived a month later, but its head, former Israeli president Ephraim Katzir, and four of its other members were arrested during a visit to a Refusenik family and expelled. The embassy vainly protested that it had not been informed of the arrests.[31]

Conclusion

The Netherlands embassy in the early 1980s became more active in behalf of Jews who wanted to emigrate, but the results of its many demarches remained meager. In cables to the Ministry of Foreign Affairs in The Hague, the embassy often expressed frustration at its inability to seriously influence the fate of the many Jews who wanted to leave the Soviet Union and were unable to obtain a *vysov*, were harassed when they tried to obtain an exit permit, or were finally refused altogether. Yet embassy officials continued to approach the Consular Department of MID about the most poignant cases, not only because they were so instructed but also out of their own convictions. At the same time, the embassy's constant pleading with the Soviet authorities and the better relations it established with the Jewish community during the bleak years of the early 1980s laid the groundwork for the more active stand Dutch diplomats were able to adopt when opportunities opened up under *perestroika* later on (see Chapter 14).

IO

Perestroika

On March 11, 1985, Mikhail Sergeyevits Gorbachev was chosen as secretary general of the Communist Party of the Soviet Union (CPSU). He was the third secretary general since Leonid Brezhnev had died on November 10, 1982; the other two—Yuri Andropov and Konstantin Chernenko—had each served in that capacity for scarcely a year. Gorbachev was by far the youngest member of the Politburo at that time: he was only fifty-four, while the average age of the others was over seventy. One may wonder what made the older members choose this "young" man—who would remove all of them from their positions of power within three years.

The Impact of Gorbachev

The most likely reason for the elevation of Gorbachev is that the other members of the Politburo realized that a new approach to the management of the country's economy was urgently needed. The Soviet economy was stagnating and far from reaching the optimistic figures that were published. There was a dire need for economic reform if the party wanted to remain in power. Andropov had been elected for the same reason in 1982, but he had died before he could carry out any of his reform plans. Although he had handpicked Gorbachev as his successor, the elderly Chernenko had been chosen instead, in a final try to move back to what the gerontocracy of the Politburo considered "normalcy." After the debacle of the leadership of the wooden and sickly Chernenko, Gorbachev, who was not only the youngest of the top leadership but also the only one with an academic degree and experience in both economic and political fields, must have seemed the logical choice. Besides, he was not known as a wild reformer, born and raised as he was in the provincial echelons of the party in Stavropol before Andropov brought him to Moscow in the autum of 1978 to become a secretary of the Central Committee.[1] In November 1979 Gorbachev became a candidate member of the Politburo; by October 1980 he was a full member, in charge of agriculture.

In view of his education and experience, Gorbachev must have been more aware than any of the other Politburo members how petrified the party had become and how stagnant the economy was under its central-ized communist command. During the first half of the 1980s, for exam-ple, the Soviet Union spent thousands of millions of dollars on grain imports from the West. About 50 percent of hard currency foreign exchange earnings, on the other hand, came from oil exports alone. The range of products the Soviets were willing or able to trade with the West was beginning to resemble that of a developing nation.[2] Gorbachev had told the Central Committee at the end of 1984: "We can only remain a world power if we put our own house in order." After consolidating his power over the party during 1985, he launched his reform plan at the Twenty-seventh Party Congress, on February 25, 1986. He called it *per-estroika* (reconstruction). As the name indicates, the plan was not meant to be a radical break with the past but a careful reform within the sys-tem. Gorbachev thought that "the possibilities of socialism had not been sufficiently exhausted."[3]

The secretary general must have realized early on that, for his reforms to have any chance, he would need, on the one hand, the cooperation of Soviet intellectuals and, on the other, improved relations with the West.[4] This realization led him to formulate the concepts of *glasnost*, or "open-ness" in public life, and "New Thinking" in foreign affairs. Both were to have considerable impact on the question of Jewish emigration. *Glasnost* would eventually lead to much greater freedom of expression than had ever been known in the Soviet Union and make public discussion about human rights, including the refusal of emigration, possible. New Think-ing introduced a flexibility in the Soviet foreign policy that later enabled the new minister of foreign affairs, Eduard Shevardnadze,[5] to include discussions on human rights in the Soviet Union in his talks with foreign colleagues, especially the U.S. secretary of state. At the funeral of his pre-decessor Chernenko, a few days after he became secretary general, Gor-bachev had been warned by U.S. Vice-President George Bush "that this issue [human rights] is extremely important to the president and the American people."[6]

But there was no sign of change in the Jewish emigration policy in either 1985 or 1986. In fact the Netherlands embassy was only able to issue Israeli visas for 1,153 persons in 1985 and 902 in 1986, among the lowest yearly totals since the early 1970s. A CSCE meeting on human rights in Ottawa in April 1985 ended in failure. The one small sign of hope was a message from the embassy to The Hague in July 1986: the Soviet foreign ministry had told the embassy that Israel had proposed a meeting of consular officials and that MID agreed to such a meeting. It was suggested that the meeting be held in Helsinki in July or August.[7] There had been frequent political contacts between Israeli and Soviet officials at the United Nations, but this was the first such contact specifically organized between consular officials.

Two officials from each side went to the Finnish capital on August 18, 1986, for a meeting that lasted only one and one-half hours. The Soviet delegation had a very limited mandate: it only wanted "clarifications" on the position of the "Russian group of people" (in Israel); the protection of the Russian Orthodox Church (meaning its properties in Israel), and the protection of Soviet interests in Israel. For those purposes the Soviet officials proposed to send a Soviet delegation to Israel to discuss "technical matters." The Israeli delegation had naturally hoped that the emigration question and possibly the restoration of at least consular relations might be discussed. But the Soviets answered that they had no permission at all to discuss what they called "political" questions. The Israelis then presented a written statement asking for clarification on the position of Jews in the Soviet Union. Would more Jews be allowed to emigrate, and what was the condition of prisoners? The Israeli delegation added that a visit of a Soviet delegation to Israel could be accepted only if an Israeli delegation would be allowed to visit the Soviet Union.[8] Nothing doing, was the answer of Gorbachev's spokesman Gerasimov the next day: "There is no Israeli property in the Soviet Union."[9] The stalemate between the two countries continued.

In the spring of 1986 a new bureau was created within MID: the Department for Humanitarian Affairs. The words "human rights" were still anathema in the Soviet Union, but the new department did raise expectations of at least some action in the humanitarian field. In August 1986 a new chapter was added to the Statute on Entering and Leaving the Soviet Union of 1970, which took effect on January 1, 1987.[10] While it introduced greater clarity on many points, it turned out to be more restrictive regarding the possibility of obtaining a permit to emigrate than even the actual practice. Exit permits were to be granted only to persons sponsored by a first-degree relative, including brother or sister. There would be no exceptions made for Jews, said the authorities. The "secrecy" and "poor relative" issues remained unchanged.

American Pressure

Meanwhile things began to stir in the relationship between the Soviet Union and the United States. George Shultz, appointed secretary of state by President Ronald Reagan in 1982, decided to push hard for observance of human rights by the Soviet Union and in particular for freer emigration of Jews. In a meeting with Soviet foreign minister Andrei Gromyko, in New York on September 28 of that year, Shultz "gave particular attention to the human rights area . . . Jews, dissidents and families divided by Soviet refusal . . . and the Helsinki watch group." Gromyko answered: "Is it so important that Mr. or Mrs. so and so can or cannot leave such and such a country? I would call it a tenth-rate question."[11] The difference between the Western concern for the rights of the individual and the basic Soviet contempt for those rights could not have been shown more clearly than in those words.

Shultz's insistence on emphasizing human rights in his discussions with the Soviet leadership was keenly supported by President Reagan, who himself brought human rights questions forward "with genuine feeling"[12] in his conversations with Soviet leaders and with Soviet ambassador Anatoly Dobrynin. Shultz rejected linkage, as Secretary of State Cyrus Vance had done (see Chapter 8), but maintained a forceful stand. In an address at the University of California he stated:

> Linkage had too often become a trap. The Soviets used it against us. In the case of the Soviet Jews, the Soviets were using human beings as pawns, encouraging us to believe that concessions to Soviet demands on issues of important substance, such as MFN-treatment for their prospective exports to the United States, would lead to better treatment of Jews in the Soviet Union or to more permits for Jewish emigration. We would, I argued, avoid that trap by addressing every issue on its merits: we would press on what was right for Soviet

Jews whether things were going well or poorly on other issues of concern. We would step up to each issue and assert our interest strongly.[13]

Shultz seemed to forget that the linkage between Jewish emigration and most-favored-nation status for Soviet exports had been created by the U.S. Congress, not by the Soviets. But his insistence on addressing the issue of the Soviet Jews "whether things were going well or poorly on other issues" was eventually to bring success, although success had to wait until Gorbachev and Shevardnadze had consolidated their New Thinking in Soviet foreign policy. The Soviet Jews owe a great deal to the conviction and persistence of George Shultz.

Shultz's first success came at the second Gorbachev-Reagan summit in Reykjavik on October 11 and 12, 1986. Shultz insisted again on a discussion of the human rights issue, and this time his strategy worked. He called the result "an outstanding break-through. The Soviets had acquiesced by agreeing to recognize human rights issues as a regular, open and legitimate part of our agenda."[14] The point was overshadowed at the time by the failure of the two leaders to agree on nuclear disarmament, but the human rights concession bore fruit inside the Soviet Union soon afterward. The most public step taken by Gorbachev was the release of Andrei Sakharov from his forced exile in Gorki on December 16, 1986, after their famous telephone conversation. Sakharov's triumphant arrival at the Yaroslavl station in Moscow on December 23 was seen, by the hundreds who welcomed him, as the beginning of a new era in which human rights would play their legitimate role in Soviet political life. They were right, although the road to that goal was not to be straight or quick or easy.

It was Gorbachev's right-hand man Alexander Yakovlev, then a secretary of the Central Committee of the CPSU, who at about the same time ordered the committee-secretariat to create a section in the Department of International Information—the Section on Humanitarian Issues and Human Rights. This was an important new departure since the Central Committee was a bastion of conservatism in the party and the party was still controlling life in the Soviet Union. It was now put in charge of a more liberal policy regarding human rights.

What caused this remarkable switch in policy? Alexander Yakovlev denies that foreign pressure had anything to do with it. "It may disappoint you but there is no direct connection between the events in

Reykjavik and the establishment of the special section in the Central Committee," he claims. "Gorbachev wanted to introduce democracy in the Soviet Union and we realized there could be no democracy without human rights."[15]

That statement is not quite convincing. The "democratization" that Gorbachev proposed at the Plenum of the Central Committee in January 1987 was a democratization within the Communist Party that as yet had little to do with Western-style democracy and would not have required greater observation of human rights. It is quite possible that the new Soviet leaders, in the first place Gorbachev himself and Shevardnadze, did already sincerely want to do something about human rights in their country. Yakovlev, who had served as Soviet ambassador to Canada and discussed the problem of Jewish emigration with Jews who demonstrated in front of his embassy in Ottawa,[16] did take the lead in the Central Committee secretariat toward a more liberal stand. But it seems unlikely that a decision to increase Jewish emigration would have been taken with such speed and at that very moment were it not for the pressure exercised by the American administration and, it should be added, by the Western and neutral participants at the third CSCE follow-up conference, which opened in Vienna on November 4, 1986. Shevardnadze surprised everyone there by proposing during the opening session that a conference on "humanitarian affairs" be held in Moscow. Gorbachev needed goodwill and credits from the West and could not afford another torrent of criticism on the Soviet human rights performance, as had been received during the previous conference in Madrid (see Chapter 7). Whatever the inner feelings of the main participants, the timing of the new measures could hardly have been coincidental. It was foreign pressure that gave the final push toward liberation of prisoners and more freedom for Jews to emigrate.[17]

The new section in the secretariat of the Central Committee began its work in January 1987, headed by Andrei Grachev. He had to "dance with the wolves," as one participant remarked,[18] because many others, in particular some hard-liners in the Politburo headed by its second in command, Yegor Ligachev, and in the KGB, remained obstinately opposed to the application of human rights and human freedom in their country. The KGB had a special department working on Jewish problems: Department 8, "on the struggle against Zionism." According to Yakovlev, "it controlled all the struggle against Zionism at the international level and promoted and spread anti-semitic sentiments all over the world, especially in the Arab countries." When a draft document containing a new law on exit and entry had been written in the secretariat of the Central Committee, the KGB came back immediately with a document twice as long and full of counterarguments.[19]

Special committees for humanitarian affairs were also set up in the other governmental bodies that dealt with Jewish emigration, including the Ministries of Foreign Affairs, the Interior, Defense, Defense Industry, and "Medium Machine Building" (responsible for nuclear armament). The heads of these committees would meet regularly in the Central Committee under the chairmanship of Yakovlev. The setup was typical of the complexity of decision making in the Soviet bureaucracy: everything had to be done by committee. It would take tremendous effort and time to reach any decisions.

For most Westerners it is hard to understand that Gorbachev, Shevardnadze, and Yakovlev could not simply order that a new liberal law on emigration be adopted. Whenever Gorbachev referred to his struggles with "opponents," there was a tendency among Western observers at the time to doubt the truth of such complaints. Hadn't the secretary general of the CPSU always been all-powerful? It must be remembered, however, that by the end of the 1960s collegial rule and consensus decision making had already become the norm within the Soviet bureaucracy. In the 1970s the Central Committee expanded and became more powerful; it was much more than a rubber-stamp. "Central Committee member and General Secretary are mutually vulnerable and mutually dependent," wrote an American observer in 1971.[20] This assessment was all the more true during the first years of Gorbachev's tenure as secretary general, when the Central Committee was still dominated by elderly members who had served as party leaders for many years. Moreover, he could not yet be completely sure of support in the Politburo, where Yegor Ligachev, although he had been brought in by Gorbachev himself, quickly developed into his conservative opponent.[21] Gorbachev is to be believed, therefore, when he claims that he did not decide everything alone.[22]

Last but not least there was always the KGB, the state within the state,[23] acting on the basis of ingrained antisemitism. KGB officials were the main opponents of reconstruction and of all reforms. Gorbachev's orders were often not carried out.[24] Could Gorbachev not have subdued this hydra? No, says Yakovlev, he depended too much on the KGB for information. "He liked information about anything, about himself, his wife, about everything which surrounded him. [KGB head Vladimir]

Kryuehkov was a sort of a Jesuit character, and he knew that weak point of Mr. Gorbachev and just supplied that information."[25]

Early in 1987 Gorbachev nevertheless decided that he had to take decisive action and for once overrule the KGB: political prisoners must be freed, and more Jews must be allowed to emigrate. In January 1987, an MID official stated in an interview that the number of permits would be "drastically" increased.[26] The Netherlands ambassador was told by a consular official of MID on February 3 that "difficult visa questions would be dealt with quicker from now on."[27] It also became clear that the first-degree relative requirement was being interpreted as applying only to new applicants, not to those who had requested an exit permit before January 1, 1977. According to an official statement, 500 additional exit permits had been granted. On February 12, Gorbachev's spokesman Gerasimov announced that 112 prisoners had been pardoned. In answer to a question he added that Joseph Begun, one of the staunchest Refuseniks, was not among them, "since he had not asked for it [a pardon]."[28] Begun was soon afterward freed anyway.[29] On February 23, the embassy could for the first time report a noticeable increase in the number of applications for Israeli visas. This was an exciting moment that thousands all over the world had been waiting for; it looked as if a second emigration wave had begun.

The Second Wave

The first figures were indeed encouraging: while visas had been issued for only 62 people in December 1986, more than 900 people were allowed to leave in April 1987—in one month as many as had left in the whole of 1986. But that figure remained the maximum monthly quota for the rest of the year. The total number of persons receiving visas in 1987 was to reach 8,563. The opponents of Jewish emigration were clearly still doing all in their power to limit the flow of permits, and the better-known Refuseniks, in particular, were not yet allowed to go. The Moscow daily *Vechernaya Moskva* even published the names of Alexander Lerner, Vladimir Slepak, and six others who would not be given exit permits because of "secrecy." It was progress that for the first time such news could be published, although it did not help the Refuseniks in question.

In March 1987 two prominent Jewish leaders, Edgar M. Bronfman, president of the World Jewish Congress, and Morris B. Abram, president of the American National Conference on Soviet Jewry, visited Moscow and succeeded in discussing with the Soviet leadership improvements in the emigration procedures for Soviet Jews. After his return, Abram reported to the Department of State that they had obtained impressive concessions. According to him the Soviets were prepared to institute direct flights from the Soviet Union to Israel via Rumania. Abram did emphasize in this connection that the Jewish community in the United States was insisting on freedom of choice for the emigrants as to their final destination. The Soviets were furthermore reported to be willing, in principle, to permit 11,000 Refuseniks to emigrate, excepting those retained under the secrecy clause. They had also hinted that the new regulations on exit and entry might not be interpreted restrictively for new applicants. Finally, they were prepared to be forthcoming on issues related to Jewish religion such as ritual slaughter and opening of synagogues.[30]

For the time being, however, none of those promises was realized, except for the more liberal interpretation of the new exit regulations.[31] Had the Jewish leaders been misled? Alexander Yakovlev remembers that he did help conclude an agreement between the Jewish delegation and the Soviet minister of aviation so that there would be direct flights from Moscow to Tel Aviv. "Everybody agreed on that," he says, "including Mr. Gorbachev." Sometime later he asked Gorbachev why nothing was happening. The answer was, "The KGB is against it."[32] Israel would have to wait for direct flights for several more years. Nevertheless the Israeli authorities decided to reciprocate the Soviet reopening of the emigration with a gesture on their part. They consented to a Soviet delegation to Israel "in the hope of reciprocity."[33] Visas were provided by the Netherlands embassy for a group of eight people, and the delegation arrived in Israel on July 12, 1987. But reciprocity was not quickly forthcoming: it took another year before a similar Israeli mission could arrive in Moscow (see Chapter 14).

Secretary of State Shultz arrived in Moscow in April 1987, for the first time taking along his assistant secretary for humanitarian affairs, Richard Schifter. Schifter had separate discussions with a Soviet counterpart, Vice-Minister Anatoly Adamishin. Nothing came out of these discussions, but a precedent had been set. When Shultz and Schifter attended a Jewish *seder* organized in the U.S. embassy compound, Shultz told the Refuseniks gathered there: "Never give up. Never give up. I can assure you: we are not going to give up." Schifter had another meeting in Moscow in August, and at that time he was able to discuss individual cases of persons wanting to emigrate to the United States. As soon as he turned to prospective emigrants for Israel, however, his interlocutors clammed up: that was no business of the United States. Schifter explained that the issue was not whether a particular person wanted to emigrate to the United States but whether the Soviet Union was prepared to abide by the provisions of the Helsinki Final Act, signed by Leonid Brezhnev on behalf of his country. When Shevardnadze visited Washington in September, he brought along the head of the Department of Humanitarian Affairs of MID, Yuri Reshetov. The Soviets had taken Schifter's point: they had decided that if a Soviet citizen wanted to separate himself from his motherland and live abroad, his case was no longer a purely domestic affair. It could, therefore, be discussed with the Americans (and with representatives of other countries). Reshetov suggested, however, that the dialogue on human rights become a two-way street— that the Soviets, in other words, would also raise human rights issues with the other side.[34] For a time this practice became standard: whenever a Western representative raised an urgent human rights case, the Soviets would try to come up with a murder case in that other country with a nonwhite defendant, or with general complaints about racial discrimination, unemployment, housing shortages, or similar social questions,[35] ridiculous or not. This practice enabled MID to assure the other participants in the Section on Humanitarian Issues and Human Rights in the Central Committee that the discussions were indeed a two-way street.

By the end of 1987 it had become clear that there was a real change in the thinking of the Soviet leaders and that the new policies were not a smoke screen. But it took long for the necessary decisions to be taken and even longer for them to be put into practice. The reason was not only opposition against the new line but also the problems Gorbachev faced when he had to translate new thoughts into concrete policies. Especially in the economic field even Gorbachev, though announcing far-reaching reforms at the Plenum of the Central Committee on June 26, 1987, hesitated much too long to agree to concepts like a truly free market or private property. He was equally hesitant to fully accept freedom of movement for Jews. On the eve of the next meeting with President Ronald Reagan in Washington in December 1987, Gorbachev maintained in an interview with an American television network that to allow Jewish Soviet citizens with "special knowledge" to emigrate would mean a brain drain for his country. That was surely a compliment for the Jews, who constituted not much more than 1 percent of the Soviet population,[36] but not helpful to Refuseniks.

Yet Foreign Minister Shevardnadze had spoken in private quite differently two months earlier in Washington. In October, at the meeting at which they reached agreement in principle to abolish all intermediate-range nuclear missiles, he had told his U.S. counterpart Shultz that Soviets would now move to expand human rights, that their overall policy had changed. Shevardnadze had acknowledged that there were no substantive barriers now for Jews who wished to leave, although he did make one important exception: those exposed to "state secrets." He even added: "Give me your lists, we'll be glad to look at them."[37] Just before the Washington summit a Freedom March organized there in behalf of Soviet Jewry was attended by some 25,000 people, providing moving evidence of the concern for Jews who wanted to leave the Soviet Union. At the summit itself Schifter was assured by the special Soviet representative for humanitarian questions, Alexy Glukhov, that the first-degree relative requirement was no longer enforced and that this new policy would remain in effect.

And indeed, once again Jewish emigration began to increase within two months after a summit (see Table 2, pages 222–23). In February 1988 for the first time in the second wave visas were issued for more than 1,000 persons. The connection with the summit was unmistakable. It is true that by that time the internal pressure, the desire among the Jews to emigrate, had greatly increased. The much larger number of exit permits granted in 1987 and the general optimism generated by *perestroika* gave many of them hope that they, too, would be able to leave the country. But the increase of the number of exit permits granted just two months after a summit cannot be a coincidence. Gorbachev had other internal problems that he undoubtedly considered more pressing than Jewish wishes to emigrate.

It is remarkable that Gorbachev hardly mentions human rights questions in his memoirs. Only when he describes his meeting with Shultz on April 28, 1988, he complains that Shultz "as usual" turned the conversation toward the theme of human rights, "as if there had not already been serious changes in this direction in the Soviet Union." He concludes that Shultz had to please his president, who liked to reduce everything to "the human rights strategy" and was afraid of losing a last trump card in the discussions with the Soviet Union.[38] Nothing could better illustrate the irritation the former-president still feels about Western insistence on his country's observance of its human rights commitments. Clearly, like Yakovlev, Gorbachev continues to pretend that human rights were

an internal question that has been solved by his country independently.[39] That a man like Shultz was genuinely concerned with the fate
of the Soviet Jews, dissidents, and Refuseniks is still beyond Gorbachev's
comprehension.

Gorbachev's attitude makes it all the more obvious that only the unre-
lenting pressure exercised by American leaders like Shultz, as well as by
the representatives of all the Western and most of the neutral and non-
aligned nations at the Vienna CSCE conference, can explain why the
gates suddenly opened so much wider for Jewish emigrants. That pressure was successful, in turn, because of the urgent need of the Soviet
Union for a general détente and agreements on nuclear and conventional
disarmament that would enable it to divert money from defense toward
the civilian economy. Shevardnadze was, in fact, quite honest in October
1987 when he said that the Soviet Union was taking actions on human
rights issues because "we judge them in our own interest."[40]

On the other hand, opponents of freer emigration were, in early 1988,
not sitting still. Refusals on grounds of secrecy increased proportionally
with the number of permissions. Often OVIR did not even bother to tell
the applicants that their applications had been refused, let alone why.
Appeal was possible to a committee of the Supreme Soviet, the parliament of the Soviet Union, but nobody knew its address or its membership, except that Andrei Gromyko chaired it.[41] One thing changed considerably, however—publicity. *Glasnost* began to work. Courageous
editors of two publications in particular—*Moscow News* and *Ogonyok*
(Little flame)—began to expose many of the evils in Soviet society,
including the emigration question. *Samizdat* publications like *Express
Khronika* had already done that for a long time, but they still lacked the
technical means for mass circulation available to the legal media that
were now joining in.

Israeli government representatives were, meanwhile, negotiating
directly with Soviet diplomats at the United Nations in New York to
obtain permission for an Israeli mission to be stationed in Moscow. The
Soviet mission had now, after all, been in Israel for more than six
months. Agreement was reached, and on March 15, 1988, the Netherlands ambassador in Moscow was instructed to request entry visas for
an Israeli "consular" mission of six persons for an initial stay of two
months. They were to be attached to the embassy of the protecting
power—the Netherlands. The Soviet answer to this request took a long
time. On April 28, the *Jerusalem Post* wrote: "The Soviets indicated that

they were refraining from issuing visas to the Israeli Consular Mission because the requested 'terms of reference' were too broad and had not been agreed upon."[42] Clearly the Israelis were trying to give a wider diplomatic scope to their mission than the Soviets were as yet willing to concede, although their own representatives in Israel were being received for diplomatic discussions in the Ministry of Foreign Affairs in Jerusalem. Not until July 28 did TASS announce that Israeli diplomats had arrived in Moscow on that day "to get acquainted with activities of the Netherlands embassy's Israeli interest section."[43]

There was practically no office space available in the already over-crowded Netherlands embassy, yet the mission was not allowed to use the former Israeli embassy building, although the rent for it had been paid since 1967. The members of the mission had to make do with establishing an office in their miserable bedrooms in the hotel Ukraina. Obviously there was still strong opposition within the Soviet foreign ministry to concessions toward the Israelis. The Arab Section, especially, was leaning over backward not to offend its Arab friends. Yet the arrival of the Israeli mission marked the beginning of an improvement in the relations between Israel and the Soviet Union and would lead to the reestablishment of relations two and one-half years later. The members of the mission all spoke Russian (two of them had actually been born in Moscow) and quickly established close relations with many Soviet Jews and Refuseniks. Their arrival was also very welcome to the Dutch consular officials, who were by then swamped by visa applications and, without Israeli help, would not have been able to handle the enormous crowds of applicants that were to face them in 1989 and 1990 (see Chapter 14).

President Reagan, visiting Moscow at the end of May 1988, was enthusiastically greeted by the local population. In the background of that visit a bizarre incident took place. Reagan (or members of his staff) had decided that during the forthcoming summit he would visit a Refusenik family. The U.S. embassy chose a pleasant, English-speaking couple, Yuri and Tatyana Zieman, that had been waiting for their exit permit for more than ten years and whose twelve-year-old daughter had recently written a letter to Reagan. They were told some ten days in advance that the president planned to visit them. The authorities immediately began to repaint their apartment building and to repave their street. But the Soviets were furious about the president's plan. While Reagan rested in Helsinki for a day before going on to Moscow, the Soviet deputy foreign minister Alexander Bessmertnykh flew to the

Finish capital to announce that the Ziemans would never receive an exit permit if Reagan would indeed pay them a visit. He was "confident" they might be able to leave if the issue were not forced.[44] The night before the appointed day the president wisely canceled it. The idea was ill conceived to begin with. Although it may well have originated in a sincere concern for the plight of Refuseniks and a desire to help them, it would have provided publicity for the American president that might have been at the expense of his hosts. By canceling the visit the Americans gained leverage to plead for exit permits for the Ziemans after Reagan's departure. On June 21, the Soviet ambassadors in Washington and The Hague, where their case had also been put forward, informed the respective foreign ministries that exit permits would be granted to the Ziemans. In making this announcement at such a high level, MID showed how proud it was of its victory over its KGB opponents. One midlevel computer expert and his wife, who taught English, had needed a very high-level diplomatic incident before they could be granted their freedom.

Human rights were once more emphasized at the summit and mentioned in the joint statement issued at the end. But many Refuseniks remained without permission. Demonstrations were held regularly in front of the Ministry of the Interior, the Supreme Soviet, and the Lenin Library, and with the same regularity the demonstrators were beaten up by ruffians obviously in the service of the KGB and trucked in for the purpose. But even a few minutes' exposure to the foreign news cameras was a victory for the undaunted demonstrators. Lists with the names and data of Refuseniks continued to be carefully compiled and handed to embassies and representatives of the foreign press. In this way the pressure on the *perestroika* leadership was kept up. Nevertheless the number of exit permits issued was once again clearly determined by foreign insistence. Around the time of the summit at the end of May, the monthly number of visas jumped from 1,289 in April to 1,730 in May and 2,064 in June, twice as high as in February. In November and December the figure doubled again (to 3,949 and 4,602 respectively). Gorbachev visited the United States in early December and spoke to the General Assembly of the United Nations.

The increase did not, however, lead to a larger immigration into Israel; in fact, the number of Soviet Jews arriving there went down compared to 1987. More and more Jews were opting for the United States after their arrival in Vienna. What the Israelis called the dropout rate reached an all-time high in July, at 92 percent.[45] This situation led not only to the high-level discussions about a Bucharest route (see Chapter 11) but also to sharper Israeli scrutiny of the *vysovs*, the invitations from Israel demanded by the Soviet emigration authorities. The Israeli mission noted that there were many false *vysovs* in circulation, which they suspected were being made in the United States. The Netherlands chargé d'affaires reported that OVIR, although undoubtedly aware of the falsifications, had not seemed to mind.[46] He added that the embassy until then had freely extended the validity of *vysovs* and inscribed the names of new brides or babies in them. Although OVIR had at various times changed its stance toward this practice, its attitude was now a very liberal one. OVIR had made clear once again that it did not care about the validity of the invitations whenever it was told to increase emigration. Those documents were no more than pretexts to maintain the fiction of family reunion (see Chapter 2). On the other hand, the Department of State concluded that "there was evidence that the Soviet authorities were holding Soviet Jews who applied [at the U.S. embassy] to go directly to the United States more strictly to the requirement that applicants be invited by a close relative in the country to which they wished to go."[47]

The Israelis now decided that the embassy should become somewhat more restrictive regarding changes in *vysovs*. New instructions permitted the validity of the Israeli documents to be extended by no more than eight months. New spouses or babies could be added only within six months of their marriage or their birth, respectively. The year of birth or the address of the applicant could be changed if a mistake had been made, but all other changes could be entered only by the Ministry of Foreign Affairs in Jerusalem. Copies of the corrected documents had to be sent to Israel.[48] Soon afterward all questions regarding changes in, and extensions of, *vysovs* were handled by the Israeli mission itself,[49] but that arrangement did not change much in the degree of control either. The dilemma remained the same: once a Soviet Jew had obtained an exit permit valid for Israel, it was humanly unthinkable that either the Israeli authorities or the Netherlands embassy would refuse him a visa and thereby prevent his emigration. At the moment the visa application was made it had, moreover, become practically impossible for the embassy or the Israeli mission to check the validity of the invitation: that document had been submitted to OVIR and was no longer available either to the applicant or to the embassy. To induce a larger percentage of the Soviet Jewish migrants to go to Israel, three methods could be applied. The Israeli government could try to induce the American Jewish organizations to cease helping Jews to come to the United States as refugees; it could demand that all migrants first travel to Bucharest and be given a visa for Israel only after their arrival there; or the U.S. government could be urged to stop the practice of automatically accepting Soviet Jews as refugees for entry into the United States. The Israeli government subsequently tried all three methods.

Conclusion

In the second half of the 1980s, as in Brezhnev's time, decisions on Jewish emigration were clearly taken as a result of both internal and external pressures. The urge of the Jews in the Soviet Union, and especially the Refuseniks, to emigrate had not diminished but had been practically ignored in the first half. When Gorbachev became secretary general of the CPSU in 1985, he was told by the Americans that improvement in Soviet relations with the United States would require improvement of the Soviet human rights record, and increased emigration of Jews would be one of the criteria. By 1987, Gorbachev had decided that internal factors, the fulfillment of his *perestroika* policies and in particular the economic situation,[50] made it imperative that he obtain better relations with the United States and therefore accept the American condition. Opposition to such a policy was strong, as it had been in Brezhnev's time, but together Gorbachev, Shevardnadze, and Yakovlev succeeded in overcoming it. Thus the increase in Jewish emigration was once again the result of an interaction of external and internal factors.

The Bucharest Route

When on May 14, 1948, David Ben-Gurion proclaimed a new state in Palestine that was to be called Israel, the very next sentence in his proclamation read: "The State of Israel will be open to the immigration of the Jews from all the countries of the dispersion." A year later he made it even more clear: "Mass-immigration—it was for this that the State was established and it is by virtue of this alone that it will stand." And later again: "Immigration is not only Israel's lifeblood—the guarantee of her security and future. It is her very essence, her soul; the sin against immigration is the one sin she cannot forgive."[1]

Israel and Immigration

Thus the immigration of Jews was and is the basic tenet of the State of Israel. No wonder that the Israeli authorities became worried when, beginning in 1971, a small number of Soviet Jews, having obtained exit permits on the basis of invitations from Israel and in the possession of visas for Israel, nevertheless chose to go elsewhere, in particular to the United States.[2] In 1974 the *noshrim* (dropouts), as the Israelis call them,[3] had already reached 18.5 percent of the total (see Table 3, pages 223–24). History seemed to repeat itself: in the 1930s only 10 percent of the Jews who succeeded in leaving Germany went to Israel.[4] What were the reasons for the choice of Soviet Jews in the 1970s?

After the Russian Revolution of 1917, a strong Zionist movement, which above all desired to assist in building a Jewish state, emerged in the Soviet Union (see Prologue). During the 1920s, however, this movement was increasingly persecuted, and by the 1930s it had been virtually wiped out. When Jewish consciousness was reawakened in the late 1960s and emigration to Israel became possible in the early 1970s, Zionist feelings were naturally also revived. An organized Zionist movement, however, was never tolerated, and anything remotely related to "propaganda for emigration" was immediately snuffed out by the KGB. Zionism was constantly equated with fascism and considered a crime. The great majority of the Soviet population, the Jews not excepted, had no idea what Zionism really meant. It is reasonable to assume that most of the dedicated Zionists such as there were at the time had either emigrated to Israel by the mid-1970s or been refused. By that time the emigrants also came more and more from the cities in the Soviet heartland; they knew less about their Jewish heritage than those who had come from territories formerly belonging to Poland or the Baltic states that had only come under Soviet control in the 1940s.[5] Dedication to Israel thus became less prevalent among the emigrating Jews just as the chance to travel to the United States as refugees was discovered.

This chance existed under the U.S. Migration and Refugee Assistance Act of 1962, through the intermediary of the office of the American Hebrew Immigrant Aid Society in Vienna. This office had been established after the Second World War to help Jews from other East European countries, in particular Czechoslovakia and Hungary, to migrate to the United States. All Jewish emigrants coming from the Soviet Union also had to use Vienna as a transit point since there were no direct connections between that country and Israel. In Vienna they were received by the Israeli Jewish Agency but could also request help from the Hebrew Immigrant Aid Society. An understanding was later worked out according to which the Jewish Agency would refer migrants to the Hebrew Immigrant Aid Society if after three or four days they persisted in their decision to go somewhere other than Israel.

Aliyah and Dropouts

Israel offered all Jews the chance to live in their own country and help build their own society, free from any antisemitism, fear of persecution, or discrimination. It was from the beginning a democratic state. But it could not, of course, match the United States in the economic sense. For those who did not feel that religious or Zionist convictions obliged them to go to Israel, the choice of the United States undeniably offered better economic prospects and a generous support program. In fact, Israel experienced major difficulties at this time in finding housing and jobs for the unexpected influx from the Soviet Union. Moreover, immigrants in Israel had to cope with a language that was new and difficult for most of them and an existence in a country surrounded by—and several times at war with—a hostile Arab world. Some Soviet Jews also feared that they would not be fully accepted there as Jews because they had a non-Jewish mother or wife. Soviet propaganda continuously emphasized the negative aspects of life in Israel to discourage emigration. It was an uneven competition: Israel had no chance to contradict this propaganda or even to present a fair picture of life in the Jewish state.

These conditions largely explain why by the middle of 1978 more than half of the Jewish emigrants from the Soviet Union chose to go to the United States rather than to Israel, a percentage that increased to over 66 percent in 1979. Not surprisingly, this phenomenon caused great anxiety in Israel and led to conflicts within the American Jewish community and between that community and Israel. As early as 1971 Representative Edward Koch of New York had introduced a bill in the U.S. House of Representatives that would have permitted some 30,000 Soviet Jews above the quota limits to enter the United States. But this proposal did not have the support of some Jewish organizations because of its detrimental effect on immigration to Israel.[6] Koch withdrew the bill when he received a promise from Attorney General John Mitchell that Jewish immigration would be expedited through the attorney general's prerogative to grant "parolee" status to Jewish immigrants from the Soviet Union.[7] This status required individual sponsors and offered fewer facilities than refugees received. As it turned out, however, resorting to parolee status was not needed because the Refugee Assistance Act for the time being offered a sufficient number of "slots" for those Jews who were able to leave the Soviet Union on Israeli visas and wanted to go to the United States.

If there was a certain amount of conflict among Jewish organizations in the United States about the dropouts, the clash between those organizations and Israel was more serious. Israeli authorities accused the Hebrew Immigrant Aid Society and the Joint Distribution Committee of "hijacking" Jews in Vienna.[8] Jews who used their Israeli visas to go to the United States or other countries instead of going to Israel were accused of cheating. It was claimed that they should have applied directly to the embassies of their countries of destination in Moscow. Not for the last time those accusers forgot that the Soviet authorities refused to issue an exit permit to anyone who did not have a guarantee of a visa for the country to which he wanted to go, or to allow anyone to pass the border who did not have a visa matching the destination mentioned on his exit permit (see Chapter 3). As we have seen, the number of Soviet Jews who obtained a regular U.S. immigration visa under the quota for the Soviet Union remained small; until 1990 it never exceeded a few hundred in any given year.

Another argument that the Israelis used against the dropout phenomenon in the 1970s and again in the 1980s deserves attention. It was claimed that Soviet authorities were vexed by the "duplicity" of Soviet Jews who applied for exit permits with invitations from Israel but in fact went elsewhere and would use this duplicity as an argument to reduce Jewish emigration. In particular the representatives of Lishka in Tel Aviv asserted on various occasions that they had received warnings to that effect from Soviet sources. But insofar as these sources were specified, they were journalists, lower-level OVIR employees, or representatives of one of the Institutes for Foreign Affairs in Moscow, and not—but for one exception much later—official spokesmen for the Soviet government. This exception was a conversation between the Soviet ambassador in Paris, Yuli Vorontsov, and the Israeli ambassador, Ovadia Sofer, in July 1985. Sofer's report, classified "confidential" but not "secret," was immediately leaked to the Israeli press. Vorontsov supposedly said that more Jews would be allowed to emigrate, provided they all went to Israel, relations with Israel were restored, and Israel gave up the Golan Heights.[9]

This report was strongly denied, however, by TASS, the Soviet news agency, and in Israel itself the *Jerusalem Post* quoted "reliable sources" as saying that the report was suspect and that what Vorontsov had supposedly said "sounded entirely out of character for the vast majority of Soviet envoys."[10] This last remark is certainly correct. The meeting undoubtedly took place, but Sofer's report does not ring true in the form in which it was published.

But were the Soviet authorities in fact very upset by the increased percentage of Soviet emigrants choosing to go to the United States instead of to Israel? The present head of Lishka, Yaakov Kedmi, still has no doubts:

> It must be remembered that the Soviets practically did not allow emigration at all. If Jews continued to go to the United States instead of Israel, the Soviets could move the Jewish

emigration down to the level of regular emigration and severely limit it, as happened in 1979 when they began to ask for evidence of close relationship between the sender of the invitation and the would-be emigrant. This was very dangerous: Israel thereafter paid for the dropout with an almost total stop of the Jewish emigration.[11]

Richard Schifter, U.S. assistant secretary of state for humanitarian affairs from 1985 to 1993, sees it differently:

I became convinced that the Jewish emigration from the beginning to the end was a function of American-Soviet relations. I remember that a Soviet diplomat said at a human rights conference: "Look, we are on the Arab side—how can we let the Jews out?" Another example is the drop in the number of exit permits after 1979 when the Soviet authorities decided on a more confrontational approach to the United States. Jewish emigration was never on the top of their agenda and was decided upon in conjunction with other foreign policy decisions. Thus the dropout rate had no influence at all.[12]

Kedmi and Schifter both recognize the great influence of American policies on the flow of the Jewish emigration, and while Kedmi emphasizes the pressure from Soviet Jews themselves, Schifter would not deny the importance of that factor. But it is clear that decisions on the volume of the emigration were taken at the highest level in the Kremlin. As we have seen in several instances, the relationship with the West in general and the United States in particular was one of the main considerations of Soviet leaders, especially whenever the internal, in particular the economic, situation made it desirable to obtain Western favors in the form of loans, trade, or technology. In those instances Jews were granted exit permits in order to favorably impress American and other Western public opinion. To obtain this effect, it mattered only that those Jews were able to leave, not where they went. In fact, American, and especially Jewish American, public opinion might be more impressed by greater numbers of Soviet Jews arriving in the United States. The drop in exit permits granted to Jews in the Soviet Union after 1979 seems to prove this point in reverse. The Soviet effort to influence American public opinion in a positive direction had failed during that year, and authorities reduced emigration sharply. The emphasis of the reduction was, at least in the beginning, on those emigrants most likely to choose the United States as destination.[13]

Insofar as Soviet leaders kept the Middle East in mind, their main purpose was to calm their Arab clients, who frequently protested the outflow of Soviet Jews to Israel. This factor, too, suggests that it was rather to the advantage of the Soviets when more and more Jewish emigrants did not choose Israel as their final destination.[14] In 1987 the Soviet diplomat (and Arabist) Sennadi Tarasov stated explicitly that Moscow was against forcing Jewish emigrants to fly first to Bucharest, from where they could only have continued their journey to Israel. "We don't want to be accused of denying these emigrants their freedom of choice regarding their destination."[15] Therefore, even if the argument was used at lower levels of Soviet officialdom that Jews should not be given exit permits for Israel since they did not really want to go to that country, it is unlikely to have been official policy.[16]

Israel Fights Back

From the beginning the Israelis were not going to accept the increasing level of dropouts without a fight. In their eyes the emigrants were abusing the invitations they had obtained and the Israeli visas they had been granted. On top of that, American authorities were giving refugee status to people who possessed a valid visa for another free country—Israel.[17] But what could be done? Direct flights between the Soviet Union and Israel would have been a solution, but until the 1990s the Soviet authorities steadfastly refused to grant permission for such flights for fear of upsetting their Arab clients. Should Israel limit its invitations to genuine Zionists? That solution was unthinkable, and in any case, how was one to determine who was a Zionist and who was not? Could American Jews be persuaded to terminate their aid to the *noshrim*?

That last solution seemed to have the best chance of success, and in early 1977 Israel began to put pressure on the American Jewish organizations involved in the reception of the Jewish emigrants. A committee of eight (later ten) had been set up toward the end of 1976 with American and Israeli representatives. It made the following recommendations:

— reorganization of the Israeli immigration departments and better housing for immigrants in Israel (a recognition that all was not well in that respect);

— termination of "unintentional rewards" for immigration into the United States (potential discrimination against Jews vis-à-vis other refugees);

— requirement that Jews desiring to go to the United States should apply directly for U.S. visas (ignoring the facts that immigration visas to the United States were available to only a very limited number of Soviet Jews every year and that Soviet authorities were unwilling to grant exit permits for any country other than Israel to Jews presenting Israeli invitations);

— termination of American Jewish aid to *noshrim* as of February 1, 1977.[18]

The last point was, of course, the most crucial, since by itself this measure might have considerably slowed down the flow of migrants to the United States. But it went too far for the majority of American Jews.

Most outspoken was, and is, the Union of Councils for Soviet Jews. Its leaders consider this question central to the Jewish movement and to Jewish survival. In their view rescuing captives is a commandment in the Torah: "You must rescue the captives, and the responsibility of saving a human life overrides concerns on any other level." They feel that as Jews they must make sure that other Jews are able to be safe and to leave a country. Thus, if Jews can migrate more freely to the West than to Israel, it should be the first task of their organization to help them.[19]

The National Conference on Soviet Jewry was usually more responsive to Israeli views, but even that organization in the end felt that it could not go against the principle of free choice of destination for the migrants. The Hebrew Immigrant Aid Society and the Joint Distribution Committee always tried to remain outside of politics, but they, too, had to accept the general mood in the American Jewish community. Their boards repudiated their representatives in the committee of ten, and their work in behalf of the dropouts was resumed after a brief period. The first Israeli attempt had failed.

In 1979 the Israelis discussed with the Netherlands Ministry of Foreign Affairs whether Soviet authorities could be asked to allow a direct air link between Moscow and Tel Aviv, perhaps to be flown by the Dutch airline KLM. The Netherlands ambassador in Moscow, asked for advice, answered that such a request would have no chance of success. The ambassador added that to plead for a form of transport that would in fact force all Jewish emigrants to depart for Israel would, in his opinion, not fall within the normal exercise of the representation of Israeli interests by the embassy. "The choice of the land of his future settlement must always be left to every emigrant."[20] But the ministry in The Hague considered that it could not refuse to pass on a specific request to the Soviet authorities if Israel asked it to do so. The embassy dutifully complied and got the expected negative answer. The assistant head of MID's Consular Department stated that it was not possible to honor the Israeli request because of the lack of diplomatic relations and "other international circumstances."[21]

No other initiatives seem to have been undertaken during 1978 and 1979, although the dropout rates continued to increase. But after the sharp decline in the number of exit permits in 1980 (see Table 2, pages 222–23, and Chapter 9), two Israeli delegates visited The Hague in May 1981 to convey great concern about the increase in the number of dropouts. They claimed to have received two warnings that Moscow could not continue to allow unlimited emigration if emigration had as its primary goal "out of the Soviet Union" instead of "to Israel." The only result of this visit appears to have been a proposal for the elimination of the question, "What is your final destination?" from the application forms used by the Netherlands embassy in Moscow.[22] In the past many applicants had honestly answered: "United States." The effect was, of course, more apparent than real, and later the old form was used again. In the following years, Jewish emigration further declined until, from 1983 to 1986, the number of cases hovered around a thousand per year. Under those circumstances discussions about the dropout rate obviously had no great priority. But the situation changed when Mikhail Gorbachev's *perestroika* opened the gates again for Soviet Jews in 1987.

A New Proposal

On December 9, 1987, the Israeli ambassador in The Hague, Suffot, presented a memorandum to the Dutch Ministry of Foreign Affairs with a new idea: the Bucharest route. The Netherlands embassy in Moscow, it was proposed, would no longer issue an immigration visa for Israel but put a stamp on the exit permit reading: "Valid only for travel to Bucharest, Rumania, for completion of Israeli immigration procedures." This procedure would be, claimed the Israelis, similar to the procedure used by the American embassy in Vienna to enable the Soviet Jewish migrants to travel to Italy in order to obtain their refugee status at the office of the U.S. Immigration and Naturalization Service in Rome (see Chapter 3). The Rumanians, said the ambassador, had already agreed.[23]

Rumania was the only member of the Warsaw Pact that had not broken diplomatic relations with Israel in 1967, and Israel had maintained a full-fledged embassy in Bucharest. Lishka had been instrumental in obtaining permission for the greater part of the Rumanian Jews to leave the country and go to Israel. It is not denied in Israel that the Rumanians were well paid for that exodus. Now the Rumanian government would once again cooperate. The Israeli prime minister Yitzhak Shamir himself met with the Rumanian president, Nicolae Ceaușescu, several times and made a deal with him.[24] Would money again have been involved? "Of course," declares a high Israeli official, "Ceaușescu was part of the game and everything in Rumania had its price." It must be remembered that Rumania was long the "darling of the West," as the only member of the Warsaw Pact that sometimes dared to deviate from Soviet points of view and refused the permanent stationing of Soviet troops on its soil.

In The Hague the Israeli memorandum was followed a day later by a personal letter from the Israeli foreign minister, Shimon Peres, to his Netherlands counterpart, Hans van den Broek. Peres claimed that the new approach was based on "new Soviet emigration regulations and practice, permitting those who wished to do so to reunite with relations in the United States, Australia, and elsewhere, without the fiction of an invitation from Israel." Peres went on:

> I find it impossible to avoid the conclusion . . . specifically spelled out by Mr. Gorbachev himself in several public forums in the United States . . . that what Moscow considers "abuse" of Israeli invitations by individuals whose destination is other than Israel . . . may undermine our efforts to convince Moscow to allow more of our brethren to leave the USSR . . . to come here. Moreover, while our primary objective is to open the gates for all who wish to leave, we cannot but uphold our specific responsibility for encouraging the fulfillment of our other commitment—enabling them to reach Israel.[25]

Here again is the assertion that "'abuse' of Israeli invitations" might be an excuse for the Soviet authorities to reduce emigration. Had Gorbachev really "spelled it out"? Unfortunately no dates or places were indicated for his alleged statements. As far as can be ascertained, Gorbachev, irritated by repeated questions on this subject during his first visit to the United States, did say something like: "They don't really want to go to Israel." But he did not connect this complaint with threats to reduce the number of exit permits. If ever such a threat was made, it certainly was never carried out.

In the Dutch Ministry of Foreign Affairs, meanwhile, officials realized that Peres's letter created a difficult choice for the minister. "Our point of departure must be," a memorandum to him said, "that we have to accede to reasonable requests from Israel. We can continue to issue Israeli visas to people who declare *expressis verbis* that they don't intend to go to Israel only as long as the Israelis do not ask us to stop that." On the other hand, "Our parliament, as well as Jewish circles, especially in the United States, will have difficulty understanding Dutch cooperation in what—rightly or wrongly—will be seen as a restriction of the Soviet Jews' ability to emigrate." Finally, the memorandum mentioned what was to become one of the important factors in the debate: "We must find out whether Peres's interpretation of the new Soviet emigration law is correct."[26]

Clearly the Dutch were far from eager to carry out the Israeli proposal. It was evident to them that Jewish migrants would not be able to change their route to another country once they arrived in Rumania. Even if they succeeded in leaving the Bucharest airport, no embassy could issue a visa within the brief period likely to be allowed in transit there. A high official in the Ministry of Foreign Affairs called it "a curious construction."[27]

Lishka had meanwhile taken a further step. The text of the *vysovs*, most of which were sent through that office directly to applicants in the Soviet Union (see Chapter 5), was changed. It now affirmed that a visa on the basis of the *vysov* could only be issued in Bucharest. The Moscow embassy sent an anxious cable about this news to The Hague but was reassured by the ministry, after consultations with the embassy in Tel Aviv, that the new annotations on the *vysovs* did not change the existing practice. The embassy could continue to issue visas for Israel without regard for the proposed destination.[28] Nevertheless the new text caused worried questions from the Jewish community in the Soviet Union and from the media, to which the embassy could answer only that "for the time being" there was no change in the way visas for Israel were being issued. No wonder that those who intended to ask for exit permits in order to go to the United States hastened their preparations and that the dropout rate started to increase sharply—from an average of 75 percent in 1987 to more than 90 percent for the first time in May and to 97 percent in October 1988.[29]

On May 20, 1988, Kol Israel, the official Israeli radio service, announced that "a decision in principle" had been taken to "prohibit the issuance of Israeli visas to Jews who want to leave the Soviet Union, but have no intention to go to Israel." The Netherlands embassy in Moscow once again asked for information, and its counterpart in Tel Aviv answered that the Israeli Ministry of Foreign Affairs had denied the announcement. But the American embassy in Tel Aviv cabled at the same time to Washington that the Israeli prime minister's office had confirmed the decision, adding that the foreign ministry was responsible for its implementation. The Israeli minister of absorption, Tzur, was reported to have said that there were technical delays in implementing the plan; he hoped that it would soon be put into operation.[30] It seems clear that the "technical delays" were due to the Dutch hesitations.

As was to be expected, the question again aroused a lively debate within the American Jewish community. In particular the Union of Councils for Soviet Jews pleaded for "retention of an alternative route for those who seek resettlement elsewhere." The organization's director Micah Naftalin, in a conversation with the director of the Bureau for Refugee Programs of the U.S. Department of State, Richard Moore, called the plan for direct flights "a public relations disaster waiting to happen." He said that his organization had tried to interest the Israelis in devising a "freedom of choice" opportunity at Tel Aviv airport, or perhaps within a few months after the Soviet Jews arrived. But, understandably, the Israelis could not accept anything like "refugees from Israel." Moore said that his bureau was also unhappy with the concept of mandatory direct flights.[31]

On June 6, 1988, a joint statement was issued by most of the interested Jewish organizations, including the National Conference on Soviet Jewry, the Union of Councils for Soviet Jews, the Hebrew Immigrant Aid Society, the American Jewish Committee, and the American Jewish Congress. The statement advocated what was called a "two-track" policy that endorsed direct flights "for those who wish to settle in Israel" but maintained the principle of freedom of choice. In a meeting with Secretary of State George Shultz, Jewish leaders headed by Morris Abram, president of the National Conference on Soviet Jewry, confirmed this

policy. Abram maintained, however, that under current Soviet regulations the free choice could be exercised at the time of application. The
Department of State explained in a cable reporting on this meeting to the
U.S. embassy in Moscow that there were two obstacles for direct settlement of Soviet Jews in the United States: the applicants would need invitations from relatives in the United States, and Soviet authorities were
applying the requirement of "close relationship" more strictly to applicants for the United States than to those for Israel.[32] It might have added
that the requirement that applicants be out of their country before
refugee status could be granted was also still an obstacle—and perhaps
the main one—for more direct migration to the United States as refugees.

On June 20, 1988, the U.S. embassy in Tel Aviv cabled to Washington
that the Israeli cabinet had the day before formally approved the decision
to set up the Bucharest route with 16 votes in favor, 2 against, and 3
abstentions. The embassy added that it was unclear how the decision
would be implemented and quoted the Israeli daily *Ha'aretz,* which
expressed the views of the opponents: "Even if we suppose that it is given
to us to impose direct flights on some *olim* [immigrants to Israel] . . .
what good will that do us? There will be immigrants here who strive to
leave. . . . The Israeli government will only have increased the potential
for emigration among the Jewish citizens of Israel."[33]

Other countries also expressed concerns, but for different reasons.
The United Kingdom proposed on July 27 that the members of the European Community approach Israeli authorities to express concern that the
freedom of choice for the emigrants would not be assured. The British
Foreign Office considered that Soviet restrictions on the freedom of
movement would be used for Israeli purposes. The Dutch Ministry of
Foreign Affairs vetoed that proposal and so informed the Israeli ambassador.[34] The proposed language of the demarche was much too harsh
and would have made the Dutch position toward the Israelis in this question untenable.

In the middle of July the prime minister of the Netherlands, Ruud
Lubbers, and the foreign minister, Hans van den Broek, paid a visit to
Israel, and were subjected to strong pressure for Dutch cooperation
regarding the Bucharest route by their Israeli colleagues Yitzhak Shamir
and Shimon Peres. The two Dutch ministers stressed their reservations.
Anything should be avoided, they said, that would make emigration of
Jews from the Soviet Union more difficult. The Netherlands, after all,
had its own principles and values to which it had traditionally adhered.

One such principle was the freedom of choice. But in the end, the Dutch ministers did promise to study the Israeli arguments further and to discuss the question with Israel again in the future.[35]

In connection with the principle of freedom of choice, it should be emphasized (and Israelis have made this point) that whereas the Universal Declaration on Human Rights of the United Nations does recognize the right of everyone to leave his country and to return to it, it does not mention a freedom to enter another country. The reason is obvious: every country wants to control the influx of immigrants, when necessary, by demanding visas. On the other hand, the freedom to leave one's country would be of little value if one would not also be free to choose one's destination.

During the ministerial discussion in Jerusalem the Dutch side also broached the idea that the U.S. government might be prepared to accept Soviet Jews as refugees *after* a stay in Israel of, for instance, one year. Of course, this idea did not have a chance. Even if the United States would stretch its definition of the term "refugee" to such an extent that an applicant would be considered for refugee status after spending a year in Israel, such a notion was, as the Union of Councils for Soviet Jews had already found out, totally unacceptable to Israel. Nevertheless, The Hague instructed its embassy in Washington to take the idea up with the Department of State. Would the United States either extend the possibility of granting the status of refugee for Soviet Jews to one year after arrival in Israel via Bucharest, or could it increase the quota for immigrants from Israel?[36] The answers from Washington were as should have been expected: a Soviet Jew arriving in Israel would no longer qualify for emigration to the United States as a refugee, and an increase in the quota would "open up a Pandora's box."[37]

Shortly afterwards, in a conversation with the Jewish leader Morris Abram, Secretary of State Shultz made clear once more where the U.S. administration stood: "The first priority is to get the Jews out; then we should consider where they should go." Shultz emphasized that the concept of choice was so deeply imbedded in him that "you won't get it out." Abram assured Shultz that the Jewish community opposed proposals, apparently supported by the Israelis, to change U.S. refugee laws that would make Soviet Jews who dropped out in Vienna ineligible for admission to the United States as refugees.[38] Shultz confirmed his stand in favor of freedom of choice to Van den Broek in a conversation at UN Headquarters on September 29. All efforts were now directed, he said, toward inducing the Soviet Union to grant exit permits directly for the United States.[39]

Finally on October 6, 1988, negotiations on the Bucharest route plan took place in The Hague. The Israelis had already requested such negotiations in July, but the Dutch side had held back. The Israeli delegation consisted of a hawk and a dove: Nehamiah Levanon, the head of Lishka, considered it a "falsehood" that Jews used a visa for a free country like Israel to obtain refugee status in the United States and was resolved to do anything to change that situation.[40] Yeshayanu Anug, deputy director general of political affairs in the Israeli Ministry of Foreign Affairs, was personally in principle against any restriction imposed by the Israeli government on the freedom of choice of the emigrants. It was important to him that as many Jews as possible should leave the Soviet Union, and he considered it better and more honorable to facilitate the possibility for Jews to leave for wherever they wanted to go.[41] Their interlocutor on the Dutch side was Director General Henry Wijnaendts.

The outcome was an agreement to try out the Bucharest route for a period of six to nine months, beginning one month after its approval by both governments. Both delegations reiterated "the right of any prospective emigrant to choose freely the country of his destination." The Israelis maintained, however, that the Soviet Union had promised to allow direct emigration to other countries and that "the fiction of all Jews emigrating to Israel enabled the Soviets to avoid acting in accordance with its promise." On this basis the Dutch side, apparently influenced by the fact that the Netherlands embassy in Moscow was, after all, only the mandatory of Israel in these matters, agreed to a trial period. If it appeared that the Bucharest route was restricting the emigration of Soviet Jews, both parties agreed that they would return to the *status quo ante*.[42]

The Israelis were satisfied, and Prime Minister Shamir and Foreign Minister Peres quickly informed the Netherlands embassy in Tel Aviv that they had approved the text.[43] But the Dutch foreign minister hesitated and decided to ask the advice of his ambassador in Moscow. That ambassador pointed out that in his view the freedom of choice was not guaranteed in the agreement and that the assurances that switching to the new system would not cause long delays for would-be emigrants were insufficient. Even if Soviet authorities were indeed prepared to issue exit permits valid for departure to the United States as refugees, there still remained the question of the *vysovs*, the invitations from relatives. The ambassador estimated that at that moment some ten thousand Jews were preparing their requests for exit permits (it became clear later that even that estimate was much too low), but on the basis of an invitation from Israel, not the United States. For those hoping to go to the United States, departure would at the very least be postponed until invitations from relatives in the United States (if such relatives could be found) could be obtained and applications made at the American embassy. Moreover, the American embassy was not equipped to handle anything like the number of applications that could then be expected, even assuming that it would be authorized to grant refugee status in Moscow. The delay of one month before the new measures would be introduced was therefore much too short. The ambassador pleaded for a gradual changeover and an assurance that alternatives would be in place beforehand.[44] Van den Broek thereupon decided to ask the Israelis for assurances concerning the speed with which applicants could be helped in Moscow. On October 18, 1988, the director general asked the Israeli ambassador for confirmation that the U.S. embassy would be able to issue the same number of visas as the Netherlands embassy was then handing out—some two thousand per month.[45]

Five days later the *Washington Post* published an article by John M. Gosko headlined: "Israel Fails in Plan to Divert Soviet Jews." While noting that Israel was still negotiating with The Hague, it stated that the Israeli effort "had foundered for the foreseeable future because of the reluctance of the Netherlands . . . to participate in a plan that effectively required recipients [of Israeli visas] to go to Israel or remain in the Soviet Union." The Reagan administration, according to the article, regarded the Israeli effort as violating freedom of choice in emigration. Morris Abram was quoted as saying: "The American Jewish community is opposed to forcing anyone to live where he doesn't want to live. The community will not support coercion." According to Gosko, Secretary of State Shultz, speaking to the Senate Judiciary Committee, had called the Israeli plan "an attempt to rig the system." The administration could not be in favor of that.[46]

The Netherlands embassy in Washington reported that according to Assistant Secretary Richard Schifter the contents of this article were "based on good knowledge." An Israeli official had confirmed, Schifter had added, that when the Bucharest route was enforced, "measures would be taken to prevent migrants from leaving the airport in Bucharest."[47]

On November 11, 1988, Israeli Ambassador Suffot presented the answers to the requests of Minister Van den Broek to the Netherlands Ministry of Foreign Affairs. The ministry concluded that the Israelis had given virtually no guarantees on the substantive questions, in particular the ability of the American embassy in Moscow to deliver sufficient refugee visas (the ministry officials seem to have more or less ignored the equally important question of the *vysovs*). "Furthermore," it was concluded, "a procedure whereby as a result of Rumanian cooperation emigrants would be isolated and not able to travel to another country than Israel could not bear examination."[48] That final conclusion summed up—albeit a little late—the essence of all the opposition to the Israeli plan.

Conclusion

While one can well understand the deep feelings of the Israelis about immigration and about what they called the dropout phenomenon—and such understanding was certainly not lacking among the Netherlands authorities involved—the idea, sometimes expressed in Israel, that in the matter of the Bucharest route the end would have justified the means, cannot be accepted. It can easily be imagined what the reaction of world opinion would have been if a Jewish emigrant, trying to reach the U.S. embassy in Bucharest, would have been forced back to the airport and the waiting plane for Israel by the Rumanian Securitate. Pressure from the U.S. administration, supported by practically the entire American Jewish community, together with the "hesitations" of the Dutch, has saved the Israelis from what Micah Naftalin correctly called "a public relations disaster waiting to happen."

12

Non-Jews Leave with Israeli Visas

It may seem strange to discuss the emigration of non-Jews in a study of the Jewish emigration from the Soviet Union. Yet, curiously, from the late 1960s onward, sometimes a few, sometimes sizable groups of non-Jews were able to leave the Soviet Union with Israeli visas—in other words, as if they were Jews and as if they were going to Israel. After 1987 their number became so considerable that at times they constituted more than 20 percent of all emigrants with Israeli visas. Since practically none of them went to Israel, they naturally influenced what the Israelis called the dropout rate, seemingly decreasing the percentage of *olim*: the emigrants actually going to Israel.

Why Were They Forced to Use Israeli Visas?

The main reason for this phenomenon was the Soviet objective to maintain the fiction of family reunion as the only reason for allowing anyone to leave the Soviet Union. Until the very end the Soviets feared the "domino effect" of allowing people to emigrate who did not have, or could not pretend to have, close relatives in the country of destination. They also found it difficult to let people go who had no visas for another country, no promise that they would be received, and who were therefore beforehand characterized as refugees—refugees from the "workers' and peasants' paradise."

Yet those same authorities at different times wanted, or even forced, people to emigrate. Emigration was apparently for Communist authorities, or more precisely the KGB, the easiest way to get rid of people who could not be "reformed" in the communist sense but whose constant persecution and arrest caused bad publicity and more and more protests in the West. The quickest manner in which to accomplish this goal was to send the candidates to the only embassy that would issue a visa imme-diately—the Netherlands embassy, which would grant an Israeli visa the same day to almost anyone showing an exit permit valid for Israel. There was another advantage for the KGB in this kind of emigration: since they were supposedly going to Israel, the emigrants would lose their Soviet citizenship (see Chapter 2). This loss meant that these "undesirables" would be unable to request Soviet passports or to return again as Soviet citizens.[1]

But what about the necessary invitation from Israel? That never seems to have presented a problem. It was, of course, not beyond the capabil-ity of the KGB to produce false *vysovs*, but sometimes even those were not needed. Several applicants admitted to the Dutch consul that they had never had an invitation and yet been issued exit permits for Israel. As early as 1969 the Netherlands embassy asked Israeli authorities for permission to issue an Israeli visa to an applicant who could not yet show an exit permit. Before an answer was received, the applicant reap-peared with an exit permit valid for Israel. The ambassador reported that he had applied the rule that anyone with such an exit permit would be granted a visa, although the man made clear he had never had an invita-tion. The automatic issuance of visas by the embassy upon presentation of a Soviet exit permit could, stressed the ambassador, lead to the grant-ing of visas to persons whom Israeli authorities might afterward consider to be "less desirable." On the other hand, it would not be a solution for the embassy to request preliminary authorization for every case, since Soviet exit permits had a limited period of validity that did not leave suf-ficient time for consultation. Moreover, he said, it was usually not possi-ble to verify whether the applicant had or had not been in possession of an Israeli *vysov*, since this document was withheld by Soviet authorities.[2] There is no record of an Israeli answer to the ambassador's report but the authorization to issue a visa to anyone presenting an exit permit valid for Israel was not withdrawn.

It was typical for the Soviet bureaucracy that while sometimes *vysovs* were dispensed with, at other times OVIR insisted, in order to maintain the fiction of family reunion as the only reason for emigration, that Israeli *vysovs* had to be presented when applications were made by non-Jews. Some non-Jewish applicants were even sent to the Netherlands embassy to request a *vysov* from Israel. A well-known non-Jewish dissident, Yulius Telesin, had left the Soviet Union with an Israeli visa in 1969. More dissidents were to follow the same path, and sometimes Jewish activists had helped them obtain invitations from Israel.[3] In many cases, on the other hand, it must be assumed that false invitations were somehow produced, either in the Soviet Union, in the United States, or elsewhere. Since OVIR held them back with the application forms, neither was available for verification by the embassy.

In 1972, the head of Lishka, Nehamiah Levanon, went to The Hague and reported that Israel was aware that Soviet authorities sometimes used "emigration to Israel" to get rid of non-Jewish dissidents, such as members of Helsinki Watch Groups. These troublemakers were allowed, or forced, to go into exile. He mentioned the case of the brother-in-law of the well-known dissident Vladimir Bukovsky, who had left the Soviet Union in this way.[4] Levanon did not propose any measures. Similarly in 1976 the Netherlands embassy reported that another dissident, Andrei Amalrik, had been sent to the embassy (clearly by the KGB) to request an invitation from Israel, although he was not Jewish. Some others, said the embassy, were "more or less forced to leave in this way."[5] Another case came up in 1980. The U.S. consul in Tel Aviv asked Israeli authorities to allow his Netherlands colleague in Moscow to issue an Israeli visa to a member of a Helsinki group. Jerusalem did authorize the Netherlands embassy to grant a visa once the applicant had an exit permit, but not to promise a visa in writing. It wished to avoid the impression that this was an Israeli initiative. That arrangement would not work, answered the embassy: "This case is not handled by OVIR but by the KGB, which refuses any oral contact with us." The Israelis then relented and authorized a written promise; the dissident left for Vienna with an Israeli visa soon after.[6] There was a suspicion in the Netherlands embassy that the KGB at times also tried to get rid of common criminals in this way; furthermore, it was well known that the KGB tried to send out spies along this route.

Christian Emigrants

While these examples concern incidental cases, more and more frequently adherents of certain Christian denominations were allowed, or even pushed, by the Soviet authorities to leave along this route. Most of them belonged to Protestant denominations such as Pentecostals or Free Baptists, which had refused to register with authorities and were therefore not recognized. After registration their preachers would have become employees of an atheist state, and that was unacceptable to these denominations. Most also refused military service. The Ukrainian Roman Catholics (Eastern rites), also called Uniates, on the other hand, were unwilling to recognize their forced incorporation by Joseph Stalin into the Russian Orthodox Church.[7] Armenian Christians formed another group.

Encouraged by the Helsinki Final Act, some members of these groups began trying to emigrate from the Soviet Union in the late 1970s. By May 1979 seven Pentecostal families had been allowed to do so, and all had had to declare Israel as their destination.[8] Two other families, becoming known as the "Siberian Seven," had by then been living in the American embassy in Moscow for almost two years. They belonged to a group of Pentecostals who had refused to register in Chernogorsk in Siberia and were subsequently persecuted, their children put in an orphanage, their church destroyed, their leaders condemned to prison camps. They finally came to the conclusion that it was not possible for them to continue living under communist rule and decided on emigration. First they thought of Israel, land of the Bible, but were told that there was no Israeli embassy in Moscow. Then they went to the American embassy. On June 27, 1977, they rushed the gate of the U.S. embassy, and all but one succeeded in getting past the Soviet militia. They were to stay in the embassy for over six years. OVIR refused to accept *vysovs* that an Alabama pastor had signed for them because he was not a relative. It finally became clear that only "emigration via Israel" could possibly resolve the dilemma that more and more became a matter of precedent for both the Soviet Union and the United States. Moscow feared that letting the Siberian Seven go would encourage many others to try and leave in the same way; Washington feared that others might also try a sit-in in the embassy.[9]

After Ronald Reagan became president, he and his secretary of state, George Shultz, talked to the Soviet ambassador, Anatoly Dobrynin, about human rights, divided families, Soviet Jewry, and Refuseniks. The president also talked "with sincere intensity" about the Pentecostals.[10] Reagan suggested a "small gesture: to grant exit permits to the seven Pentecostals." The Soviet leaders hesitated, since to them the American request "looked distinctly odd."[11] At Shultz's urging, Israel authorized the Netherlands embassy to issue a visa to the members of the group,[12] in particular to a woman, Lydia Vaschenko, who had been taken from the embassy to a hospital after a hunger strike. Jerusalem also hesitated, however, to allow her to actually enter the country; it, too, feared setting a precedent. The group in the embassy, on the other hand, not trusting their authorities, insisted that they would not leave their haven until informed of Mrs. Vaschenko's safe arrival in Israel. Finally the head of the American delegation at the CSCE follow-up conference in Madrid, Max Kampelman, discussed the question with a member of the Soviet delegation, General Sergei Kondrachev, who clearly represented the KGB. Kondrachev recommended that Mrs. Vaschenko be received in Israel and that all other members of the two families also apply for Israeli visas. That way, he said, "the decisions could be made in certain quarters in Moscow rather than in other less favorable ones." This plan was finally accepted by all parties. Mrs. Vaschenko arrived in Israel and sent invitations to the others; they all left the Soviet Union on July 18, 1983.[13]

During the early 1980s emigration on Israeli visas was at a very low ebb and so there was not much chance for members of Christian denominations to use this escape route. The situation of many was desperate. Their pastors were arrested, their makeshift churches bulldozed, and their young men condemned to long prison terms for refusing to serve in the armed forces. No wonder that when emigration on a larger scale became possible for Jews again in 1987, Christians remembered the example of the Siberian Seven. Increasing numbers somehow obtained *vysovs*, which were accepted by OVIR. All exit permits were stamped "valid for Israel," and so an Israeli visa was affixed by the Netherlands embassy.

Did the Netherlands consular officers ever doubt whether applicants were Jewish? Of course they did. When a blond and blue-eyed family with ten children and a non-Jewish name applied for visas for Israel, the officers naturally had misgivings. The embassy once cabled to The Hague: "We know that non-Jews are still being pushed out—or helped out—of the country this way. But when the Soviet authorities accept them, there is nothing further we can do about it. Applicants give up all their papers and so it is no longer possible to see whether they are Jews or not."[14] The only way to find out would have been to ask, and that the Dutch could not and would not do. The question would have opened up a hornet's nest: even in Israel itself there is no agreement on who is a Jew and who is not.[15] Perhaps even more important, as long as the only way for these Christians to escape communist persecution was to take the Israeli emigration route, it would have been against the humanitarian principles of the Dutch to block it. After all, it was only a technical question: the Christians would be received in Vienna by Christian church organizations, first the World Council of Churches, later Caritas, and helped along to enter the United States (or sometimes other countries, in particular Canada) and consequently not be a burden for Israel.

There is one curious case on file in which the Netherlands embassy asked for preliminary authorization for the issuance of an Israeli visa to a non-Jew because the applicant had a criminal record. In 1987 the Soviets suddenly gave an exit permit to a certain Jonas Simokaikis, who had tried to hijack an airplane fifteen years earlier. Hijacking had meanwhile been declared an international crime, and so the embassy decided to ask for instructions. France had offered to receive him, but the Soviets refused an exit permit valid for that country. The Israelis showed their willingness to help and authorized a visa, but before it could be issued, the French had persuaded the Soviets to grant an exit for France after all and so the man traveled there directly.[16]

Yet, as noted before, the non-Jewish emigrants traveling on Israeli visas undeniably increased what the Israelis called the dropout rate. For that reason the Israeli mission, after its arrival in Moscow, criticized the misuse of Israeli visas. After the mission itself took over the handling of invitations that needed corrections or changes, Pentecostals complained that they had been refused such changes. It was hardly a secret that Israeli *vysovs* were fabricated by Pentecostals in Ladispoli, near Rome in Italy, where Jews and Christians alike were waiting for appointments with the U.S. Immigration and Naturalization Service. Request for such *vysovs* and the necessary data were usually transmitted by phone from the Soviet Union. On one occasion a Soviet official at the Presidium of the Supreme Soviet of the Ukraine provided a Pentecostal emigrant with the correct Ladispoli telephone number.[17]

The Israeli mission further suggested to the Netherlands ambassador that he urge the Soviet authorities to end their practice of incorrectly indicating the destination as Israel on exit permits for applicants who did not want to go there and were not Jewish. The ambassador recognized that the way the Israeli visas were being used was improper. If other countries would have consented to grant them visas directly, instead of using the refugee status, and the Soviets agreed to issue exit permits to applicants for their real destination other than Israel, the problem would not have arisen. But except for those few applicants to whom the United States could promise a regular immigration visa, that was not yet the case, so the Christian sect members would, in effect, have been deprived of their way out. The ambassador therefore answered that he could make the requested demarche with the Soviet authorities only upon instructions from the Israeli government through The Hague.[18] Those instructions did not come, perhaps because the Israelis realized the problem, perhaps because the Americans argued against it both in Jerusalem and in The Hague.[19] One month later the Netherlands ambassador in Moscow was invited to visit Israel and was received there by Prime Minister Yitzhak Shamir, who then resolved the matter with these words: "I am not against saving also non-Jews from the Soviet Union [with Israeli visas] if that is the only possibility. We will not make a point of it."[20]

How large was the percentage of non-Jews among the holders of Israeli visas leaving the Soviet Union? According to figures from the U.S. Department of State, the total number of persons departing the Soviet Union in 1988 was 22,403 (the Netherlands embassy reported visas issued for 26,183, however) of which 3,438 (15.3 percent) were Pentecostals. The highest monthly percentage was over 23 percent in December 1988.[21] The Refugee Data Center in New York, which tabulates refugee arrivals in the United States, did not record religion or ethnic background until 1988. The data for that year are still unreliable, since 78.8 percent of the Soviet refugee arrivals are listed as of "unknown religion." By 1990, on the other hand, there were few refugees arriving anymore who had left the Soviet Union on Israeli visas. Only for 1989, therefore, do more precise figures exist. They show that in that year 74.25 percent of arriving Soviet refugees were classified as "Jewish," almost 2 percent as "unknown," and the rest under various Christian denominations. The largest Christian groups were the Pentecostals (8,819, or 18.2 percent) and the Armenian Christians (3.7 percent).[22] It must be added, however, that the total number of Soviet refugee arrivals registered by the Refugee Data Center is much lower than Israeli figures. The figures from the center can, therefore, only give an indication, but they are in line with the estimate of just over 15 percent Pentecostals in 1988.

By early 1989 the cost of moving Pentecostals through the Vienna-Rome pipeline had become a serious problem for the United States, since the voluntary agencies handling their lodging, food, and transportation were being refunded in whole or in part by the U.S. government. Solutions were discussed parallel to the discussion of the Jewish migration along the same route. It was proposed to process all Pentecostals in Vienna, and a maximum of thirty days was imposed on any refunds to voluntary agencies.[23] But in the end the Pentecostal problem merged with the Jewish one: after November 6, 1989, the Israel route was closed to the members of Christian denominations since Israeli visas were no longer accepted by the United States as a basis for the granting of the refugee status (see Chapter 13). But by then OVIR was already giving many Christians permission for direct emigration.[24] All processing of Pentecostals now shifted to the American embassy in Moscow. Some of them received preferential treatment equal to that of Refuseniks, being provided by the embassy with letters of appointment that enabled them to apply for refugee status in Rome. Others were given first preference as soon as the new refugee procedures were in place. In 1990, the number of admissions of Pentecostals in the United States was given as 7,615.[25]

Conclusion

Until 1990, sizable numbers of non-Jews left the Soviet Union with exit permits for Israel stamped with Israeli visas by the Netherlands embassy. The Soviet authorities were clearly aware of this emigration and in fact often encouraged, if not forced, "unruly citizens" who could not be reformed into the communist mold to take the "Israel route." An internal factor, the impossibility of reforming these people, interacted with an external one, the bad impression the constant harassment of these Christians was making abroad.

While some Israeli authorities regretted the use of false invitations and the misuse of their visas and—understandably from their point of view—the apparent effect of this phenomenon on the dropout rates, the Israeli prime minister in the end recognized that it was more humane, and better for his country's public image, to accept it.

13

Trouble for Refugee Status in the United States

Suddenly, toward the end of 1988, some Soviet Jews were for the first time denied refugee status by the office of the U.S. Immigration and Naturalization Service (INS) in Rome. The INS began to question applicants individually and express doubt whether they were, as the law demanded, "in immediate fear of persecution" or of a "well-founded fear of persecution." During November, 7 percent of the applicants were denied refugee status; in December the percentage increased to 8.5 percent; in January 1989, it was 19 percent. Altogether, 649 persons were refused entry as refugees into the United States between October 24, 1988, and January 25, 1989.[1] A shock wave went through the Jewish organizations in the United States. Lawyers were immediately dispatched to Rome to lend assistance.[2]

The INS action was due to the explosive increase in the number of applicants. Immigration officials foresaw that the quota for Soviet refugees under the Refugee Relief Act in fiscal year 1989 would not be sufficient and the INS decided, apparently on its own, to apply the rules more strictly. The Soviet Jews (as well as a number of non-Jewish emigrants from the Soviet Union, especially Pentecostals) who were denied refugee status were told they could enter the United States as parolees. But that status meant they would not be eligible for financial support from the U.S. government and had to obtain private guarantees (see Chapter 3). Most were therefore unable to accept the offer or refused it. The Department of State pointed out to the INS that it was not applying the law correctly. The Supreme Court had decided that it was sufficient if a group had a well-founded fear of persecution; it was not necessary to prove that there was, for every individual member of the group, real persecution or a fear of it.[3] But Secretary of State George Shultz admitted to Jewish leaders that "lack of money and slots had disrupted the refugee program and that changing conditions meant that all Soviet emigres did not automatically qualify for refugee status." The percentage of denials continued to rise, reaching 40 percent in April 1989. In September 1989 there were some five thousand people still waiting in Rome who had refused to accept parolee status.[4] Those originally rejected were later allowed to reapply for refugee status; those accepted in the United States on parole after August 14, 1988, could apply for adjustment of their status to that of an alien admitted for permanent residence.[5] Some had meanwhile returned to the Soviet Union.[6]

It was a first warning of things to come. The American refugee program was not geared to receive Soviet Jews in the numbers that now had to be expected (see Table 3, pages 223–24).

The U.S. Perspective

In the beginning of 1989, exit permits were granted to most of the old leaders of the Refusenik movement who had still been refused the year before. Some Refuseniks who still lacked a permit now formed a new organization with the unlikely name Public Council to Aid the Work of OVIR in the City of Moscow. Its head, Dr. Leonid Stonov, hardly imagined that within a year he would indeed be allowed to meet with officials of MID and OVIR.[7]

From March 1989 on, the Netherlands embassy began to issue more visas per month than it had done even in the top year of 1979. More than 90 percent of the emigrants with Israeli visas were now choosing the road to the United States. American officials as well as the voluntary agencies, in particular the Hebrew Immigrant Aid Society, realized that the United States had neither the resources nor the legal authority to process and receive all those Soviet emigrants in a timely fashion. On the other hand, human rights in the Soviet Union were still being restricted, and human concerns therefore remained an important guide for U.S. policy.[8]

The first consideration was to effect savings in the existing program. The Hebrew Immigrant Aid Society began by proposing to process all refugees in Vienna, eliminating the costly detour via Rome. But according to the American embassy in Moscow, this change would achieve only half of what was needed. On February 7, 1989, it proposed to process in

Moscow all Soviets intending to "divert" to the United States via Western Europe. This solution, said the embassy, would go far toward regain-
ing control over the refugee program, and it would also mean huge
savings. Applicants would be able to wait at home for the decision on
their application for admission to the United States as refugees. After
receiving notice that admission would be granted, they could request exit
permits from OVIR. Applicants might continue a more or less normal
life, even if exit permits were in the end refused. They would no longer
have to be financially supported in Vienna and Rome. Subsidies for
transportation costs would be lower and in many cases could be eliminated entirely, as long as emigrants could pay for their trip to the United
States themselves in rubles. And finally, the new system would eliminate
what the embassy called the "charade" of obtaining an exit permit and
a visa for a country to which the emigrant had no intention of going—
Israel.[9]

The plan of the U.S. embassy in Moscow would require Soviet cooperation. As long as the existing Soviet legislation was in force, OVIR
would have to accept invitations from the United States even if they were
not sent by direct relatives, as it did in practice as far as Israeli invitations
were concerned. As long as the need for an exit permit was not legally
abolished altogether, an even better arrangement would be that permission to enter another country would be accepted in place of an invitation. There was hope that new Soviet legislation being prepared would
be more liberal, but the embassy feared that the need for exit permits
would almost certainly be maintained. It was thought that Soviet
authorities would see the political advantage in reducing the number of
applications to OVIR and shifting the onus of refusal to the country of
entry. Curiously, the embassy proposal did not mention the difficulty of
granting refugee status to applicants still living in their own country.
Apparently it was assumed that the president's authority under the Immigration and Nationality Act to accept as refugees persons still in their
own country would be used.

The embassy's proposal was accepted by the Department of State. But
the department also realized that, even assuming Soviet cooperation
could be obtained, limited personnel, space, and resources in the old U.S.
embassy building in Moscow would pose serious difficulties. Therefore
it was estimated that the shift would take from twelve to eighteen
months.[10] It would bring savings in money but not resolve the main difficulty: that there were not enough refugee slots or financial resources to

accommodate the enormous increase in applications from Soviet emigrants—not only Jews but also Pentecostals and some Armenians as well.
The new secretary of state in the administration of President George
Bush, James Baker, told Jewish leaders in early March that the refugee
situation was one of the biggest budgetary problems he faced as secretary. At present the department was "robbing Peter to pay Paul" by bor-
rowing refugee slots from other regions.[11] A new Policy Coordinating
Committee on U.S. Policy on Soviet Refugees was set up in the State
Department. A memorandum drafted for the first meeting of this committee noted that there were "firmly held differences" over the question
of how best to regulate the flow of Soviet refugees and how to influence
INS's determination of who was a refugee. These differences existed not
only within the department but also in other agencies and in political
interest groups. Three policy options were identified:

> Option 1. The attorney general could be provided with factual back-
> ground on the treatment of Soviet Jews (and Pentecostals) to see
> whether a *prima facie* case of qualifying for refugee status existed.
> This was believed still to be the case and therefore the proposal would
> lead to a much lower number of denials. But this option also included
> the proposal to stop processing applicants with other offers of reset-
> tlement (i.e., visas for Israel) as of July 1, 1989, and to encourage
> other countries, such as Israel, Canada, and Australia, to accept them.
> This proposal would, it was maintained, bring the processing of
> Soviet refugees in line with overall refugee policy. As it stood, Soviet
> refugees were being treated more favorably than others.
>
> Option 2. A moratorium would be declared as of October 1, 1989
> (the beginning of fiscal year 1990) on refugee applications. In the
> meantime changes in Soviet emigration requirements would be sought
> and the Vienna-Rome pipeline would be "seriously restricted."
>
> Option 3. The open-door policy would be continued until after the
> 1991 Moscow Human Rights Conference, but the INS interview
> process would continue to control the flow of refugees.[12]

It should be emphasized that continued reliance on INS screening to
limit the number of refugees (as envisaged in option 3) would have per-
petuated elements of confusion and uncertainty if not discrimination.
How would an INS adjudicator who had never been to the Soviet Union
and did not speak Russian (more interpreters were urgently requested in

March)[13] ascertain whether a Jewish applicant from, for instance, Bukhara had a more genuine fear of persecution than one from Moscow or Odessa, or vice versa? Besides, the applicants had already left their country with the purpose of coming to the United States. Refusal would force them to go where they did not want to go—or even to return to the Soviet Union. Option 3 would also have entailed a heavy additional allocation of funds, which would have had to be approved by Congress. But options 1 and 2 would undoubtedly expose the administration to severe criticism. The secretary of state had a difficult decision to make and therefore decided to consult with the Congress and public interest groups before concluding what should be done.[14]

In May 1989, Assistant Secretary of State Richard Schifter traveled to Moscow and warned the Netherlands ambassador that the U.S. government was preparing new legislative measures regarding the reception of refugees that might severely restrict the migration of Soviet Jews to the United States. There were funds for 43,000 refugees, which he hoped might be just enough until the end of the fiscal year on October 1. (The cost of transportation and resettlement averaged $7,000 per person.)[15] Schifter further indicated the possibility that the United States would put those already possessing a visa for a third country in the lowest-priority (sixth) category, a step that might cut Jewish emigration to the United States in half.[16] The tremendous surge in visa applications at the Netherlands embassy during the summer of 1989 (from 5,000 in April to almost 10,000 in August) indicated that rumors had also reached those who hoped to go to the United States as refugees. Yet those involved with migration issues on both sides of the ocean continued to hope that the flow of Jewish migration would not be interrupted and that the U.S. administration would somehow find the necessary authorization and funds. But as it turned out, budgetary constraints, although the direct trigger for action, were not the only reason for the coming change.

During the summer informal meetings took place in Washington between administration officials and representatives of Jewish organizations. The officials pointed out that an estimated 50,000 Jews were expected to migrate to the United States in 1989 and that the number might well double in 1990, exceeding the annual total of 90,000 refugees from all over the world that could be accepted under existing laws. The administration could have sought a revision of the legal and budgetary provisions determining that maximum. However, there was doubt that sufficient congressional support for such revision could be found. There was also doubt within the Jewish organizations that they would be able to raise the additional funds they had always provided for the settlement of Soviet Jews within the United States, let alone make up for the short-fall in official allocations.

The reasons for both doubts were the same: the situation for the Jews in the Soviet Union had improved. Could one really maintain that in the Gorbachev era Jews were still in such immediate danger of persecution that they were entitled to absorb the greater part, if not the whole, of the quota for refugees accepted by the United States? Would not the advocates for refugees from other areas begin to protest? Would members of Congress under those circumstances be prepared to allocate the large additional sums required? And would the Jewish communities that had until now liberally contributed the large funds needed for the resettlement of their brethren still be willing to do so and even increase their contributions?

It was in many ways an embarrassing situation for those, both in the administration and in the Jewish community, who had struggled for so long to induce the Soviet Union to let its Jewish citizens go. They were well aware that the proposed changes in U.S. policy would "turn away thousands of Soviet Jews who had hoped to begin a new life in the United States."[17] Finally the National Conference on Soviet Jewry, the Council of Jewish Federations, and other Jewish organizations agreed with the administration that, even if the total number of refugees that could enter the United States were to be increased to 120,000, a higher number for Soviet Jewish refugees than the then available 40,000 was not sustainable. There was after all, said the representative of the National Conference, another country willing to accept them.[18] The Union of Councils for Soviet Jews angrily refused to go along.[19] Did Israeli pressure play a role? Some of the administration officials involved have denied it,[20] and that denial is probably correct in the direct sense. However, there can be no doubt that Israeli representatives in the United States did all they could to influence public opinion and in particular the Jewish community in the direction of restricting the flow of Soviet Jews to the United States.

Interagency discussions meanwhile continued. A revised memorandum of July 3, 1989, pointed strongly toward the solution Schifter had already indicated in Moscow: refugee admissions in practice to be limited to the relatives of American citizens and others to be encouraged to seek resettlement elsewhere (mainly in Israel, of course, although Australia and Canada were also mentioned). This revision would bring U.S. policy for Soviet refugees in line with "worldwide practice," except that the possibility of accepting additional Soviet immigrants as parolees would be maintained. The memorandum also proposed an announcement to be made on August 1 that the INS office in Rome would soon be closed and that those receiving visas after October 1 would need an appointment date for the Rome office before leaving Moscow.[21]

No conclusions were reached, however, at the meeting on July 7, when the memorandum was discussed, and it was not until August 29 that the final meeting took place.[22]

The United States Restricts Entry of Jewish Refugees

The discussions on a new policy regarding Jewish refugees were leaked to the American press in the beginning of September 1989 and published in the *New York Times* on September 3, and in the *Washington Post* on September 7 and in greater detail on September 12. On September 13 the Netherlands embassy in Washington was officially informed that "the administration will tomorrow take the decision no longer to process refugee status requests from immigrants in the possession of an Israeli visa issued by the Netherlands embassy after September 30."[23] Congress was informed the next day in a hearing. The administration stated that it proposed to increase the ceiling for Soviet refugees for the fiscal year 1990 to 50,000. Of these, 40,000 would be "fully funded" and 10,000 would be "available for private funding." The 50,000 Soviet refugees were to include not only Jews but also Armenians and members of religious sects, mostly Pentecostals. The offices in Rome and Vienna would be closed, and a processing center would be established in Washington to assist the U.S. embassy in Moscow. In Rome and Vienna some 20,000 persons were "in various stages of refugee processing" and more than 40,000 applicants were already waiting for an interview with the U.S. embassy in Moscow.[24]

This decision caused a tremendous shock in Moscow—despite previous warnings. Thousands of Jews who had earlier received notice from OVIR that permission to emigrate had been granted had delayed collecting their permits since they had affairs to settle and the validity of the permits, once collected, was short. Many who had received exit permits and were planning to go to the United States were waiting, as had been common practice, until the last moment to go to Moscow and obtain their Israeli visas. Worse was the situation for many thousands who were in the various stages of the long process between obtaining an invitation and applying for an exit permit. Suddenly they realized that they had only a few days left if they hoped to enter the United States as refugees with an Israeli visa. To make a new application directly at the American embassy would mean starting emigration procedures all over again, and it was well known that this embassy was as yet far from equipped to handle the now impending volume of applications.

The Netherlands ambassador in Moscow, while recognizing that the United States was entitled to change its policy and take the new measures, regretted above all that so little warning time was given. He expected a last-minute rush on his Consular Section and therefore proposed that the cutoff date of September 30 not be the date the embassy granted the Israeli visa but the date OVIR issued the exit permit. This change would make an orderly processing possible, especially for emigrants a distance from Moscow. It would also clearly put the onus for delays where it belonged—on the local OVIR offices.[25] This suggestion was supported by the American embassy and accepted by the U.S. authorities.[26] Even so, the volume of applications almost overwhelmed the Consular Section (where the Israeli officials continued to assist loyally). In the last week of September visas were issued for 7,620 persons— more than 1,500 per day. Each document had to receive final approval from and be personally stamped and signed by a Dutch official.

On September 15, Deputy Secretary of State Laurence Eagleburger testified before the U.S. Congress that "50,000 Soviets would be admitted in fiscal 1990 within a total of 125,000 refugees worldwide." He added that the U.S. embassy in Moscow would now handle applications on a priority basis, just like "regular" immigrants under the Immigration Act, the first priority being given to those with relatives in the United States.[27] This provision was a new blow to many applicants, as the majority of Soviet Jews had no, or at most only distant, relatives in the United States from previous migrations. Moreover, invitations could be sent only by those who possessed U.S. citizenship, and thus many recent immigrants did not yet qualify. All in all, the new priority meant that many Soviet Jews would not be given a chance to emigrate to the United States—if at all—for a long time to come. Exceptions were made, fortunately, for Jewish dissidents and Refuseniks (and for Pentecostals). The United States would continue to receive them as refugees; they would get letters of appointment on the basis of which they could travel to Vienna and Rome and quickly obtain refugee status there.[28]

There was a brief concern within the Israeli mission in Moscow that some holders of Israeli visas, even if they no longer qualified for entry into the United States, would still go with a transit visa to Austria and either try to reach another country or stay in the camp there.[29] To prevent these possibilities, Israeli officials in Moscow revived the idea of a Bucharest route and it proposed that the Netherlands embassy would no longer issue Israeli entry visas but stamp on the exit permits: "Valid for travel only to Bucharest or Budapest to complete immigration procedures for Israel." This time the answer from the Ministry of Foreign Affairs in The Hague was unequivocal: "The task of interest-representation does not include issuing *laissez-passers* for Rumania or Hungary; their own Embassies can do that." However, a second Israeli proposal was accepted. All applicants for an Israeli visa would now have to present a ticket valid for travel to Israel. Both the ambassador and the foreign ministry considered that applicants now had a free choice: to apply either directly to the U.S. embassy (that this route might take a very long time did not alter the principle) or to the embassy representing Israel. If they chose the latter, it was now not unreasonable for the Israelis to demand proof that emigrants did have the possibility—in fact, the intention—to go there.[30]

For a while it seemed that such proof would become easier to obtain, as an agreement was finally reached on direct flights from Moscow to Tel Aviv. This agreement was initiated in talks at UN Headquarters in New York between Soviet Foreign Minister Eduard Shevardnadze and his new Israeli colleague Moshe Arens. They agreed on political and commercial contacts between the two countries and on the principle of direct flights. Cultural exchanges would also be encouraged, and the Soviet Union would even make it possible to place a phone call from the Consular Section directly to Israel (previously phone calls could be made to anywhere in the world, except to Israel).[31] On December 7, Reuter's announced that the Israeli airline El Al had signed an agreement for direct flights between Tel Aviv and Moscow, to begin in early 1990. Soviet-Israeli relations were clearly improving, but resumption of official relations, if only at the consular level, was not yet in the offing. The direct flights did not materialize either (see Chapter 14).

After October 1, 1989, it became clear that many more exit permits were still in circulation than either the Netherlands embassy or the American authorities had foreseen. Some dated from long before September. Now all turned up. The estimate of between 1,000 and 2,000 valid permits proved much too low. On October 6 the embassy reported that it was still issuing visas for several thousand persons per week. The American embassy in Moscow had already proposed a second cutoff date: visas issued after October 31, whatever the date of the exit permit, would no longer be accepted for American refugee status. The U.S. embassy in The Hague passed this proposal on to the Netherlands Ministry of Foreign Affairs.[32] To move this date further back might, it was feared, encourage antedating or falsification of exit permits. The Netherlands embassy in Moscow did accept that a new cutoff date might be needed but pleaded for ample warning time.[33] Some antedating was indeed discovered, reported the embassy during October, although the number remained small in comparison to the total number of applications. Nevertheless the U.S. administration, when it was informed that visas had been issued in October for more than 11,000 persons, decided on November 1 that the second cutoff date would be November 6. The decision was announced the following afternoon in Moscow, so only one working day—Friday, November 3—remained for applicants with valid exits to obtain visas that would still entitle them to American refugee status. Out of deference to the Israelis, the Netherlands Consular Section did not work on the next day, a Saturday, but overtime on Sunday November 5 enabled another 390 persons to obtain visas. They were often stragglers from faraway in the Soviet Union who had been alerted at the last moment by announcements on Radio Liberty, which also broadcast the fact that the Consular Section would be open that Sunday. The last stamp was handed out twenty minutes before midnight.[34] An era had ended.

Conclusion

The measures taken by the American administration in the autumn of 1989 made it impossible for Soviet Jews to more or less automatically obtain refugee status and enter the United States as refugees. It did not stop migration under that status, but it did limit the total yearly number of Soviet Jews entering the United States to about 40,000 (the rest of the 50,000 quota was taken up by Pentecostals, Armenians, and some others). In fact, the refugee program became a converted immigration program: only close relatives of American citizens could henceforth hope to qualify, and the necessary procedures delayed even their departure considerably.

The immediate reason for these measures may have been that funds for receiving the refugees were exhausted. But it is clear that the real cause for the change in policy was the recognition by the U.S. administration and the majority of American Jewish organizations that under Gorbachev the situation of Soviet Jews was no longer so precarious as to generate the political and financial support needed for a continuation of the old policy.

There is no indication that the Americans officially discussed the change beforehand with the Israelis. It is nevertheless evident that this change was immensely pleasing to the Israelis and that they had been exercising pressure behind the scenes in this direction. The Netherlands representatives were given some indications of what was about to come, but the warning time for the general public was, due to the long internal decision-making process within the U.S. administration, too short.

The Jews who wanted to leave the Soviet Union but did not have close relatives in the United States now faced the choice of staying put or going to Israel.

14

The Last Years

Inevitably the American decision not to grant the refugee status more or less automatically to Soviet Jews wanting to go to the United States caused a slump in applications for Israeli visas in Moscow. The Jews who still wanted to leave the Soviet Union for the United States had a difficult choice to make—stay home, leave for Israel instead, or settle for a long wait and an uncertain chance of eventually going to the United States. After the cutoff date of November 6, Israeli visas were issued during the rest of that month for only some 800 persons. The American embassy, meanwhile, had begun to distribute application forms under the new procedure. Jews, Armenians, Pentecostals, and Baptists, but many other Soviet citizens as well, lined up in endless rows in front of the embassy—often, as they said, just to try their chance. By early December more than 200,000 forms had been handed out and about half of them returned and sent (unopened) to the processing center in Washington, D.C. Even if the center quickly determined the *prima facie* eligibility of applicants, it might take the ten examiners assigned to the U.S. embassy in Moscow for this purpose up to two years to give each a hearing. Even then, only those having close relatives in the United States would, in practice, have a chance. U.S. Ambassador Robert Barry, who visited Moscow, told the Netherlands ambassador that a sufficient number of slots within the quota would be reserved for long-term Refuseniks. For the rest, he said, the process would remain "a tragic lottery."[1]

The Israeli mission estimated, at the same time, that some 100,000 invitations to come to Israel were in the hands of Soviet Jews. Would they use them? The hesitation lasted for two months. During December, Israeli visas were issued for a slightly higher number of persons than in

November: 3,355, bringing the total for 1989 to 83,666. But in January 1990, the Jews had clearly come to a decision. Applicants began to appear in unprecedented numbers in the Bolshaya Ordinka street where the Netherlands Consular Section and the Israeli mission were now located. The year 1990 was to see by far the largest number of Jews ever to leave the Soviet Union and the largest number of Soviet immigrants ever to enter Israel within one year.

Aliyah

Thus in 1990 the Soviet Jews were once again "voting with their feet," notwithstanding the fact that the majority of Jews still left in the Soviet Union were highly assimilated and had on the whole no strong Zionist feelings. Why did they, nevertheless, choose *aliyah* (literally, "ascent") to Israel?

As always, various considerations contributed to their decision, but many Jews were undoubtedly responding to the prevailing situation in the Soviet Union. The political atmosphere was tense in early 1990. Mikhail Gorbachev abolished the monopoly of the Communist Party in February, causing a lot of opposition. Soviet troops, trying to subdue demonstrations and dissidence in Vilnius, Tbilisi, and Baku, made many victims. In all the Soviet satellites in Eastern Europe, new leaders had come to power during 1989, and they were introducing democratic reforms. The Warsaw Pact, for so long the Soviet defense bastion, now existed in name only. The internal economic situation in the Soviet Union went from bad to worse, and the lines in front of the almost empty shops became even longer than normal. As had so often happened in Russia in times of tension, antisemitism increased, and even rumors about the possibility of pogroms were rife.[2] In January some Jews inquired whether the Netherlands embassy would be able to protect them in case a pogrom materialized. The ambassador answered that nobody in acute danger of his life would be left standing at the door. But he added that a right of asylum in a foreign embassy, as known in Latin America, did not exist in Europe.[3] Some two hundred delegates from the new Congress of People's Deputies chosen in May 1989 urged Gorbachev to publicly denounce antisemitism. Apparently fearing for his popularity, he did not do so.[4]

Nevertheless, there were endeavors to revive the Jewish cultural life that had existed so richly in czarist Russia and even at times under communist rule. A Jewish cultural center was opened in Moscow in

February 1989 and named after the murdered Jewish actor Shlomo Mikhoels. The opening of a congress of a Union of Jewish Organizations in the Soviet Union in Moscow on December 16, 1989, was a great occasion, but it was marred by a demonstration by members of the new nationalistic and antisemitic organization Pamyat, who shouted anti-Jewish slogans.[5] *Glasnost* had permitted suppressed antisemitic instincts to appear.[6] As *Pravda* wrote on July 22, 1990, "Judophobia has become popular . . . and prompts Jews to emigrate." Many Jews simply did not believe that a revival of Jewish culture could happen in Russia. The revival of antisemitism, on the other hand, was all too apparent.

Under those circumstances, it was not surprising that more and more Jews decided to go to a country that was "theirs." It was to some extent a cumulative process. Whenever members of one family decided to go, their relatives lost their closest contacts and felt less secure. The more Jews who left from a community, the more lonely and isolated were the ones left behind. And so the visa numbers jumped to 9,735 in February and 19,026 in March, the highest ever. The travel situation remained difficult because direct flights, although promised to El Al, were still not permitted. The Hungarian airline Malev offered to bring emigrants directly to Israel by charter flight, but it canceled the first flight at the last moment when threats were received from the Islamic Jihad movement.[7] Emigrants after that traveled by train or plane, and sometimes even by bus, to Bucharest, Budapest, or Warsaw, where they could board El Al flights to Tel Aviv.[8]

Why Gorbachev Let Them Go

Why did Soviet authorities at this time decide to let so many Jewish citizens leave in an exodus that, up to then, they had so assiduously tried to stop, or at least to limit?

One reason was that the internal political situation in the Soviet Union had radically changed. The new Congress of People's Deputies counted among its members a number of noncommunists and indeed former dissidents such as Andrei Sakharov. Even some of the communists had turned into progressive reformists. The Congress began trying to exert more influence. One of its two chambers in particular, again called the Supreme Soviet, became more like a real parliament, almost continually in session and exercising legislative authority. Inspired by Sakharov, more and more members began to criticize the human rights violations of the authorities and especially the KGB. The pressure for better observance of the obligations undertaken in the Helsinki Process tended in particular toward greater freedom of movement and thus to a more liberal emigration policy. Yet the direct influence of this parliament was still limited, and real power was being concentrated more and more into the hands of one man: President Gorbachev. He made his decisions on Jewish emigration on the same basis as he made other decisions—the maintenance of his own power within the country and of his country's influence in the world. Application of human rights obligations followed from these considerations and was not a goal in itself.

Externally, on the other hand, the year 1990 was the year in which the Soviet Union lost its defensive cordon—the Warsaw Pact—while the two Germanies were united in one country that was to remain a member of NATO. Those developments were very hard for the leadership of the Soviet Union and its people to accept. Gorbachev and Eduard Shevardnadze desperately tried to save what they could of Soviet influence in international politics and especially of the power balance in Europe. They demanded a change in the NATO strategy and the termination of the military confrontation in a declaration by the members of the former Warsaw Pact and of NATO that they were no longer considering each other as enemies.[9] Such a declaration would at least give them a rationale for accepting the withdrawal of the Soviet troops from East Germany and the countries that had belonged to the Warsaw Pact. They also wanted the CSCE to become more institutionalized and thus assure them a role in future decisions about security in Europe.

The CSCE follow-up conference in Vienna ended successfully in January 1989. Its concluding document stated that there should be time limits for decisions on applications for emigration, a possibility for appeals against "poor relative" refusals, a review of "secrecy" refusals every six months, and formal notification of secrecy designations in the future. The participating states promised that laws and regulations would conform with their obligations under international law and CSCE commitments. (It would take the Soviet Union, however, more than two years to carry out this promise.) There was further agreement on creating a mechanism for the resolution of questions regarding the "human dimension" (i.e., individual hardship cases). This mechanism allowed complaints regarding the human dimension to be brought officially to the attention of another state through diplomatic channels. The state receiving such a complaint had an obligation to answer it; if that answer was deemed insufficient, bilateral consultations might follow. In the end a case could even be brought before a Conference on the Human Dimension. Three such conferences were to be held: in Paris in 1989, in Copenhagen in 1990, and in Moscow in 1991.[10] Just before the end of the Reagan administration Secretary of State George Shultz, aided by Assistant Secretary Richard Schifter, had succeeded, against considerable opposition, in giving the U.S. delegation the green light to accept the wish of the Soviet delegation and insert the Moscow conference in the concluding document and thus to bring the Vienna conference to an end. In return, MID promised a major effort to reduce the Refusenik list.[11]

At the Copenhagen conference in June 1990 the Soviet delegation became even more cooperative regarding human rights. The external pressure was having its full effect. The delegation had allowed the spokesman of the Refuseniks, Leonid Stonov—to his immense surprise— to travel to Copenhagen from Moscow to take part in the public discussions that the nongovernmental organizations held in the margin of the conference. The head of the U.S. delegation, Max Kampelman, stated that the conference's concluding document was "the most significant advance in the Helsinki process since the agreement itself came into being."[12] The Soviet delegation reported home a little proudly: "The success of the Copenhagen forum became possible . . . thanks to democratic changes in Europe, our policy of restructuring, and new approaches to the issues of human rights and democracy in the Soviet Union." Later it stated, "The shift of our line from confrontation to cooperation received a positive response." All was not yet well, however, because the Soviet delegation pointed out that

> with such an on the whole favorable background, a certain inflexibility on the Soviet side in solving a number of practical issues (Refuseniks, people convicted for political reasons, misuse of psychiatry) continues to have an irritating effect on the Western public. . . . The discussion in Copenhagen shows that timely adoption in the Soviet Union of laws on exit and entrance, freedom of conscience and political organization . . . will increase the prestige of the Soviet Union. . . . It is necessary to introduce without delay a draft law on psychiatric care.[13]

After Copenhagen, European politics went into high gear. In July, in London, NATO did indeed decide to change its strategy and to accept both the idea of a declaration of nonenmity and a limitation of the strength of the German army. Gorbachev and Shevardnadze thereupon gave Chancellor Helmut Kohl of the Federal Republic of Germany the go-ahead for unification of his country, with continued membership of NATO. Negotiations began during the same month in Vienna on a Charter for a New Europe, as it was eventually called. It was signed in Paris in November and provided for a limited institutionalization of the CSCE.

Against this background, a Soviet failure to observe its human rights obligations would clearly have been very detrimental to the maintenance of its vulnerable international position. It would have been unthinkable for the Soviet government to create new difficulties for the departure of its Jews at that particular moment. In fact, the Soviet leadership decided at this time to accept the principle of a right to emigration; there were to be no further numerical limitations.[14]

Thus a completely new situation in Europe in 1989–91 had made it essential for the Soviet Union to obtain political understandings with the West, and the West had made it clear at the Soviet-American summits as well as at the CSCE conferences in Vienna and Copenhagen that maintenance of human rights obligations would be a prerequisite for such understandings. At the same time, the internal economic situation in the Soviet Union was deteriorating, making Western help a dire necessity. Once more the Soviet decision to allow increased Jewish emigration was based on an interaction of external and internal considerations.

A More Active Role for the Netherlands Embassy

During the bleak years of 1985 and 1986 the Netherlands embassy, in striking contrast with the policy of the early 1970s, had become more active in maintaining contacts with dissidents and Refuseniks and in making representations about them to Soviet authorities. Among the Jewish activists who were then still imprisoned was Joseph Begun. A diplomatic note about his case was sent to MID by the embassy in January 1985, at the request of the Israeli authorities.[15] In March, for the first time, the head of the Consular Section paid a visit to Mrs. Irina Begun at her apartment to talk with her and with relatives. He promised the embassy would continue to try and obtain improvements in Begun's situation.[16] Irina Begun had meanwhile decided to go on a hunger strike to show her solidarity with her husband. Some of her friends wished to join her but, being Orthodox Jews, wanted to be certain that such action was permissible. Stretching the limits of interest representation, the embassy transmitted their query to the chief rabbinate in Jerusalem.[17] The answer assured the Orthodox Jews that it would be all right to join in. In May, Irina Begun—whether because of her hunger strike or because of actions undertaken by the embassy—received a letter from her husband, the first in a long time. He wrote that he was in the Chestopol prison camp and that his health was "not bad."[18]

In June 1985 the British embassy proposed that some Western embassies send representatives to the trial of a Jew accused of economic crimes, and the Netherlands embassy questioned the Ministry of Foreign Affairs in The Hague whether it should participate. The answer came in the traditional style: "It would be of interest if *other* Western countries would attend, but as far as the attendance of your own embassy is concerned, you should underline your special position."[19] In the end, at the request of the family, there were no foreign observers at the trial at all. The judgment was surprisingly mild—a suspended sentence of two years.[20] The reason became clear when shortly afterward the man appeared twice on Soviet television and accused the Dutch consul Anton Schellekens by name who, he said, "had urged him in a truly provocative way to leave his fatherland." Two diplomats from other countries and three foreign correspondents were also named. It was, said the Netherlands ambassador, "undoubtedly a warning to dissidents and Refuseniks against contacts with foreigners at the beginning of the Youth Festival" that was about to start in Moscow.[21] The man later explained to his friends that he had made the accusations under heavy pressure from the KGB and had been threatened with prosecution under Article 64 (treason).[22] The Netherlands diplomat in question does not seem to have suffered any harm from the accusations against him.

Although there was no major modification of Soviet policy regarding Jewish emigration immediately after Mikhail Gorbachev announced his policy of *perestroika* on February 25, 1986 (see Chapter 10), the embassy nevertheless detected signs of a change. That same month Anatoly Sharansky, after complicated negotiations with the American administration, had been released from prison and put on the bridge to West Berlin and to freedom (see Chapter 4). In August 1986 Sharansky's mother, Ida Milgrom, and his brother and family received exit permits and were issued Israeli visas by the Netherlands embassy.[23] Shortly afterward visas were also issued to Refuseniks Leonid Wainshstein, who had waited for fourteen years, and Benjamin Bogomolny, after twenty years.

The latter held, according to the embassy, the all-time record: he had begun applying in 1966.[24]

At the end of November 1986 the Dutch prime minister, Ruud Lubbers, together with Foreign Minister Hans van den Broek, paid an official visit to Moscow. The briefing that the Netherlands Ministry of Foreign Affairs prepared for them on the question of humanitarian cases was still couched in the old language:

> There is no possibility to develop independent initiatives in the framework of the representation of Israeli interests. Private requests [to intervene with the Soviet authorities] can only be honored if Israeli authorities have been consulted and have approved. In case of specific requests from [the Netherlands] parliament to intervene in behalf of Jewish Soviet citizens in jail or having been refused exit permits, one cannot overlook the interaction between such Dutch steps and the function the embassy in Moscow fulfills in the representation of Israeli interests and the special position which this function creates for the Netherlands.[25]

But by that time the foreign minister was ahead of his staff. In 1984 he had made a personal plea in behalf of Sharansky, at the end of a conversation with his Soviet colleague Andrei Gromyko in Stockholm. He had met with Sharansky's wife, Avital, who had begged him to plead her husband's case. Van den Broek complied, but Gromyko's answer was clear: "Don't dirty your mouth with that name!" Undeterred, Van den Broek presented Gromyko with a list of "urgent cases" during a later conversation in New York. These actions had had no repercussions on the representation of Israeli interests by the Netherlands embassy. For the visit to Moscow a similar list had been prepared. It contained mostly names of Jewish Refuseniks, but also some cases of Christians who wanted to leave. At the end of his conversation with the new Soviet foreign minister, Eduard Shevardnadze, Van den Broek took him aside and handed him the list. Shevardnadze accepted it. Lubbers and Van den Broek also had a meeting with Gorbachev, but there the subject of dissidents and Refuseniks was not brought up.[26]

More signs of relaxation in the Soviet policies regarding migration came up early in 1987. In January, the Netherlands ambassador made a personal plea with a vice-minister of foreign affairs regarding three cases in which former emigrants wanted to visit seriously ill relatives or attend funerals in the Soviet Union. This time he was given some hope, and indeed a few days later one entry visa was granted to an Israeli for a visit with his sick father in the Soviet Union. The Soviets were at last beginning to show some compassion.[27] The ambassador was also told that difficult visa questions would be dealt with more quickly from now on, owing to Gorbachev's new policy of *uskorenye* (speedup). Nevertheless the other two requests remained unanswered.[28] Still, a month later a new request for another Israeli was granted within one day. In March there was a general increase in visa applications, which meant that more exit permits had been granted. The embassy could also report that Joseph Begun had been freed and that he had applied for a visa at the Consular Section,[29] one of the clearest signs the Soviets could have given of a change in their policy.

The Netherlands ambassador now decided it might also be time to change the attitude of the embassy toward contacts with dissidents and Refuseniks. For a few years the head of the Consular Section had had contacts with Refuseniks, but meetings took place only outside the embassy. The ambassador was convinced that a diplomat had the right and even the duty to try and meet with citizens of the country in which he worked, including dissidents in opposition. More and more Soviet citizens, on the other hand, clearly wanted to have such contacts and were willing to take the risks. Moreover, the strict policies forbidding Soviet citizens to meet with foreigners appeared to be softening. There now seemed to be a recognition among Soviet officials that human rights obligations would have to be observed if Gorbachev's new policies were to have any chance of success in the Western world. Such an attitude provided an opening for foreign embassies that had to be tested by the Dutch embassy as well. If lists of humanitarian cases were to be presented regularly to the authorities, the embassy had to obtain reliable information directly. Besides, precisely because the embassy represented Israel, it was well placed to help keep up the spirits of the Refuseniks and offer them a place to meet with Dutch and other foreign diplomats and journalists, with visitors from the West, and last but not least among themselves.

The ambassador approached his foreign minister personally, giving his arguments but also pointing out that the new line would mean a 180 degree turn from the old policy. Van den Broek did not hesitate to give his consent. The head of the Consular Section was encouraged to intensify his contacts; the ambassador and his wife themselves began to invite first Refuseniks and then also other dissidents to the embassy.[30]

Meetings between dissidents and Westerners had until then been organized mainly by the American embassy. In their residence, Spaso House, the U.S. ambassador Arthur Hartman and his wife cleverly began to give live concerts, lectures, and weekly showings of the latest American films. A mixture of guests was invited—Soviet officials as well as dissidents and Refuseniks, foreign diplomats and journalists as well as Soviet artists, film critics, and others. Furthermore, American embassy staff members were allowed to organize a *seder*, a Jewish Passover ceremony, to which Jewish dissidents and Refuseniks were invited. These gatherings had also become possible through a change in embassy policy undertaken as a personal initiative by the ambassador and allowed by the State Department.

It worked: guests from all the invited circles came and mixed. The KGB clearly did not like it; in the beginning guests were constantly harassed and had their names ominously noted down by the militia guards in front of the residence. Once the strings of the ambassador's Steinway were found to have been cut just before a recital by the Refusenik pianist Vladimir Feltsman. But the recital was given, and the film showings continued. One result was that the Soviets sent fewer officials to receptions at the embassy, because "they might be confronted with dissidents there." But the contingent of officials allowed to visit parties at any Western embassy was carefully controlled and limited anyway. The Americans faced that problem in their own particular fashion: they made sure that their guest speakers or soloists or the American films were so interesting to the Soviets, either politically or artistically, that many could not or would not afford to miss meeting, hearing, or seeing them.[31] The irritation of the KGB may have contributed to the Soviet decision to withdraw all Russian household personnel from the U.S. residence at the end of 1986, although this act was mainly in retaliation for the expulsion by the Americans of a number of Soviet spies working at the UN secretariat in New York. Ambassador Hartman was replaced by Jack Matlock in February 1987. Matlock maintained many contacts with dissidents and Refuseniks and gave *seders*, but he did not continue the weekly film showings.

The Netherlands embassy opened its doors to Refuseniks for the first time in April 1987 to host a reception after the first public concert the pianist Feltsman had been allowed to give in Moscow since he had applied for an exit permit many years before. After some anxious moments of doubt whether the Refuseniks and their friends would dare to come and whether the militia would let them pass, some thirty guests showed up. It was the first of what grew to be regular meetings in the embassy of prominent Refuseniks, dissidents of various kinds, and Westerners. There was never a sign that any of the participants was more than usually harassed because of his or her participation in these events, nor was the embassy more than usually hindered in its work for either Israeli or the Netherlands interests. *Perestroika* and *glasnost* developed just quickly enough to make this result possible.[32]

The embassy meanwhile tried to follow up on the most tragic cases of refusal on the list that Minister Van den Broek had submitted in October 1986. It contained the names of fifty-two persons, but by May 1987, only nine had been given permission to leave. An Israeli list had also been introduced by the Dutch, but it fared no better. In June, after a long wait, the ambassador was finally received by Soviet Vice-Minister Anatoly Adamishin to discuss these cases. The ambassador was told that "the law was the law." That law might be changed, but not to please the Netherlands or any other Western nation. These questions remained internal affairs of the Soviet Union. Humanitarian questions should not burden the good bilateral relations. The ambassador, on his part, made clear that in view of the lively interest of Dutch public opinion and of the Dutch parliament, humanitarian questions could not be separated from Dutch foreign policy. He emphasized some particularly poignant cases such as the situation of the Gudava family from Georgia. The husband had permission to go, but his pregnant wife was still refused. As usual, no promises were made, and the ambassador left MID wondering whether his efforts had borne any fruit. But when ten days later the Gudavas presented their exit permits at the embassy and he could personally hand them their Israeli visas, there was at least some satisfaction.[33] The departure, at about the same time, of Vladimir Feltsman and his wife was undoubtedly mainly due to American pressure but gave pleasure to all their Western friends as well.

The embassy tried to help in other ways. Toward the end of 1987 some five hundred requests for *vysovs* were sent by diplomatic pouch to Israel every month.[34] The Hague, on the other hand, now allowed the embassy to distribute Hebrew grammars and dictionaries to the emigrants, although the ministry still balked at the distribution of a beautifully illustrated Israeli calendar.[35] The embassy confirmed that the grammars and dictionaries would be welcome: "The time that teachers of Hebrew were condemned to labor camps appears to be behind us."[36]

Visa applicants were now lining up in front of the embassy by the hundreds every morning. The Russian assistants complained of the heat and the crush in their much too small office. Scuffles sometimes broke out between applicants for Israeli visas and those who wanted visitor's or transit visas for the Netherlands. The two groups finally had to be given separate entrances. The arrival of an Israeli consular mission in July 1988 (see Chapter 10) made the overcrowding of the Consular Section even worse, but the Israelis did provide very welcome help. The Israelis admirably accepted their difficult position: they had no official status or identity cards, although the embassy time and again insisted that they be given such cards. They had a makeshift office in a hotel but did most of their work in the overcrowded Dutch Consular Office; Dutch facilities had to be used for their communications. Repeated requests by the Netherlands ambassador for permission to use the former Israeli embassy building were met with silence.[37]

Much business was carried out, of necessity, in the street. Application forms were handed out and filled in and the exit permits returned there after the visas had been stamped on them. It was primitive but it worked: every visa request was still honored the same day. Soon the members of the Israeli mission began to examine *vysovs* themselves, to see whether requests for extensions or changes could be granted. They handled all questions regarding the transmission of documents and arranged for a direct courier service (under Dutch seal) for that purpose to their embassy in Vienna. They dealt with applications for visitor's visas and were naturally giving out all possible information at the reception desk. The Israeli mission also relieved their Dutch colleagues of the task of giving financial aid to emigrants,[38] but that had become a minor duty anyway since during the 1980s the provision of support had gradually been taken over by two organizations, one from outside and one from inside the Soviet Union.[39]

Late in 1988 the situation suddenly improved for the Israeli mission. Curiously, the reason was a terrorist attack. On December 2, 1988, several terrorists kidnapped a group of schoolchildren in the city of Kazan. In exchange for the release of the children, they obtained an airplane and forced the crew to fly to Israel, apparently believing they would not be extradited by that country. The Israeli government wisely decided to send them straight back to Moscow. This cooperation seemed to provide Soviet Foreign Minister Shevardnadze with just the excuse he needed to overcome the resistance of the KGB and MID's Arabists against concessions to the Israelis. He received the head of the Israeli mission, Aryeh Levin, personally and told him he was now allowed to have political consultations in MID.[40] Perhaps even more important was that, a month later, the former Israeli embassy building was put at the disposal of the Netherlands embassy.[41] The necessary repairs of the building at Bolshaya Ordinka street, which had stood empty for twenty-two years, took—as always in the Soviet Union—a long time, but on June 5, 1989, it was open for business, albeit still under the escutcheon of the Netherlands.[42] The Dutch Consular Section and the Israeli mission now finally had sufficient space to work properly and receive visa applicants. It was just in time, for the crowds of applicants could not possibly have been handled in and outside the building of the Netherlands embassy for much longer.

In 1988 the number of exit permits granted by OVIR increased by leaps and bounds, but many new refusals were also handed out while some of the "old" Refuseniks were still waiting. Lists of urgent cases were therefore continuously drawn up and presented by the Netherlands ambassador or his deputy to the newly established Department of Humanitarian Affairs in MID. Many high-level Western visitors and several other embassies did the same. They all faced the question already raised by a Netherlands ambassador in the 1970s: How do we know we are dealing with the most urgent cases and not leaving out others equally or more deserving of our support? In consultations between the Ministry of Foreign Affairs in The Hague and the embassy in Moscow, the Netherlands reached the conclusion that in the enormous Soviet Union there simply was no reliable way to determine which cases were the most urgent. The only solution was to include the names that were received, after checking the reliability of the data as much as possible. Whenever new urgent cases were brought to the attention of Dutch officials, sometimes in The Hague, more often in Moscow, they, too, would be included in the next list.

One case frequently discussed with MID concerned the mother of a well-known Refusenik, Igor Uspensky. When he and his family finally got permission to leave in the summer of 1989, he was informed that this permission did not extend to his mother, the by-then seventy-seven-year-old widow Irina Voronkevich (who was not Jewish).[43] So she had to stay behind with a grandson in Moscow while the rest of the family moved to Israel. She might or might not have worked in a secret biology laboratory, but obviously she had had nothing to do with it for many years. When her case still had not been resolved in the spring of 1990, the Netherlands embassy, after consulting its foreign ministry and urged on by the Netherlands Academy of Sciences,[44] brought it officially to the attention of the Soviet government under the human dimension mechanism newly adopted in Vienna. When the answer was still negative, a bilateral consultation was held in the margin of the Copenhagen conference on the human dimension in May. Mrs. Voronkevich was finally allowed an exit permit for a visit to her family in Israel in the autumn of 1990—from which, of course, she did not return to Moscow.[45] It had been one of the most curious Refusenik cases that the embassy dealt with. Even the officials at MID had to concede that it was ridiculous to hold a seventy-seven-year-old grandmother for security reasons. But they were still unable to break the opposition undoubtedly coming from the KGB. Was it a roundabout way of punishing the Refusenik son? When the KGB finally had to give in, it did so in a typically backhanded way (which was not unique) by still refusing an exit permit for emigration to Israel and only allowing a tourist visit—small-minded to the last.

Relations Restored, the Task of the Netherlands Ends

The enormous increase in the number of visa applications, meanwhile, almost overwhelmed the staff of the Israeli consular mission and the Dutch Consular Section working together in the former Israeli chancery. In the spring of 1990 the Netherlands ambassador had to ask the Ministry of Foreign Affairs in The Hague for urgent help. He reported that an average of 915 visas for emigration to Israel were now being issued daily. On top of that came several dozen visitor's visas. It had become possible to obtain exit permits for tourism to Israel, and many Jews who could afford it were traveling to that country, either just to visit relatives or to explore it for possible immigration later. Furthermore, there were always corrections of *vysovs* from Israel to be signed. Several hundred were handled every day. The members of the Israeli mission and the Russian assistants prepared these documents, but the final stamp and signature still had to be given by a Dutch official. Dutch visitor's and transit visas increasingly became an additional burden, as travel to the Netherlands had also greatly expanded. It was not unusual that more than 2,000 signatures and stamps had to be affixed in a single day, and only two Dutch staff members were officially assigned for that task. Two others helped out from time to time but could not be detached permanently from their regular work. For the consul and his assistant these almost mechanical tasks became more and more unbearable, physically and psychologically. An additional assistant and a seal-signature stamp-machine were urgently requested.[46] Help was promised but took several months to arrive.

Naturally the Soviet authorities were now urged even more insistently by the Israelis to reestablish direct relations with Israel. In January 1990 TASS still found it necessary to expressly deny that such relations were in the offing. It said that the Soviets were ready to hold talks on "adjusting the status of both groups." There were questions about their functions, periods of stay, and numerical strength. But speculations about raising their status were "groundless."[47] The resistance from the pro-Arab sections in MID was still too strong and was not finally overcome until September of that year. After the Netherlands embassy had issued in July and August Israeli visas for an incredible number of 54,000 emigrants, direct discussions between the Soviet and Israeli foreign ministers Eduard Shevardnadze and David Levy at the UN General Assembly in New York on October 30, 1990, at last led to an agreement to establish consular relations. Consulates general would be opened in Tel Aviv and Moscow. Details were to be further discussed, and the Dutch representation of Israeli interests was to remain in force until those discussions were finished. Direct flights between Moscow and Tel Aviv were finally to be allowed.[48]

The further discussions took time, but on December 25, 1990, the head of the Israeli mission Aryeh Levin finally presented his letter of introduction as consul general to Foreign Minister Shevardnadze in person. That event was very unusual: the Soviet foreign minister was not in the habit of personally receiving credentials even from full-fledged ambassadors, let alone from a consul general. Levin also received his *exequatur* very quickly—two days later. The Israeli flag was raised on the Israeli chancery on January 3, 1991. The representation of Israeli interests by the Netherlands embassy had come to an end. Or had it?

On January 7, 1991, Israeli Prime Minister Yitzhak Shamir addressed a letter to Dutch Prime Minister Ruud Lubbers in which he expressed the gratitude and appreciation of his government to the Netherlands for having "faithfully and devotedly represented the affairs of the State of Israel in the Soviet Union." He continued:

> For more than twenty-three years, your service in Moscow on our behalf wrote a glowing page in the annals of the Jewish people. The government of the Netherlands bore the heavy burden during the dark and bitter years of Jewish oppression.

You worked as our faithful partner in championing the rights of Soviet Jews and the ingathering of our Jewish brethren from the Soviet Union.

The people of Israel recognize that your involvement on our behalf, beyond routine representation of diplomatic interests, made possible a process of historic dimensions, involving the emigration of hundreds of thousands of Soviet Jews. We would like to record and convey our special gratitude to the ambassadors and other personnel at your Moscow embassy who, over the years, rendered this signal humanitarian service to our people.

At this fateful time, as masses of Soviet Jews arrive in their Homeland, we send our deepest thanks to the People and Government of the Netherlands.

Shamir had had no doubt that the interest representation had ended, as his letter began with the sentence: "On the occasion of the reestablishment of formal relations between the Soviet Union and Israel and the termination of the representation of Israel's interests by the embassy of the Netherlands . . . "[49] But did the establishment of consular relations indeed mean that the consul general could take care of "formal relations"? Had not only the consular but also the diplomatic task of the Netherlands embassy ended?

It was a question of mostly theoretical interest. As we have seen, the Netherlands embassy hardly ever acted for Israel in anything that could be called the diplomatic sense. Consul General Levin, who in the Israeli foreign service had the internal rank of ambassador, had already been given the right to have discussions on political subjects in the Soviet foreign ministry. Yet the question remained whether the Soviet authorities should be formally notified that the representation by the Netherlands had ended. The Netherlands ambassador had submitted that question for the first time to The Hague on October 16, 1990. Consul General Levin, he reported, had expressed the belief that a consul general could act for his country in the diplomatic sense. Was this correct, and would the embassy's task therefore end completely? Though the question was repeated on December 31, it remained unanswered for almost four months. Even then the answer was wrong (and Levin had been right). The Hague maintained that after Shamir's letter no further action was required to end the interest representation.[50] The legal adviser at the

Netherlands Ministry of Foreign Affairs had overlooked Article 17 of the Vienna Convention on Consular Relations, which states that "in a State where the sending State has no diplomatic mission and is not represented by a diplomatic mission of a third state, a consular officer may, with the consent of the receiving state, be authorized to perform diplomatic acts."[51] In the end the Soviet authorities were never asked for such consent nor informed of the termination of the task of the Netherlands embassy. But since the new Israeli consul general did already have permission to perform what were in fact diplomatic acts, he could continue to do so until full diplomatic relations were restored between the Soviet Union and Israel, and he became an ambassador also in name, on October 25, 1991. The task of the Netherlands thus did fully end on January 3, 1991.

The Exodus Goes On

During 1990, Jewish emigration from the Soviet Union continued at an enormous rate: 184,847 persons left the Soviet Union with a visa for Israel that year, and all but 166 of them arrived in that country. At the same time direct emigration to the United States under the Refugee Act of 1980 and the new procedures established in 1989 (see Chapter 13) was beginning. The Hebrew Immigrant Aid Society estimated that a total of 26,717 Soviet Jews arrived in the United States and Canada in 1990. Thus in one year some 212,000 Soviet Jews had left their country; more than 187,000 were to follow in 1991 and more than 100,000 in each of the next four years.[52]

One would have expected that all Refuseniks would now have been allowed to leave. But this was not the case although their number did decrease considerably.[53] Some cases remained unresolved, and new refusals were reported. Uncertainty remained because there was still no new law on exit from and entrance into the country. As early as May 1989 a draft had been prepared and a spokesman of MID had informed U.S. Assistant Secretary of State Richard Schifter of a plan to issue a decree regarding emigration. It would abolish the requirement of permission for emigration from relatives and limit the duration of refusals for reasons of secrecy to five years. The decree was to be promulgated by the Presidium of the Supreme Soviet just before the new Congress of People's Deputies would convene on May 25, 1989.[54] But the newly chosen members of the Congress objected and requested henceforward to follow parliamentary procedures.[55] For the old Presidium to promulgate such an important decree just before the new Congress was to meet would indeed have been highly undemocratic. The decree was not issued, and the question remained in suspense.

Schifter's report and the continued increase in emigration figures nevertheless induced President George Bush to inform Congress in May 1989 that he intended to waive the Jackson-Vanik Amendment. Among the American Jewish organizations, the National Conference on Soviet Jewry agreed in June and the American Jewish Congress in August. Only the Union of Councils for Soviet Jews remained opposed. The president finally offered a trade package including most-favored-nation status (and thus a waiver) to President Gorbachev at their summit conference in Malta in December 1989, on condition that the Soviet Congress of People's Deputies pass the new emigration law. The Americans were once again assured that it would be passed, this time by May 31, 1990, the opening date of a new summit between Bush and Gorbachev in Washington. But again the Soviet Congress failed even to discuss the matter.[56] At the summit Gorbachev said that the new emigration law would soon be passed, not as a concession to the Americans but as a "logical consequence of our *perestroika.*"[57] However, before President Bush agreed to sign the trade agreement, Gorbachev had to accept a public anouncement by Bush that he would not submit it to the Senate before the Soviet Congress passed the emigration law.[58] It was the maximum Bush could do under the obligations imposed on him by the Jackson-Vanik Amendment. A few days later, at the opening of the Copenhagen CSCE conference on humanitarian affairs, Foreign Minister Shevardnadze repeated that the Soviet Union "would not back off from its commitment to a new emigration law."[59]

When that law still had not been passed by December 1990, Bush finally decided that it was necessary to waive certain provisions of the amendment in order to be able to ship large quantities of food to the Soviet Union on credit, to alleviate threatening shortages. Most-favored-nation status and the trade agreement were not part of Bush's action.[60]

Not until May 20, 1991, did the Congress of People's Deputies finally adopt a new law on exit and entry. It guarantees the right of every citizen to leave (either temporarily or permanently) and to enter the Soviet Union on the basis of passports for foreign travel. The "poor-relatives clause" is reduced to a notarized statement that there are no demands outstanding for alimony payments to parents or minor children. In cases where such a statement is refused, an appeal can be lodged with a court. Secrecy as ground for refusal is in principle limited to five years, although it can be extended by a commission to be formed by the government. Here, too, appeal to a court is made possible under certain conditions. Moreover, citizens are to be informed at the beginning of their employment about restrictions for travel on the basis of the possession of "information constituting a state secret."[61]

Nevertheless during the last summit between Presidents Bush and Gorbachev in July 1991, the U.S. president handed his Soviet colleague a list of ninety-five Refusenik cases that still had not been resolved. Assistant Secretary of State Schifter asked the Netherlands embassy to support U.S. demarches in this respect and remarked that since the new law was not yet being applied, secrecy restrictions of more than five years were still in effect and appeals against vetoes by relatives could still not be launched in the courts.[62]

In fact, a Resolution on the Promulgation of the Entry and Exit Law had been adopted the same day as the law itself. It provided that its main parts would not come into force until January 1, 1993. This delay may have been due to a compromise in the Congress of People's Deputies with conservative opponents, although there were also said to be practical difficulties with the manufacture of passports in the quantities suddenly required.[63] The resolution did stipulate that the provision abolishing the decree of February 17, 1967 (according to which Jewish emigrants lost their citizenship automatically upon leaving the Soviet Union, see Chapter 2), would come into force on July 1, 1991. Under certain circumstances, specified in the Law on USSR Citizenship, the lost citizenship could even be restored. For the first time in twenty-four years Jewish emigrants no longer had to travel as stateless persons possessing only a three-page exit permit: they could now apply for ordinary Soviet passports. The decree of August 3, 1972, on the diploma fee (see Chapter 6) was also finally abolished. The Soviet press remarked that the adoption of the new law was a historic occasion, but added cynically that the countries that had insisted on this law for years were now "hastily throwing up barriers to keep Soviet citizens out."[64]

Conclusion

It is very doubtful that the Soviet leadership ever expected the Jewish emigration to turn into the enormous exodus it in fact became. According to an American source, by October 1995 a total of 984,396 Jews had left what used to be the Soviet Union with Israeli visas since 1967.[65] Since the change in U.S. regulations of September 30, 1989, approximately 225,000 Jews had by then gone directly to the United States, either as refugees or as regular immigrants;[66] their number must be added to the total.

The various statistical bases are too different to permit adding up the numbers with precision. Yet it is safe to assume that from 1967 through October 1995, about 1,200,000 Jews left the territories that used to constitute the Soviet Union, either with visas for Israel, or, from 1990, as refugees under the U.S. Refugee Assistance Program. More than 786,000 of them went to Israel and about 430,000, including at least 15,000 non-Jews, to the West, in great majority to the United States.

Epilogue

To leave one's native country for good is always a traumatic experience. In the Soviet Union the harassment of prospective emigrants, which made their applications and their departure a hell; the refusal of exit permits and sometimes even the withdrawal of already issued ones, unexpectedly forcing people to stay; the enormous sums of money demanded from the emigrants before departure; the overzealous customs control of their last possessions; and, for those with Israel as their marked destination, the automatic loss of citizenship—all made this exodus into a drama that moved Western public opinion for many years and time and again influenced bilateral and multilateral foreign policy.

The evolutions up and down in the number of exit permits granted to Jews were never published, let alone publicly explained by the Soviet authorities. Jews would suddenly become aware that permits were being granted, or find their chance to leave suddenly restricted or virtually suspended just as they were preparing to go. This uncertainty, plus the irrational refusal of permits based on unpublished legal provisions without the possibility of appeal to an independent judicial authority, caused deep suffering to a great many Soviet Jews between 1967 and 1991. The Universal Declaration on Human Rights was not observed; the Helsinki Final Act of the Conference on Security and Cooperation in Europe and its follow-up meetings could provide some palliative measures and later help individual cases, but these did not basically alter the defenseless position of the Jewish victims of Soviet arbitrariness until just before the final collapse of the Soviet Union. And yet Jews continued to leave the Soviet Union in whatever numbers were allowed; during the period covered by this book, 1967 until the end of 1990, the Jewish community there lost about a quarter of its members through emigration; five years later it may have been one-half.[1]

The Jewish desire to emigrate from the Soviet Union was prompted as much by a distaste for the living in dishonesty forced upon them by the communist state as by anti-Jewish discrimination, by a general sense of hopelessness regarding their future in their country as much as by anti-semitism. It was enormously stimulated by the founding of a Jewish state in Israel, especially after that state had prevailed in the Six-Day War in 1967. The Jews themselves then began to stir and to demand their right to leave. The surprising decision of the Soviet authorities from 1971 onward and again after 1987 to indeed grant permission—at first to a small and then to an ever-increasing number of Jews—was prompted by an interaction of internal and external factors.

The Soviet Jews "did not dwell alone." Their internal pressure found a response in Israel as well as with active Jewish organizations in the West, initially especially in the United States. In turn those organizations, often with the semisecret Israeli Lishka in the background, succeeded first in inducing Western public opinion and then also non-Jewish Western organizations and Western governments to demand from the Soviet government observance of human rights provisions regarding free movement and the granting of exit permits to Jews.

The conclusion must be, however, that Israeli and Western pressure was successful only when the internal situation, in particular economic stagnation acerbated by low oil prices or bad harvests, forced the communist leadership to make concessions in order to obtain Western credits and technology. When the internal economic situation improved, the oil prices increased, or hoped-for political or economic concessions were not forthcoming, the "tap" could be closed as quickly as it had been opened.

The Netherlands played an unassuming role in this drama from the moment it agreed to represent Israeli interests in 1967. The Dutch in general greatly sympathized with the fate of Soviet Jews, and embassy officials tried to expedite their departure as much as they could. At first the authorities in The Hague were convinced that the embassy should not maintain contacts with the Jewish community or with Refusenik leaders for fear it might be prevented from continuing its work for Israel. For the same reason diplomatic steps for dissidents or Refuseniks were never carried out in the name of the Netherlands, but always in that of Israel. In the 1980s this policy changed: the embassy was directed to plead for

Refuseniks and prisoners in the name of the Netherlands itself; it later began making direct contacts with Refuseniks and dissidents; and it finally became one of the main forums in Moscow for meetings of Refuseniks, dissidents, Western diplomats, and foreign journalists.

Direct assistance to individual Jews was extended by numerous non-governmental organizations, Jewish and non-Jewish. Volunteers from many countries acted as couriers and established communications. Courageous Jews inside the Soviet Union made sure that Western public opinion remained aware of the fate of the Soviet Jews in general and Refuseniks in particular. Many paid for their actions with imprisonment or internal exile. Protests in their behalf were lodged by the Israeli government (through the intermediary of, and later often together with, the Netherlands) as well as by the American and many other governments. Those demarches were at first usually rejected and seemed useless, but more often than not the Soviet authorities in the end proved sensitive to Western pressure, especially if exerted on a high level.

Hundreds of thousands of Jews who left the Soviet Union are now trying to rebuild their lives in a new homeland. Most will succeed there (and if not they, then their children); some will not; most will stay there; and some will want to go back, or go elsewhere—thus has it always been with mass-scale emigration. But the departure of the Jews from the Soviet Union was more than just an emigration: it was—and still is—a mass exodus of a nation that, although it never possessed its own territory, did once have a rich cultural life and its own language, literature, and religion. Whether some of that can be revived and salvaged in the cities of the former Soviet Union is becoming more and more doubtful.

One can only wish that the migrants will find in their new land the happiness and prosperity they hoped for when they left the land of their birth and a new fulfillment of their cultural, political, or religious desires. That is what, after their long ordeal, they richly deserve.

Appendix

Table 1

Number of Persons for Whom Visas for Israel Were Issued by the
Netherlands Embassy in Moscow, 1967–1990

1967[a]	ca. 116
1968[b]	230
1969	2,808
1970[b]	935
1971	ca. 14,000
1972	31,413
1973	34,778
1974	20,146
1975	13,209
1976	14,064
1977	17,146
1978	30,579
1979	50,461
1980	20,342
1981	9,127
1982	2,561
1983	1,344
1984	890
1985	1,153
1986	902
1987	8,563
1988	26,183
1989	83,666
1990[c]	141,572

Source: Netherlands embassy Moscow, in reports to the Ministry of Foreign Affairs, The Hague.
[a] After June 10, 1967, date of the breaking off of relations between the Soviet Union and Israel.
[b] Uncertain.
[c] For eight months only; later figures have not been preserved in the Dutch files.

Table 2

Number of Persons for Whom Visas for Israel Were Issued by the Netherlands Embassy in Moscow, 1973–1990, per Month

1973		Mar.	1,085	Apr.	2,002	May	133
Sept.	3,659	Apr.	1,243	May	2,131	June	118
Oct.	4,266[a]	May	1,230	June	1,489	July	175
Nov.	3,498	June	1,496	July	680	Aug.	150
Dec.	—	July	1,300	Aug.	1,040	Sept.	108
1974		Aug.	1,513	Sept.	1,693	Oct.	60
Jan.	2,209	Sept.	1,913	Oct.	952	Nov.	65
Feb.	1,620	Oct.	1,555	Nov.	690	Dec.	98[b]
	—	Nov.	1,656[b]	Dec.	966	**1984**	
Nov.	1,511	Dec.	1,865	**1981**		Jan.	99
Dec.	1,423	**1978**		Jan.	910	Feb.	83
1975		Jan.	1,946	Feb.	2,342	Mar.	51
Jan.	1,208	Feb.	2,131	Mar.	710[b]	Apr.	109
Feb.	1,038	Mar.	1,835	Apr.	916[d]	May	77
Mar.	825	Apr.	1,870	May	905	June	82
Apr.	1,291	May	1,919	June	855	July	77
May	879	June	1,943	July	728	Aug.	65
June	1,012	July	2,211	Aug.	348	Sept.	61
July	980	Aug.	2,540	Sept.	509	Oct.	51
Aug.	946	Sept.	2,845	Oct.	290	Nov.	54
Sept.	1,099	Oct.	4,021	Nov.	218	Dec.	81
Oct.	1,460	Nov.	3,427	Dec.	396	**1985**	
Nov.	1,223	Dec.	3,891	**1982**		Jan.	—
Dec.	1,248	**1979**		Jan.	257[e]	Feb.	94
1976		Jan.	4,040	Feb.	290	Mar.	94
Jan.	1,064	Feb.	4,126	Mar.	301	Apr.	158
Feb.	1,227	Mar.	4,029	Apr.	217	May	—
Mar.	1,345	Apr.	4,187	May	194	June	—
Apr.	1,007	May	4,499[c]	June	239	July	—
May	1,234	June	4,332	July	171	Aug.	73
June	907	July	4,191	Aug.	260	Sept.	—
July	884	Aug.	4,861	Sept.	205	Oct.	136
Aug.	849[b]	Sept.	4,423	Oct.	153	Nov.	102
Sept.	1,138	Oct.	4,867	Nov.	162	Dec.	—
Oct.	1,416	Nov.	3,616	Dec.	112	**1986**	
Nov.	1,683	Dec.	3,300	**1983**		Jan.	104
Dec.	1,310	**1980**		Jan.	108	Feb.	51
1977		Jan.	3,271	Feb.	112	Mar.	46
Jan.	1,294	Feb.	2,868	Mar.	96	Apr.	75
Feb.	1,023	Mar.	2,868	Apr.	121	May	42

Table 2 (*continued*)

June	61	July	761	Aug.	2,261	Sept.	16,619
July	49	Aug.	785	Sept.	2,443	Oct.	11,669[f]
Aug.	100	Sept.	896	Oct.	3,032	Nov.	2,084
Sept.	109	Oct.	902	Nov.	3,949	Dec.	3,355
Oct.	122	Nov.	857	Dec.	4,602		
Nov.	81	Dec.	811			**1990**	
Dec.	62			**1989**		Jan.	5,813
		1988		Jan.	3,528	Feb.	9,735
1987		Jan.	722	Feb.	4,777	Mar.	19,026
Jan.	136	Feb.	1,012	Mar.	6,021	Apr.	13,939
Feb.	255	Mar.	1,115	Apr.	5,022	May	19,472
Mar.	576	Apr.	1,289	May	5,801	June	19,378
Apr.	903	May	1,730	June	6,712	July	27,777
May	760	June	2,064	July	8,115	Aug.	26,435
June	921	July	1,914	Aug.	9,963		

Source: Netherlands embassy, Moscow, in reports to the Ministry of Foreign Affairs, intermittently from September 1973, regularly from November 1974. No further data found after August 1990.

[a] War in Middle East.
[b] Missing, computed from yearly total.
[c] 200,000th visa issued May 28.
[d] Computed from weekly figures, April–December 1981.
[e] Computed from monthly figures.
[f] Automatic refugee status ended by the United States.

Table 3

Soviet Jewish Emigration through Vienna to Israel, the United States, and Elsewhere, 1967–1990

Year	Israeli Visas Issued[a]	Vienna Arrivals[b]	Emigrants to Israel[b]		to the U.S. and Elsewhere[b]	
			Number	Percent	Number	Percent
1967	1,162[b]		1,162			
1968	230[a]		223			
1969	2,808		2,979			
1970	935		1,027			
1971	ca. 14,000	13,022	12,966	99.6%	56	0.4%
1972	31,413	31,681	31,432	99.2%	249	0.8%
1973	34,778	34,733	33,283	95.9%	1,450	4.1%
1974	20,146	20,944	17,065	81.5%	3,879	18.5%
1975	13,209	13,221	8,293	62.7%	4,929	37.3%
1976	14,064	14,261	7,258	50.9%	7,003	49.1%

Table 3 *(continued)*

Year	Israeli Visas Issued[a]	Vienna Arrivals[b]	Emigrants to Israel[b]		to the U.S. and Elsewhere[b]	
			Number	Percent	Number	Percent
1977	17,146	16,736	8,253	49.3%	8,483	50.7%
1978	30,379	28,865	11,998	41.7%	16,876	58.3%
1979	50,461	51,333	17,277	33.7%	34,056	66.3%
1980	20,342	21,471	7,393	34.4%	14,078	65.6%
1981	9,127	9,448	1,757	18.6%	7,691	81.4%
1982	2,561	2,692	731	27.1%	1,961	72.9%
1983	1,344	1,314	378	28.8%	936	71.2%
1984	890	895	335	37.4%	560	62.6%
1985	1,153	1,140	348	30.5%	792	69.5%
1986	902	914	206	22.5%	708	77.6%
1987	8,563	8,155	2,072	25.4%	6,083	74.6%
1988	26,183	22,403	2,173	9.7%	20,230	90.3%
1989	83,666	85,140	12,721	14.9%	72,419	85.1%
1990	—	184,847	184,681	100.0%	166	0%

Note: It should be kept in mind that the number of persons for whom visas were issued in Moscow does not have to be the same as the number of arrivals in Vienna. Recipients of visas did not always leave immediately, often not in the year in which they had received them, and sometimes not at all.

Jewish Emigration from the (Former) Soviet Union, 1990–1995 According to Israeli Statistics[c]

Year	Emigrants to Israel	to Western Countries[d]	Total
1990	184,681	28,000	212,700
1991	146,542	41,400	187,600
1992	64,790	50,900	115,700
1993	66,145	41,800	107,900
1994	68,079	38,200	106,300
1995[e]	51,535	28,000	79,500
Total	581,772	228,300	810,700

[a] *Source:* Netherlands embassy, Moscow. Minor children were inscribed in the exit permit of one of their parents and not given individual visas, but they were counted separately in the statistics by the embassy and by the other agencies.

[b] *Source:* Israeli official statistics.

[c] Provided by Lishka, November 7, 1995.

[d] Estimates only; include the United States, Canada, Germany, and other countries.

[e] To November 1.

Table 4

Netherlands Ambassadors in Moscow, 1967–1991

1965–70	Jonkheer Gerard Beelaerts van Blokland
1970–74	Age Robert Tammenoms Bakker
1974–77	Jonkheer Jan Louis Reinier Huydecoper van Nigtevecht
1977–80	Kasper Willem Reinink
1980–86	Frans Joseph Theodoor Johannes van Agt
1986–90	Petrus Buwalda
1990–93	Joris Michael Vos

Table 5

Heads of the Consular Section of the Netherlands Embassy in Moscow,
1967–1991

1966–69	Johan W. Semijns de Vries van Doesburg
1969–70	Marius P. van Soest
1970–72	Henri J. Heinemann
1972–74	Lambertus J. Count de Marchant et d'Ansembourg
1974–77	Laurentius V. M. van Gorp
1977–79	Govert van Vliet
1979–80	Frans van Lunteren
1981–84	Hermanus van der Schalk
1984–85	Antonius M. L. H. Schellekens
1985–86	Markus D. Rosenberg Polak
1986–89	Robbert E. M. van Lanschot
1989	Frantisek Z. R. Wijchers
1989–90	Hans C. Wesseling
1990–92	Wouter H. J. van Rijckevorsel

Notes

Sources for this study are primarily the messages sent to and from the Netherlands embassy in Moscow and the Netherlands Ministry of Foreign Affairs in The Hague. These and most other documents regarding the protection of Israeli interests in the Soviet Union are filed in the ministry under code 912.3, Belangen Behartiging Israel (BBI, or Interest Representation Israel). They have been numbered continuously from part 1, beginning on June 10, 1967, through part 76, which ends on December 31, 1986. From 1987 on they are under the same classification but numbered per year in roman numerals; for example, for 1987 from number I through number XXIV. The last file on BBI is for 1990, but it in fact runs until March 1, 1991. The archives of the embassy for this period have also been transferred to the ministry's archives and are stored there in separate boxes under the same code. Communications filed under different codes are so noted.

Messages about BBI were normally sent by cable and in code, first transmitted by telex, later by wireless when the embassy was provided with its own transmitter. All codes from the ministry were signed with the name of the current minister of foreign affairs when he was in The Hague or with CELER (in Latin, "quick") if he was not. The file copy identifies the desk where the text originated and the name of the drafter. Cables from the embassy were signed with the name of the ambassador or the chargé d'affaires (see Tables 4 and 5, page 225, for lists of officials). Since computers were considered too unsafe from a security point of view, they were not provided to the Netherlands embassy in Moscow during the period covered by this book.

The author is responsible for the translation of the messages from Dutch into English.

Whenever the notes refer to "embassy," the Netherlands embassy in Moscow is meant. Other embassies are specified. "The Hague" stands for the Netherlands Ministry of Foreign Affairs in that city, the seat of the Dutch governmment.

Messages to and from the U.S. Department of State and internal memoranda from that department have been quoted from documents on microfiche in its Documents Section, Washington, D.C. Some had already been declassified; others were released under the Freedom of Information Act at the request of the author (case ID: 9303630).

All interviews cited in the notes were conducted by the author. A complete list of interviewees follows the Bibliography.

The title of this book is derived from Numbers 23:9: "Lo, the people shall dwell alone" and was first used by Hanan Bar-on, former Israeli ambassador to the Netherlands. The epigraph, by Natasha Rapoport, is quoted in David Remnick, *Lenin's Tomb* (New York: Random House, 1993), 99.

Introduction

1. From 1967 to January 1, 1991, the Netherlands embassy issued Israeli visas for 568,241 persons, but at least 10,000 of them were not Jews. The official census of the Soviet Union in 1959 registered 2,267,814 Jews, or 1.1 percent of the total Soviet population.

Prologue

1. Benjamin Z. Goldberg, *The Jewish Problem in the Soviet Union: An Analysis and a Solution* (New York: Crown, 1961), 4–5; Richard Pipes, *The Formation of the Soviet Union*, rev. ed. (Cambridge, Mass.: Harvard University Press, 1964), 7.

2. Benjamin Pinkus, *The Jews of the Soviet Union, 1917–1923* (Cambridge: Cambridge University Press, 1988), 1–5; Jules Brutzkus, *Les origines du Judaism russe* (Geneva, 1946).

3. Goldberg, *Jewish Problem*; Pinkus, *Jews of the Soviet Union*; Brutzkus, *Les origines du Judaism russe*. Others claim that most of the Jews of Eastern Europe are in fact descendants of the Khazar refugees, while only a minority came from Western Europe. See Arthur Koestler, *The Thirteenth Tribe: The Khazar Empire and Its Heritage* (New York: Random House, 1976).

4. Robert J. Brym, *The Jewish Intelligentsia and Russian Marxism* (London: Macmillan Press, 1972), 9–11.

5. Ibid., 15.

6. Pinkus, *Jews of the Soviet Union*, 8, Elizabeth's decree quoted on 7.

7. Fitzroy Maclean, *Holy Russia* (London: Weidenfeld & Nicholson, 1978), 90.

8. Catherine's decree quoted in Pinkus, *Jews of the Soviet Union*, 12.

9. Catherine's edict, 1791, quoted in ibid.

10. E.g., Fuks-Mansfeld, *Het Onvoltooid Verleden* (The unfinished past), ed. A. M. Gerrits and H. Rankema (Utrecht, 1993), 18.

11. Pinkus, *Jews of the Soviet Union*, 15.

12. Nora Levin, *The Jews in the Soviet Union since 1917* (New York: New York University Press, 1988), 3.

13. Goldberg, *Jewish Problem*, 4.

14. Regulation regarding the Jews, December 9, 1804, quoted in Pinkus, *Jews of the Soviet Union*, 15.

15. Jewish Regulations, May 31, 1835, quoted in ibid., 19.

16. Maclean, *Holy Russia*, 120; Pinkus, *Jews of the Soviet Union*, 22.

17. Pipes calls them *peuples allogènes. Formation of the Soviet Union*, 5.

18. At the urging of the British Parliament, the ambassador of the United Kingdom in St. Petersburg was instructed to "look after the persecuted Jews." He was joined in a demarche by the chargé d'affaires of the United States and the minister of the Netherlands. Public Record Office, London, file Foreign Office 65, no. 115.

19. Goldberg, *Jewish Problem*, 6.

20. Mordechai Altshuler, *Soviet Jewry since the Second World War* (New York: Greenwood Press, 1987), 2.

21. Interview with Mordechai Altshuler, professor at Hebrew University, Jerusalem, March 11, 1994.

22. Pinkus, *Jews of the Soviet Union*, 27–29. The *Protocols of the Elders of Zion* were condemned as a forgery in a trial in Bern in 1934. Equally odious was *The Jewish Question* published by an organization called the Black Hundred in St. Petersburg in 1906. That did not prevent the Soviet embassy in Paris from printing an article clearly based on this publication in its September 22, 1972, issue of the magazine *U.R.S.S.* The nominal French editor of the magazine was condemned by a French court on April 24, 1973. See Emanuel Litvinov, *Soviet Antisemitism: The Paris Trial* (London: Wildwood House, 1974), 111.

23. Chaim Potok, *Wanderings* (New York: Knopf, 1978).

24. Michael Davitt, quoted in Ronald Sanders, *Shores of Refuge* (New York: Holt, 1988), 269.

25. Ibid., 43. The Hebrew Immigrant Aid Society was disbanded and founded again several times but has eventually become the most important organization helping Jewish immigrants to the United States. It is still doing so.

26. Pinkus, *Jews of the Soviet Union*, 33.

27. Levin, *Jews in the Soviet Union*, 28; Pinkus, *Jews of the Soviet Union*, 31.

28. Goldberg, *Jewish Problem*, 8; Pipes, *Formation of the Soviet Union*, 6.

29. Levin, *Jews in the Soviet Union*, 4.

30. Ibid., 5; Pipes, *Formation of the Soviet Union*, 28. It is interesting that this idea of extraterritorial autonomy is now applied to the Flemish and Walloon nationals and the German speakers in Brussels.

31. Pinkus, *Jews of the Soviet Union*, 52; Levin, *Jews in the Soviet Union*, 16; Z. R. Dittrich and A. P. van Goudoever, *De Geschiedenis van de Sovjet Unie* (The history of the Soviet Union) (The Hague: SDU, 1991), 79.

32. Josef Stalin, "Marxism and the National Colonial Question," quoted in Levin, *Jews in the Soviet Union*, 16.

33. Pipes, *Formation of the Soviet Union*, 38; Pinkus, *Jews of the Soviet Union*, 50.

34. Levin, *Jews in the Soviet Union*, 3.

35. Balfour Declaration, November 2, 1917, quoted in Sanders, *Shores of Refuge*, 299.

36. Edward Drachman, *Challenging the Kremlin: The Soviet Jewish Movement for Freedom* (New York: Paragon House, 1991), 8, 16.

37. Alex De Jonge, *Stalin and the Shaping of the Soviet Union* (Glasgow: Collins, 1986), 168.

38. Levin, *Jews in the Soviet Union*, 38.

39. Pinkus, *Jews of the Soviet Union*, 58.

40. Ibid., 78.

41. Levin, *Jews in the Soviet Union*, 43.

42. Ibid., 66ff.

43. De Jonge, *Stalin and the Shaping of the Soviet Union*, 218.

44. Lazar Kaganovich was finally ousted by Nikita Khrushchev in 1957 as belonging to an "antiparty group" but was still alive in 1990 at age ninety-six. Drachman, *Challenging the Kremlin*, 9.

45. Levin, *Jews in the Soviet Union*, 150.

46. M. I. Kalinin's declaration, November 1926, quoted in Pinkus, *Jews of the Soviet Union*, 72.

47. Interview with Asher Ostrin, Joint Distribution Committee, Jerusalem, March 22, 1994. See also Sanders, *Shores of Refuge*, 368.

48. Goldberg, *Jewish Problem*, 172; Levin, *Jews in the Soviet Union*, 282; Pinkus, *Jews of the Soviet Union*, 72.

49. Levin, *Jews in the Soviet Union*, 300; Pinkus, *Jews of the Soviet Union*, 75.

50. The law of April 1929 has been described as "nothing short of a wholesale onslaught against religion." Drachman, *Challenging the Kremlin*, 19.

51. Levin, *Jews in the Soviet Union*, 276.

52. Ibid., 223, 224; Drachman, *Challenging the Kremlin*, 24.

53. Pinkus, *Jews of the Soviet Union*, 80.

54. Levin, *Jews in the Soviet Union*, 224; Pinkus, *Jews of the Soviet Union*, 80–83.

55. Altshuler, *Soviet Jewry since the Second World War*, 2–4.

56. Levin, *Jews in the Soviet Union*, 348, 372.

57. Jozien J. Driessen, "Joden in Rusland: De Integratie van een Minderheid" (Jews in Russia: The integration of a minority), in *Het Onvoltooid Verleden*, ed. Gerrits and Rankema, 139.

58. Levin, *Jews in the Soviet Union*, 401–2.

59. Altshuler, *Soviet Jewry in the Second World War*, 4.

60. Levin, *Jews in the Soviet Union*, 469, 381.

61. Pinkus, *Jews of the Soviet Union*, 140.

62. Arnold Krammer, *The Forgotten Friendship* (Urbana: University of Illinois Press, 1974), 202. See also Avigdor Dagan, *Moscow and Jerusalem: Twenty Years of Relations between Israel and the USSR* (London: Abelard Schuman, 1970), 21: "None of the authors seems to be entirely satisfied."

63. Andrei Gromyko unfortunately does not mention this issue in his memoirs. See Andrei Gromyko, *Memories from Stalin to Gorbachev* (London: Arrow Books, 1989).

64. Krammer, *Forgotten Friendship*, 16; Pinkus, *Jews of the Soviet Union*, 166.

65. Andrei Gromyko, quoted in Krammer, *Forgotten Friendship*, 21.

66. Krammer mentions this possibility. Ibid., 31. Dagan, *Moscow and Jerusalem*, 22, also concludes that the Soviet Union "had only one concern: the elimination of British and Western influence in . . . the area."

67. Krammer, *Forgotten Friendship*, 16.

68. Jon Kimche and David Kimche, *Both Sides of the Hill* (London: Secker & Warburg, 1960), 275; Krammer, *Forgotten Friendship*, 40.

69. Krammer, *Forgotten Friendship*, 144.

70. David Ben-Gurion, interview with Sulzberger, *New York Times*, March 20, 1950. See also Krammer, *Forgotten Friendship*, 173.

71. The first immigration visa was issued by the Israeli legation on June 19, 1951, to a seventy-six-year-old woman. Krammer, *Forgotten Friendship*, 159. Krammer adds that only a single emigration permit for Israel was granted by the Soviet government for more than a decade afterward, but the Netherlands ambassador in Moscow reported in a letter to The Hague on February 20, 1953, that there had been about fifteen cases in 1952. He added that only older Soviet citizens—by exception—received permission to join their families in Israel.

72. Andrei Gromyko, UN General Assembly records, quoted in Krammer, *Forgotten Friendship*, 51.

73. Golda Meir, *My Life* (London: Weidenfeld & Nicolson, 1975), 205.

74. It was called an accident, but research in Russian archives has now confirmed the suspicion that Shlomo Mikhoels was murdered by the State Security Service.

75. Levin, *Jews in the Soviet Union*, 500–504; Pinkus, *Jews of the Soviet Union*, 141–49; Goldberg, *Jewish Problem*, 103; Judd L. Teller, *The Kremlin, the Jews and the Middle East* (New York: Thomas Yoschoff, 1957), 80.

76. Svetlana Alleluyeva, *Letters to a Friend* (London: Hutchinson, 1967), 206.

77. *Nomenclatura* is the name given to the privileged leadership of the Soviet Communist Party by the Yugoslav author Milovan Djilas.

78. See, e.g., the memoirs of the last survivor, Jakov Rapoport, in Jakov Rapoport and Natasha Rapoport, *Het Dokterscomplot* (The doctors' plot, Dutch translation from the Russian) (Amsterdam: G. A. van Oorschot, 1990).

79. De Jonge, *Stalin and the Shaping of the Soviet Union*, 500–502.

80. Rapoport and Rapoport, *Het Dokterscomplot*, 200.

81. Moshe Sharet, letter to Netherlands minister for foreign affairs, February 19, 1953, code 912.3, file 4140.

82. Director, African and Middle Eastern Affairs, Ministry of Foreign Affairs, The Hague, internal memorandum concerning conversation with Israeli envoy, June 4, 1953, code 912.3, file 4140.

83. Netherlands legation, Jerusalem, to The Hague, July 20, 1953.

84. Krammer, *Forgotten Friendship*, 195.

85. Netherlands legation, Jerusalem, letter to The Hague, October 9, 1953.

86. Pinkus, *Jews of the Soviet Union*, 246. Nikita Khrushchev denied being antisemitic in his memoirs, but he did engage in antisemitic actions. Drachman, *Challenging the Kremlin*, 30.

87. Dittrich and Van Goudoever, *De Geschiedenis van de Sovjet Unie*, 139.

88. Pinkus, *Jews of the Soviet Union*, 286.

89. Embassy to The Hague, December 17, 1962.

90. Drachman, *Challenging the Kremlin*, 35, 179.

91. The Hague to embassy, June 10, 1967; embassy to The Hague, June 12, 1967.

92. M. A. Janner, *La Puissance protectrice en droit international d'après les expériences faites par la Suisse pendant la seconde quère mondiale* (Bâle: Helling et Lichtenhahn, 1948), 89: "Bienqu'il n'existe pas d'obligation stricte à cet égard, la courtoisie internationale commande de l'accepter la réprésentation d'interêts étrangers" (Although a strict obligation in this respect does not exist, international courtesy demands that the representation of the interest of foreigners be accepted).

93. Compare the statement by Queen Beatrix to the Israeli parliament, March 1995.

94. Pinkus, *Jews of the Soviet Union*, 252.

95. Embassy to The Hague, August 21, 1967.

96. See the Vienna Convention on Diplomatic Relations, April 1961, Article 39, subsection 2.

97. Embassy to The Hague, June 13, 1967. The provision in question is Article 45.

98. Embassy to The Hague, June 13, 1967.

99. Embassy to The Hague, July 11, 1967.

100. The Hague to embassy, August 15, 1967.

101. Embassy to The Hague, September 4, 1967.

102. The Hague to embassy, June 17, 1967, and responses, June 20, 21, 1967.

Chapter 1, The Second Exodus, the First Wave

1. Embassy to The Hague, September 5, 1968.

2. Pinkus, *Jews of the Soviet Union*, 245.

3. The Soviet Union was probably the only country in the world where the Hebrew language was illegal. Jews were arrested and persecuted for studying and teaching Hebrew. Soviet customs did not permit the import of any document containing a Hebrew character. Handwritten Hebrew-Russian dictionaries were in use. Interviews by author.

4. Boris Kochubyevski, quoted in Leonard Schroeter, *The Last Exodus*, 2d ed. (Seattle: Weidenfeld, 1979), 45–47.

5. Embassy to The Hague, January 9, 1969.

6. Yasha Kazakov, quoted in Schroeter, *Last Exodus*, 88–90.

7. William W. Orbach, *The American Movement to Aid Soviet Jews* (Amherst: University of Massachusetts Press, 1979), 45; Schroeter, *Last Exodus*, 128.

8. Embassy to The Hague, June 15, 22, 1970.

9. Schroeter, *Last Exodus*, 186, claims that the Israeli government knew about the attempt in advance and did what it could to discourage the effort, but later denied any knowledge of it.

10. Embassy to The Hague, July 30, 1970.

11. Schroeter, *Last Exodus*, 144; Ludmilla Alexeyeva, *Soviet Dissent* (Middletown, Conn.: Wesleyan University Press, 1985), 181.

12. Schroeter, *Last Exodus*, 173.

13. Embassy to The Hague, December 26, 1970, code 911.30: "Joden in de Soviet Unie" (Jews in the Soviet Union), part 2, 1968–74.

14. Schroeter, *Last Exodus*, 173, 176.

15. Drachman, *Challenging the Kremlin*, 189.

16. Schroeter, *Last Exodus*, 177.

17. Laurie P. Salitan, *Politics and Nationality in Contemporary Soviet-Jewish Emigration, 1968–89* (New York: St. Martin's Press, 1992), 32.

18. Bureau of Eastern European Affairs, Ministry of Foreign Affairs, The Hague, internal memorandum, March 22, 1971.

19. Embassy to The Hague, April 2, 1971.

20. Interview with H. J. Heinemann, former head, Consular Section, Netherlands embassy, Moscow, in The Hague, April 11, 1995.

21. Interview with Yuri Zieman, former Refusenik, Boston, in Washington, D.C., October 30, 1993.

22. Interview with Dmitri Simes, senior associate at the Carnegie Endowment for International Peace, Washington, D.C., December 3, 1993.

23. Interview with Emanuel Lurye, former Refusenik, Lod, Israel, March 12, 1994. Pinkus, *Jews of the Soviet Union*, 307, cites "surveys made in Israel and other countries . . . [in which also] a high percentage stated that anti-semitism existed but that they had not been personally afflicted by it and that it had not influenced their decision to emigrate."

24. Rapoport and Rapoport, *Het Dokterscomplot*.

25. The KGB frequently targeted Refuseniks, promising exit permits "soon" in exchange for compliance with its wishes. See also Chapter 4, note 4.

26. Altshuler, *Soviet Jewry since the Second World War*, 12, 230–31.

27. Victor Zaslavsky and Robert J. Brym, *Soviet-Jewish Emigration and Soviet Nationality Policy* (New York: St. Martin's Press, 1983), give a more extensive exposition of the various motives than can be provided here. Unfortunately their book is marred by their constant effort to prove their preconceived theories. See also Pinkus, *Jews of the Soviet Union*, 307ff.

28. Zaslavsky and Brym, *Soviet-Jewish Emigration*, 50.

29. Elie Wiesel, *De Joden der Stilte* (The Jews of silence, Dutch translation from the French) (Hilversum: Gooi & Sticht, 1985), 108.

30. Interviews with former Refuseniks, including Yuri Zieman and Evgeny Lein, Jerusalem, March 21, 1994.

31. Schroeter, *Last Exodus*, 126. In an interview in Jerusalem, March 14, 1994, the former Israeli prime minister Yitzhak Shamir stated: "Up till the early 1970s the Israeli government followed a policy of not speaking about it and not saying anything against the Soviets."

32. Dan Raviv and Yossi Melman, *Every Spie a Prince* (Boston: Houghton Mifflin, 1990), 38–39.

33. Interview with Yaakov Kedmi, head of Lishka, Tel Aviv, March 6, 1994; Schroeter, *Last Exodus*, 126. This office was given the Hebrew code name *Nativ*

(the route). Aryeh Levin, *Envoy to Moscow* (London: Frank B. Cass, 1996), 16.

34. Nehamiah Levanon had been working for Aliyah B. He was posted as an agricultural attaché to the Israeli embassy in Moscow in the early 1950s but was expelled by the Soviet authorities in 1955. Interview, Washington, D.C., October 31, 1993; see also Raviv and Melman, *Every Spie a Prince*, 226.

35. Schroeter, *Last Exodus*, 127.

36. The Hague to embassy, October 7, 1969.

37. Embassy to The Hague, October 16, 1969.

38. See Wiesel, *Joden der Stilte*, 119; interviews with Refuseniks, including Valery Soyfer, Washington, D.C., November 16, 1993. Nora Levin, however, believes that "Western interest has stigmatized and isolated Refuseniks, causing many of them to be helpless and in great jeopardy." *Jews in the Soviet Union,* 789.

39. Orbach calls this decision "a dramatic reversal of policy." *American Movement*, 49. Yitzhak Shamir was among those who had asked for the change. Interview.

40. Schroeter, *Last Exodus*, 128–30.

41. Orbach, *American Movement*, 29; Maurice Friedberg, *Why They Left* (New York: Academic Committee on Soviet Jewry, 1972), introd.

42. Orbach, *American Movement*. Interviews with Jacob Birnbaum, head of Student Struggle for Soviet Jewry, New York, October 20, 1993, and Lynn Singer, executive director of the Long Island Committee for Soviet Jewry, Washington, D.C., December 5, 1993.

43. Birnbaum, interview.

44. Nahum Goldman, quoted in Louis H. Weinstein, "Soviet Jewry and the American Jewish Community," *American Jewish History* 77, no. 4 (June 1988): 603.

45. Wiesel, *Joden der Stilte*, 109.

46. Davies, statement to Subcommittee on Europe, Senate Committee on Foreign Relations, November 9, 1971.

47. Interviews with Mark Levin, executive director, and Robin Saipe, communities Coordinator, of the National Conference on Soviet Jewry, New York, October 14, 1993.

48. Schroeter, *Last Exodus*, 187–88.

49. Orbach, *American Movement*, 188; interviews with Pamela Cohen, Chicago, October 4, 1993, Leonid Stonov, Chicago, October 4, 1993, and Lynn Singer, New York, December 5, 1993, all of the Union of Councils for Soviet Jews. For reports on these contacts in the 1980s, see Yury Tarnopolsky, *Memoirs of 1984* (New York: University Press of America, 1993), and Nancy Rosenfeld, *Unfinished Journey* (New York: University Press of America, 1993).

50. Representatives of this school are Robert T. Brym, Victor Zaslavsky, and Laurie Salitan. See, e.g., Zaslavsky and Brym, *Soviet Jewish Emigration*, 66; Robert T. Brym, "Soviet-Jewish Emigration: A Statistical Test of Two Theories," *Soviet Jewish Affairs* 18, no. 3 (1988): 104; Salitan, *Politics and Nationality*, chap. 5.

51. Drachman, *Challenging the Kremlin*, 36, 38.

52. The most vocal proponent of the second school is Robert Freedman. See "Soviet Jewry and Soviet-American Relations," in *Soviet Jewry in the Decisive Decade, 1971–1980*, ed. Robert O. Freedman (Durham, N.C.: Duke University Press, 1984); "Soviet Policy toward the United States and Israel in the Gorbachev Era: Jewish Emigration and Soviet Politics," in *The Decline of the Soviet Union and the Middle East*, ed. Paul Maranz and David Goldberg (Boulder, Colo.: Westview Press, 1994), 53–95; and interview, Baltimore, October 15, 1993.

53. Salitan, *Politics and Nationality*, 84.

54. These include former U.S. secretary of state Henry Kissinger (interview, New York, January 10, 1994), former assistant secretaries of state Richard Schifter and Arthur Hartman (interviews, Washington, D.C., September 30, and December 2, 1993) and former Refuseniks such as Alexander Lerner (interview, Rehovot, March 16, 1994).

55. Drachman, *Challenging the Kremlin*, 38.

56. Drachman, who first states, "The central thesis of this study is that constant pressure by Soviet Jewish leaders and their supporters succeeded in forcing the Kremlin to look more closely at the Jewish question," later also concludes: "Evidence suggests that . . . interplay [between foreign and domestic policies] determines decisions on emigration." Ibid., 36, 186.

57. Henry Kissinger, *The White House Years* (London: Weidenfeld & Nicolson, 1979), 1271.

58. Kissinger, interview.

59. Anatoly Dobrynin, *In Confidence* (New York: Times Books, Random House, 1995), 268.

60. Henry Kissinger, *Diplomacy* (London: Simon & Schuster, 1994), 753.

61. Kissinger, interview.

62. Dobrynin, *In Confidence*, 268.

63. Ibid.

64. Salitan, *Politics and Nationality*, 33.

65. Abba Eban, *My Country: The Story of Modern Israel* (London: Random House, 1972): "The Jewish emigration could also be used as a 'subtle form of blackmail' towards the Arab world."

Chapter 2, The Ten Circles of Hell

1. David Zilberman, quoted by Geoffrey Wigoder in *Jerusalem Post*, December 1, 1971.

2. Letter from a group of Jewish activists in Moscow to U.S. Congress, 1976, quoted in Drachman, *Challenging the Kremlin*, 54 n. 10.

3. Alexander Lerner, *Change of Heart* (Minneapolis: Lerner Publications, 1992), 185. Dobrynin, *In Confidence*, 267, states: "During the period of Stalin's tyranny anyone who wanted to emigrate was considered a 'traitor to the Motherland.' After Stalin's death . . . the government was still very reluctant to permit Soviet citizens to leave."

4. Drachman, *Challenging the Kremlin*, 53.

5. The following discussion is based primarily on interviews with former emigrants.

6. The Soviet Union had abstained when the Universal Declaration on Human Rights was adopted in 1948 but was bound by it through the ratification of the International Covenant on Civil and Political Rights in 1973, which incorporated the provisions of the Universal Declaration.

7. Anti-Zionist Committee, press conference, Moscow, April 21, 1983, quoted in Drachman, *Challenging the Kremlin*, 98.

8. Kedmi, interview.

9. The document was called a visa by the Soviet authorities, but "exit permit" is used here to indicate that what was involved was not a stamp in a passport but a separate document.

10. Internal passports were not handed out by OVIR but distributed by the local militia. Those passports, instituted in 1932, had a line ("the fifth line") identifying nationality. For Jews, this was *Yevrit*. See Mervyn Matthews, *The Passport Society: Controlling Movement in Russia and the USSR* (Oxford, 1933).

11. See Stephen J. Roth, *The Helsinki Final Act and Soviet Jewry* (London: Institute of Jewish Affairs, 1976), 19.

12. Interview of leading Jewish activists with Albert Ivanov, head of the administrative committee of the Communist Party of the Soviet Union, quoted in Stephen J. Roth, "Facing the Belgrade Meeting: Helsinki—Two Years After," *Soviet Jewish Affairs* 7, no. 1 (1977): 12.

13. The first such case was reported by the Netherlands embassy to The Hague in a cable of January 6, 1970: an applicant was refused an exit permit because he lacked the approval of his father and his former wife.

14. Roth, "Facing the Belgrade Meeting," 11.

15. Ibid., quoting a document signed by Jewish activists in the Soviet Union and sent to the Twenty-fifth Congress of the CPSU.

16. Embassy to The Hague, October 30, 1970.

17. Embassy to The Hague, May 18, 1989.

18. A text mentioning this sum was published in a Soviet document entitled "On Additions and Changes in the Decree of the Council of People's Commissars of April 29, 1942, no. 598, Concerning State Tax Rates," September 22, 1970, no. 803. It read: "An application for renunciation of USSR citizenship requires payment by . . . persons planning to leave for a capitalist country—500 rubles." The text appears in *White Book of Exodus*, a collection of appeals, protests, and other documents compiled by Jews in the Soviet Union, published by the American National Conference on Soviet Jewry (New York: NCSJ, 1972).

19. This fee was later lowered to 260 rubles in response to the Helsinki Final Act. Embassy to The Hague, January 21, 1976. See Chapter 7.

20. *The Position of Soviet Jewry, 1983–1985*, published on behalf of the International Council of the World Conference on Soviet Jewry (London: Institute of Jewish Affairs, 1986), 18.

Chapter 3, Migration to the United States on Israeli Visas

1. Immigration and Nationality Act, June 27, 1952, 66 Stat. 163, U.S. Code vol. 8, sec. 203; Immigration and Nationality Act Amendments, October 3, 1965, Public Law 89-236, 79 Statutes at Large, 911.

2. Immigration and Nationality Act Amendments, 1976, Public Law 94-571, 90 Statutes at Large, 2073. See also U.S. House of Representatives, Committee on the Judiciary, *Immigration and Nationality Act*, 102d Cong., 2d sess., Committee Print 6, 9th ed., April 1992.

3. Migration and Refugee Assistance Act, 1962, 76 Statutes at Large, 121.

4. Refugee Act, 1980, 94 Statutes at Large, 109. See also Levin, *Jews in the Soviet Union*, chap. 32, n. 39. The Refugee Act of 1980 redefined "refugees" and eliminated refugees as a category of the preference system.

5. The Geneva Convention Relating to the Status of Refugees was passed in Geneva on July 28, 1951. The United States is not a party to this convention. However, the United States is a party to the Protocol Relating to the Status of Refugees, adopted in New York on January 31, 1967, which incorporates the definition of the Geneva Convention. Both texts are in the Committee Print cited in n. 2, above.

6. The president did use this authorization for certain refugees from Southeast Asia. In 1988 an amendment was submitted by Senator Frank Lautenberg of New Jersey that would serve in lieu of a presidential determination. It was adopted as part of the Foreign Operations Export Financing and Related Programs Appropriations Act of 1989 (Public Law 100-461) on October 1, 1988.

7. Interviews with Martin A. Wenick and Dale Stolov of the Hebrew Immigrant Aid Society, New York, October 20, 1993; Kedmi, interview.

8. U.S. embassy, Vienna, to U.S. Department of State, Washington, D.C., February 7, 1973.

9. Embassy to The Hague, February 28, 1974.

10. The Hague to embassy, April 5, 1974.

11. The Hague to embassy, April 27, 1987.

12. Ministry of Foreign Affairs, The Hague, letter to Israeli embassy, The Hague, August 14, 1987.

Chapter 4, Refuseniks

1. Embassy to The Hague, April 21, 1969.

2. The word "Refusenik" was coined after the Russian word *otkaznik*. In 1939 the poet Marina Tsvetayeva wrote a famous poem about the German invasion in Czechoslovakia emphasizing her refusal, *otkaz*, to accept that event. *Otkaznik* then became the name for Jews who were refused permission to emigrate. The term was translated into English by combining the English "refused" with the Russian ending *-nik*, already known in the West from such words as "Sputnik" and "Beatnik." In the beginning the form "Refusednik" also occurred. It is not clear who thought of the term first. The Netherlands embassy began using it in its reporting in 1974.

3. A Fund for Aid to Jewish Repatriates was mentioned in a cable from the embassy to The Hague, July 5, 1979.

4. Interviews with former Refuseniks Zieman and Igor Uspensky, Jerusalem, March 21, 1994. Cf. Natan Sharansky, *Fear No Evil* (New York: Random House, 1988), 94; and Drachman, *Challenging the Kremlin*, 132.

5. Interviews with former Refuseniks Lerner Rehovot, March 16, 1994, and Naum Meiman, Tel Aviv, March 6, 1994.

6. Interview with Tatyana Zieman, former Refusenik, Boston, in The Hague, April 2, 1995.

7. Z. Alexander, "Immigration to Israel from the USSR," *Israel Yearbook on Human Rights* 7, suppl. (1977): 307.

8. Stephen Roth, ed., *Human Contacts: Reunion of Families and Soviet Jewry* (London: Institute of Jewish Affairs, for the International Council of the World Conference on Soviet Jewry, 1986).

9. *Jewish Chronicle* (London), February 10, 1989.

10. The following account is based mainly on the interview with Lerner, and on Lerner, *Change of Heart.*

11. Alexeyeva, *Soviet Dissent,* 184.

12. Interview with Valery Soyfer, former Refusenik, now professor at George Mason University, Oakton, Va., November 30, 1994.

13. Lein, interview. Lein, who organized the seminars in Leningrad, was arrested soon afterward and condemned on trumped-up charges to two years' imprisonment in Siberia.

14. The following account is based mainly on an interview with Sharansky, Jerusalem, March 17, 1994, and on Sharansky, *Fear No Evil.* All quotations are from the interview unless otherwise noted.

15. "Thoughts about Progress, Peaceful Co-Existence, and Intellectual Freedom" constituted the beginning of Andrei Sakharov's long struggle for human dignity in the Soviet Union. He wrote about the dangers of thermonuclear annihilation, ecological self-poisoning, hunger, and other subjects, reinforced by the antithesis between the socialist and the capitalist camps. He pleaded for a convergence between the two systems and for an "open society" in his own country. The text was smuggled to the West by the Dutch journalist (and later professor at Amsterdam University) Karel van het Reve and first published in the Amsterdam daily *Het Parool.* See Sakharov, *Mijn Leven* (Dutch translation from the Russian) (Amsterdam: Meulenhof, 1990), 336.

16. Sharansky, *Fear No Evil,* 224.

Chapter 5, The Dutch Role in the Seventies

1. The Netherlands had had no diplomatic relations with the Soviet Union after 1918 until they were established by a protocol signed in London on July 10, 1942. The first Netherlands ambassador presented his credentials on September 18, 1943. See the brochures *BZ en de Tweede Wereldoorlog* (The Ministry of Foreign Affairs and the Second World War), published by the Ministry of Foreign Affairs in April 1995, and *Netherlands Embassy Building in Moscow, 100 Years,* published by the embassy in 1988.

2. The Hague to embassy, March 9, 1968, and September 30, 1969.

3. Handwritten note by Netherlands ambassador in Moscow on internal memorandum by the head of the Consular Section, March 3, 1971.

4. Embassy to The Hague, April 14, 1971.

5. It is interesting in this connection that when Soviet authorities decided in 1971 to increase the number of emigrants to about 30,000 per year, the embassy

was given an advance warning by the Soviet journalist Victor Louis, who was generally believed to work for the KGB. Apparently the KGB wanted to make sure the embassy would be able to handle the increase. Heinemann, interview.

6. Confirmed in interview with Count L. J. R. de Marchant et d'Ansembourg, former Netherlands ambassador and head of the Consular Section, Moscow, in The Hague, January 31, 1996.

7. Heinemann, interview. See also embassy, internal memorandum, March 3, 1971.

8. Embassy to The Hague, September 4, 1972. In 1949 the Israeli embassy in Moscow had received a similar warning. See Levin, *Jews in the Soviet Union*, 485.

9. Interview with L. V. M. van Gorp, former head of the Consular Section, Moscow, in The Hague, February 19, 1993.

10. Middle Eastern and African Affairs Department, Ministry of Foreign Affairs, The Hague, memorandum concerning visit of Minister Max Van der Stoel to Israel, April 8, 1975.

11. Embassy to The Hague, October 24, 1974.

12. Embassy to The Hague, March 5, 1970.

13. Embassy to The Hague, May 5 and 15, and June 24, 1970.

14. Associated Press, press release from Jerusalem, March 17, 1971.

15. Embassy to The Hague, July 16, 1971.

16. The Hague to embassy, July 26, 1971.

17. Embassy to The Hague, November 30, 1971.

18. Ministry of Foreign Affairs, The Hague, internal memorandum, January 4, 1972.

19. Ministry of Foreign Affairs, The Hague, internal memorandum, October 6, 1972.

20. The ambassador reported that one of his interlocutors had used a French expression: *ne côtoyez pas les bords* (don't skirt the limits). See ambassador to The Hague, letter, December 14, 1972.

21. The Hague, letter to ambassador, December 21, 1972. There is no further evidence in the Dutch files about this change in policy. Former foreign minister W. K. N. Schmelzer does not recall it but believes it possible that Israeli Foreign Minister Abba Eban had come back to the question during his consultations with his Dutch colleague at the United Nations that autumn. Interview with W. K. N. Schmelzer, former Netherlands minister of foreign affairs, March 2, 1995.

22. Directorate of European Affairs, Ministry of Foreign Affairs, The Hague, internal memorandum, September 4, 1973.

23. Embassy to The Hague, January 21, 1971.

24. Embassy to The Hague, February 1, 1977.

25. See, e.g., embassy to The Hague, October 24, 1974.

26. Alexander, "Immigration to Israel from the USSR," 305, claims that the *vysov* had to arrive by mail in an envelope bearing a post office stamp. This requirement may have been in force during a particular period or by a particular OVIR office, but the Netherlands embassy never reported such a requirement; certainly almost all *vysovs* originating in the embassy were passed on by hand.

27. Embassy to The Hague, June 21, 1968.

28. Embassy to The Hague, October 30, 1970.

29. The Hague to embassy, November 9, 1970.

30. Embassy to The Hague, December 1, 1970.

31. The Hague to embassy, April 22, 1971.

32. Interview with Godert van Vliet, former head of the Consular Section, Moscow, in The Hague, April 18, 1994.

33. Usually the Israeli government did not demand full reimbursement if the money loaned had been spent for emigration to Israel. Kedmi, interview.

34. Embassy to The Hague, June 12 and 23, 1972.

35. The Hague to embassy July 10, 1972, and response, July 13, 1972.

36. Embassy to The Hague, August 26, 1974.

37. Embassy to The Hague, March 4, 1976.

38. Information provided by H. J. Hazewinkel, who at the time worked in the Bureau for Eastern European Affairs in the Ministry of Foreign Affairs, The Hague, February 7, 1996.

39. The Hague to Netherlands embassy, Vatican City, July 30, 1976.

40. Van Gorp, interview. Some officials in The Hague would privately express understanding for the leniency of their colleagues in Moscow. Heinemann, interview.

41. Embassy to The Hague, April 25, 1973, in answer to criticism voiced to the Netherlands minister of the interior during a visit to Israel.

42. Van Vliet, interview.

43. Embassy to The Hague, August 21, 1968.

44. Van Vliet, interview.

45. Embassy to The Hague, October 24, 1974.

46. In 1972 the ambassador reported that he thought "it would not be desirable to take further steps" in cases where exit permits already granted had been withdrawn on the basis that "certain facts had not been divulged by the applicants." Steps would "*a priori* be futile," it was thought, "the more so since an intervention from our side could be motivated only on humanitarian grounds." Embassy to The Hague, March 26, 1972. It should be remembered that this analysis was made well before the Helsinki Final Act, which was signed in 1975.

47. Van Vliet, interview.

48. Minister of Foreign Affairs, The Hague, to the Netherlands Israelian Churches, September 17, 1972: "You will understand that the government wishes to avoid any risk that such an important and humanitarian task as the representation of Israeli interests could be endangered."

49. Director general of political affairs, Ministry of Foreign Affairs, The Hague, internal memorandum, May 17, 1972.

50. The letter concerned Professor Levitch. File, part x, no. 5383.

51. Directorate of Middle Eastern and African Affairs, Ministry of Foreign Affairs, retrospective internal memorandum, September 15, 1972.

52. Schmelzer, interview.

53. The Hague to embassy, October 2, 1975.

54. Embassy to The Hague, October 3, 1975.

55. Ministry of Foreign Affairs, The Hague, internal memorandum by head of the European Directorate, August 15, 1977.

56. Embassy to The Hague, July 19, 1979. See also Chapter 9.

57. See, e.g., letter from embassy to The Hague, February 27, 1978.

58. See, e.g., embassy to The Hague, January 6, 1969.

59. Embassy to The Hague, June 7, 1968.

60. Embassy to The Hague, January 28, 1975.

61. The Hague to embassy, October 20, 1982; embassy to The Hague, October 21, 1982.

62. Van Gorp, interview.

63. A typical example is a letter sent on March 3, 1977, by the Netherlands Ministry of Foreign Affairs to a Dutch woman in answer to a request (copy in file, part 27). It states:

1. The Netherlands task for Israel does not include approaching Soviet citizens of Jewish origin in order to encourage them to emigrate.

2. We provide intermediary to or on behalf of Soviet citizens who want to emigrate to Israel only if we are officially asked to do so or if they have already received permission to leave the Soviet Union to go to Israel.

3. The Netherlands does not undertake independent initiatives, but only at the request of Israel.

4. No information is given about the representation of Israeli interests.
This letter repeated an answer already given in 1973 to a parliamentary question; the policy had remained unchanged.

Chapter 6, An Amazing Spectacle: The Jackson-Vanik Amendment

1. See Paula Stern, *The Water's Edge: Domestic Politics and the Making of American Foreign Policy,* Contributions in Political Science 15 (Westport, Conn.: Greenwood Press, 1979), introd.

2. Kissinger, *White House Years,* 1202.

3. Stern, *Water's Edge,* 14.

4. Kissinger, *White House Years,* 1271.

5. Levanon, interview. The full text of the decree "On Reimbursement of Government Expenses on Education by Citizens of the USSR Departing for Permanent Residence Abroad," August 3, 1972, is in Drachman, *Challenging the Kremlin,* 418–21.

6. Though often called "exit tax," the term "diploma fee" has been chosen here as more descriptive and to distinguish it from other taxes and fees demanded by Soviet authorities from prospective emigrants.

7. Alexander, "Immigration to Israel from the USSR," 293.

8. Dobrynin, *In Confidence,* 268.

9. According to Stern, *Water's Edge,* 65, Leonid Brezhnev made this comment to George Schulz, then secretary of the treasury, during a visit to Moscow. The expression is also reported by the columnist Marquis Childs in the *Washington Post,* March 13, 1973.

10. Kissinger, *White House Years*, 1271.

11. Henry Kissinger, *Years of Upheaval* (London: Weidenfeld & Nicolson, 1982), 249.

12. Embassy to The Hague, July 22, 1971: "Rumors have it that emigrants to Israel would, in addition to existing fees, have to pay 1,600 rubles to 4,000 rubles for 'education received.'"

13. Dobrynin, *In Confidence*, 268.

14. Stern, *Water's Edge*, 19.

15. Kissinger, *White House Years*, 1271.

16. Kissinger, *Diplomacy*, 753.

17. Salitan, *Politics and Nationality*, 40. Secretary of State William Rogers also said in a conversation with Jewish leaders, "The Soviets had to protect themselves against a brain-drain." U.S. Department of State, Washington, D.C., internal memorandum on conversation between Secretary of State William Rogers and Jewish leaders, August 18, 1972.

18. Both texts distributed by the Permanent Mission of Israel to the United Nations in New York.

19. Dobrynin, *In Confidence*, 268, agrees: "Moscow was more likely to change its practices if not openly challenged." It is interesting that a similar answer was given by Secretary of State Philander C. Knox to the U.S. Congress in 1911, when it urged him to protest to the czarist government about pogroms against the Jews. Congress then nevertheless abrogated the U.S.-Russian Treaty of Commerce and Navigation. Drachman, *Challenging the Kremlin*, 33.

20. U.S. Department of State, Washington, D.C., internal memorandum, August 18, 1972.

21. Memorandum of conversation between Assistant Secretary Walt Stoessel and Soviet Chargé Yuli Vorontsov, September 20, 1972.

22. Yitzhak Rabin, quoted by Evans and Novak, *Washington Post*, March 19, 1973, 21.

23. Levanon, interview.

24. Birnbaum, interview; Singer, interview.

25. Stern, *Water's Edge*, 32.

26. U.S. Department of State, Washington, D.C., internal memorandum, August 18, 1972.

27. The Hague to embassy, August 25, 1972.

28. Embassy to The Hague, August 28, 1972, and response, September 1, 1972.

29. Interview with Richard Perle, former assistant to Senator Henry Jackson, November 8, 1993.

30. Ibid.

31. Stern, *Water's Edge*, 19. Stern also states that Perle was already working on an amendment to the trade bill in July, that is, before the diploma fee decree. Perle, interview, denies this.

32. See the full text of Henry Jackson's speech in the *Congressional Record*, September 27, 1993, 32428.

33. *Congressional Record*, 1972, 33428, 33658. The text was slightly, but not essentially, changed by the time it was enacted in 1974.

34. Stern, *Water's Edge*, 42; Colin Shindler, *Exit Visa* (London: Bachman & Turner, 1978), 41. They disagree on the date.

35. Kissinger, *Years of Upheaval*, 249, 996.

36. Cohen, interview.

37. Shindler, *Exit Visa*, 58; embassy to The Hague, January 13, 1973.

38. Embassy to The Hague, February 15, 1973.

39. Dobrynin, *In Confidence*, 269, claims that he and Andrei Gromyko had convinced Leonid Brezhnev and the Politburo to annul the fee.

40. Embassy to The Hague, March 30, 1973.

41. The diploma fee was officially abolished only as of July 1, 1991, with the resolution promulgating a new entry and exit law.

42. Office of Senator Henry Jackson, press release, March 15, 1973, Jackson Papers, University of Washington Libraries, Seattle, Washington, Jackson's Black Book, no. 21.

43. U.S. Department of State, Washington, D.C., memorandum of a conversation with officials of the newly opened Office of the National Conference on Soviet Jewry in Washington, D.C., March 28, 1973.

44. Kissinger, *Years of Upheaval*, 253. The full text of the statement is in Kissinger's backnotes, 1234.

45. Dobrynin, *In Confidence*, 269.

46. Kissinger, *Years of Upheaval*, 253.

47. Jackson, quoted in Stern, *Water's Edge*, 69.

48. Perle, interview. See also Charles Horner, "Human Rights and the Jackson Amendment," in *Staying the Course: Henry M. Jackson and National Security*, ed. Dorothy Fosdick (Seattle: University of Washington Press, 1987), 119.

49. Kissinger, *Years of Upheaval*, 254.

50. Dobrynin, *In Confidence*, 269.

51. Kissinger, *Years of Upheaval*, 254.

52. Stern, *Water's Edge*, 81.

53. Shindler, *Exit Visa*, 63–64; Stern, *Water's Edge*, 82, Dobrynin, *In Confidence*, 270.

54. Andrei Sakharov, *My Life* (New York: Knopf, 1990). The letter is reprinted in his *Sakharov Speaks* (New York, 1974) and in the *Congressional Record*, Senate, December 13, 1974, 39786. Sakharov had written at the suggestion of Dmitri Simes, who had recently migrated to the United States from Moscow. Interview. It was transmitted by Sharansky. Interview.

55. Kissinger, *Years of Upheaval*, 989.

56. Ibid., 992–98; Stern, *Water's Edge*, 113.

57. Kissinger, *Years of Upheaval*, 986.

58. Dobrynin, *In Confidence*, 312, 334.

59. Interview with Adlai E. Stevenson III, former senator, Chicago, October 4, 1994.

60. William Korey, "The Story of the Jackson Amendment," *Midstream: A Monthly Jewish Review*, March 1975. See also *American Jewish Yearbook, 1976* (1975), 162.

61. Perle, interview; Kissinger, interview. In a letter to the author, December 17, 1993, Stevenson wrote: "I mentioned it to Kissinger, explaining that in time I hoped the Stevenson amendment approach could replace the Jackson/Vanik linkage to free emigration. I also argued that it would strengthen his hand in negotiations with the Soviet Union as he could explain that concessions, i.e. credits, had to be justified to the Congress. While Kissinger did not protest, he didn't approve it either."

62. Kissinger, *Years of Upheaval*, 996.

63. Perle, interview; embassy to The Hague, October 24, 1974.

64. Full texts of all the letters are in the *Congressional Record*, Senate, December 13, 1974, 39785.

65. Dobrynin, *In Confidence*, 335.

66. Stern, *Water's Edge*, 158, 160.

67. Jackson, quoted in ibid., 163–64. The senator must have added these words extemporaneously; they are not in the written text of his statement.

68. Andrei Gromyko quoted in Shindler, *Exit Visa*, 105–6.

69. Jackson was furious when he realized what had happened. In a speech to the National Conference on Soviet Jewry on May 17, 1976, he said: "The Secretary of State never informed me of the existence of such a letter, much less of its contents. The withholding of that crucial document must surely rank among the shabbiest deceits ever perpetrated by a Secretary of State on the Congress of the United States." In *Henry Jackson and World Affairs: Selected Speeches, 1953–1983*, ed. Dorothy Fosdick (Seattle: University of Washington Press, 1990). Fosdick adds: "Kissinger apologized to the Senator for lying to him and to the Congress. Jackson reported this apology to his staff, but Kissinger has never, to my knowledge, put it on the public record."

70. Stern, *Water's Edge*, 170. See also *American Jewish Yearbook, 1976*.

71. Quoted in Stern, *Water's Edge*, 180.

72. Russell Long, quoted in Korey, "Story of the Jackson Amendment," 30.

73. Gerald Ford and Henry Kissinger, quoted in Stern, *Water's Edge*, 189–90.

74. The repeal was enacted as part of the Continuing Resolution on Foreign Operations, Public Law 102-266, sec. 121.

75. Office of Senator Jackson, press release, Jackson Papers, Jackson's Black Book, no. 21.

76. Sharansky, *Fear No Evil*, 83, 190. Sharansky's support for the Jackson-Vanik Amendment was used against him by the KGB in his trial.

77. Charles Horner, in *Staying the Course*, 109.

78. Hartman, interview.

79. Simes, interview. See also Stern, *Water's Edge*; and interview with Paula Stern, former member of the International Trade Commission, Washington, D.C., November 17, 1993. Dobrynin claims that President Gerald Ford had been very angered by Jackson's conduct and believed that the senator had "behaved like a swine," a point he wanted passed on to Brezhnev and Gromyko. *In Confidence*, 335.

80. Kissinger, quoted by Korey, "Story of the Jackson Amendment," 31.

81. Stevenson, interview.

82. Adlai E. Stevenson III and Alton Frye, "Trading with Communists," *Foreign Affairs* 68, no. 2 (Spring 1989).

83. Korey, "Story of the Jackson Amendment." Cf. *American Jewish Yearbook, 1976.*

84. In interviews Perle claimed that the contents of the press conference were cleared with Kissinger beforehand (which seems unlikely), and Kissinger in turn denied that he even knew about the press conference before it took place (which is not very plausible). The truth probably lies in the middle.

85. Shindler, *Exit Visa,* 109; Korey, "Story of the Jackson Amendment."

86. Kissinger, *Years of Upheaval,* 998.

87. Stern, *Water's Edge,* 179; Peter M. E. Volten, *Brezhnev's "Peace Program": Success or Failure?* (Boulder, Colo.: Westview Press, 1982), 115–16; Dobrynin, *In Confidence,* 337.

88. Stern, *Water's Edge,* 40; and Stern, interview.

Chapter 7, Helsinki:
The Conference on Security and Cooperation in Europe

1. Roth, *The Helsinki Final Act and Soviet Jewry,* 3.

2. Kissinger, *Diplomacy,* 758.

3. See William Korey, *The Promises We Keep: Human Rights, the Helsinki Process, and American Foreign Policy* (New York: Institute of East-West Studies, 1993). This is the most comprehensive study of the CSCE process that has appeared so far, and it has served as an important source for the present chapter.

4. Kissinger, interview.

5. Max Van der Stoel, "The Heart of the Matter: The Human Dimensions of the CSCE," *Helsinki Monitor* (Utrecht) 6, no. 3 (1995): 24.

6. James Goodby, in "Human Rights: Challenge to the Bipolar Order" (unpublished manuscript), relates that the head of the U.S. delegation to the preparatory talks in Helsinki, George Vest, was shocked to hear from colleagues that in a conversation with members of the NATO Council in San Clemente in June 1973, Kissinger had virtually dismissed the idea of a European security conference. The Netherlands embassy in Washington, D.C., quoted him as having said: "I do not believe that the Soviet Union is going to be eased out of Eastern Europe by some sort of declaration." When Vest asked Assistant Secretary of State for European Affairs Walt Stoessel what his role in Helsinki should be in view of Kissinger's negative attitude, Stoessel advised him in a private letter (not in an official cable) to go on as he had done before, i.e., supporting the efforts of the Western allies in the field of freer movement. Ambassador George Vest, head of the U.S. delegation to the Helsinki preparatory conference, confirmed these exchanges in an interview, Washington, D.C., December 14, 1993.

7. Korey, *Promises We Keep,* prologue.

8. Kissinger, interview.

9. José D. Ingles, *A Study of Discrimination with Respect to the Right of Everyone to Leave Any Country, Including His Own, and to Return to His Own Country* (New York: United Nations, 1963).

10. See Goodby, "Human Rights," confirmed by Vest, interview, and Hartman, interview.

11. Communiqué of the Ministerial Meeting of the North Atlantic Council, NATO Headquarters Brussels, December 7, 1969.

12. See, e.g., U.S. Mission to NATO, to secretary of state, U.S. Department of State, Washington, D.C., March 26, 1971.

13. U.S. Department of State, Washington, D.C., to all European diplomatic posts, "Public Affairs Guidance on CSCE," November 16, 1972.

14. William Korey, who was lobbying on behalf of Jewish organizations in Washington at the time, acknowledged this in an interview, Washington, D.C., November 24, 1993: "We did not focus on 'freer movement' until the Final Act had been adopted in 1975."

15 Hartman, interview.

16. See Kissinger, *Diplomacy,* 759.

17. Helsinki Final Act, in *From Helsinki to Vienna: Basic Documents of the Helsinki Process,* ed. Arie Bloed (Dordrecht: Martinus Nijhoff, 1990), 6. All subsequent quotations from the Helsinki Final Act are from this source.

18. Drachman, *Challenging the Kremlin,* 52, maintains that these provisions constituted a severe limitation compared to the International Convenant on Civil and Political Rights, which the Soviet Union had ratified in 1973. In practice, however, it did not make much difference. As we have seen, the Soviet authorities would disregard restrictions when it suited them. Whenever they wanted to limit emigration again, they had restrictive provisions and harassments at their disposal. The important thing was that detailed provisions on freer movement were spelled out in a joint document signed by the highest Soviet leader himself.

19. See Korey, *Promises We Keep,* 8; Roth, *Helsinki Final Act,* 6.

20. Dobrynin, *In Confidence,* 346.

21. Roth, "Facing the Belgrade Meeting," 4; William Korey, *Human Rights and the Helsinki Accord,* Headline Series 264 (New York: Foreign Policy Association, 1983), 20; Van der Stoel, "Heart of the Matter," 25.

22. Korey, *Human Rights and the Helsinki Accord,* 23.

23. Goodby, "Human Rights." The same opinion was expressed by Vest, interview.

24. Dobrynin, *In Confidence,* 346, writes: "It gradually became a manifesto of the dissident and liberal movement, a development totally beyond the imagination of the Soviet leadership."

25. A predecessor group, called For the Protection of the Human Rights, had been formed in Moscow in 1969 by participants in the demonstration against the invasion of Czechoslovakia in 1968 and others. Ludmilla Alexeyeva, Malyeva Landa, Tatyana Villekanova, Tatyana Khadarovich, General Pyotr Grigorenko, and Sergei Kovalev were among the members. After several arrests and Kovalev's condemnation to a seven-year imprisonment in 1974, the group ceased to exist. Interviews with Sergei Kovalev, Malyeva Landa, and Larissa Bogaraz, all Moscow, October 10, 1994.

26. Korey, *Promises We Keep,* 44. See also Alexeyeva, *Soviet Dissent,* 187.

27. Bogaraz, interview.

28. Alexeyeva, *Soviet Dissent,* 186.

29. Levin, *Jews in the Soviet Union,* 55, writes: "Had anything been gained in separating the Jewish emigration issue from the human rights movement? . . . If it had been possible in the early period to delimit the Jewish struggle and differentiate it from the general human rights struggle, it had not been possible to delimit its consequences. The Jewish activists, whether inside or outside the human rights movement, had become in the Soviet view, the greatest enemies of the regime."

30. Sharansky, interview. See also Chapter 4.

31. Leonid Brezhnev, quoted in Roth, *Helsinki Final Act,* 14.

32. Korey, *Promises We Keep,* prologue, xxi. See also Drachman, *Challenging the Kremlin,* 370. Dobrynin also acknowledges that "from the very start, the Politburo's acceptance of the Helsinki humanitarian principles implied some non-compliance." *In Confidence,* 346.

33. Roth, "Facing the Belgrade Meeting," 7.

34. U.S. Congress, Helsinki Commission, *Implementation of the Final Act of the Conference on Security and Cooperation in Europe: Findings and Recommendations Two Years after Helsinki* (Washington, D.C.: U.S. Government Printing Office, 1977).

35. Embassy to The Hague, February 1, 1977.

36. Korey, *Promises We Keep,* 77, 97–99.

37. Ibid., 91; Arthur Goldberg, quoted in Max M. Kampelman, *Three Years at the East-West Divide* (New York: Freedom House, 1983), 1.

38. Korey, *Promises We Keep,* 144. Richard Schifter, then head of the U.S. delegation to the CSCE conference on human dimensions in Ottawa, remarked in 1985: It "does not stand to reason that tense international relations are met with the punishment of a country's own citizens. Would this not mean that a government holds its own people hostage, treating them well or poorly depending on the way other countries treat it in international affairs?" As quoted in Vojtech Mastny, *Helsinki, Human Rights and European Security: Analysis and Documentation* (Durham, N.C.: Duke University Press, 1986), 285.

39. Concluding Document of the Madrid Follow-up Meeting, September 6, *1983,* in *Basic Documents,* ed. Bloed, 131. See also Korey, *Promises We Keep,* 159; Kampelman, *Three Years,* 116.

40. Goodby, "Human Rights."

41. Dobrynin, *In Confidence,* 347.

42. Charter of Paris for a New Europe, November 21, 1990, chapter "A New Era of Democracy, Peace and Unity," preamble, *Conference over Veiligheid en Samenwerking* (The Hague: Ministerie van Buitenlandse Zaken, 1990), 45B.

Chapter 8, Down and Up in the Seventies

1. Kissinger, *Years of Upheaval,* 992.

2. Exit permits were usually valid for thirty days (see Chapter 2). Sometimes an extension would be granted, frequently not. The Israeli visas were often requested at the last moment, since applicants were practically sure that any

holder of an exit permit for Israel would be granted a visa and that this visa would be issued the same day. Those coming from outlying areas would therefore often arrive in Moscow, get their visas, and leave for Vienna from the Moscow airport or station the next day.

3. Embassy to The Hague, May 20, 1974. Cf. Shindler, *Exit Visa,* 121, who claims that during the first four months of 1976, 13,000 invitations were sent, yet only some 4,000 exit permits were issued.

4. Embassy to The Hague, March 30, 1973.

5. Volten, *Brezhnev's "Peace Program,"* 187.

6. Shindler, *Exit Visa,* 110.

7. A contrary opinion is formulated by Igor Birman in *Soviet Jewish Affairs* 9, no. 1, quoted by Zaslavsky and Brym, *Soviet-Jewish Emigration,* 75: "The decline in emigration in the mid-1970s was caused less by Soviet reaction to deteriorating relations with the U.S.A. than by changing emigré attitude towards emigration to Israel accompanied by a relatively slow growth in the numbers emigrating to other countries, due to adjustment and absorption difficulties in recession afflicted North-America." This analysis is not convincing, however, especially in view of the high demand for *vysovs*; embassy reports also contradict such a conclusion.

8. President Jimmy Carter, press conference, February 8, 1977.

9. Ibid.

10. Mark Garrison, "Hopes Raised and Dashed," *Bulletin of the Cold War International History Project* (Woodrow Wilson Center, Washington, D.C.) 5 (Spring 1995): 140.

11. Sharansky, interview: "At some moment towards the end of 1976–early 1977, because of many factors, international factors, the Soviet regime decided that it was time to take a stance."

12. The letters have been published in the *Bulletin of the Cold War International Project* 5 (Spring 1995): 140–60.

13. Salitan, *Politics and Nationality,* 93.

14. Robert O. Freedman, "Jewish Emigration as a Factor in Soviet Foreign Policy toward the United States and Israel in the Gorbachev Era," in *Decline of the Soviet Union and the Middle East,* ed. Marantz and Goldberg, 53–94. See also Freedman, *The Soviet Union and the Carter Administration* (Pittsburgh: University Press, 1987), 5.

15. See B. P. Pockney, *Soviet Statistics since 1950* (Dartmouth, N.H., 1991), 264.

16. Drachman, *Challenging the Kremlin,* 375.

17. Cyrus Vance, *Hard Choices* (New York: Scribner's, 1983), 105.

18. Orbach, *The American Movement,* 153; Freedman, *Soviet Union and the Carter Administration,* 17. See also Jimmy Carter, *Keeping Faith* (New York: Bantam, 1982), 202.

19. Cohen, interview.

20. Embassy to The Hague, November 29, 1978.

21. Drachman, *Challenging the Kremlin,* 375.

22. U.S. Department of State, Washington, D.C., internal memorandum to the secretary of state, April 12, 1979.

23. U.S. Department of State, Washington, D.C., to U.S. embassy, Moscow, April 29, 1979. It should be noted how much weaker these demands were than the results Kissinger had obtained in 1974 (see Chapter 6): no precise indication of the emigration level is demanded or given, nor are harassment or hardship cases mentioned.

24. Drachman, *Challenging the Kremlin,* 376–77.

25. Henry Jackson, commencement address at the Hebrew University of Jerusalem, July 2, 1979, quoted in press release, Office of Senator Jackson, July 2, 1979, Jackson Papers.

26. Office of Senator Jackson, press release, November 15, 1979, Jackson Papers.

27. Perle, interview.

28. *Federal Register* 44, 61167.

29. Drachman, *Challenging the Kremlin,* 377.

Chapter 9, The Bleak Years

1. The World Conference on Soviet Jewry claims in *The Position of Soviet Jewry, 1977–80* (New York: WCSJ, 1980), 5: "Well before Afghanistan, a new policy was noticeable, particularly in the Ukraine, Moldavia and Uzbekistan, where invitations were not accepted unless they came from 'first degree' relatives. Insufficient kinship of the 'invitor' was used sporadically as a pretext for refusal in the past, but never on a wide scale. It was first applied broadly in Odessa in May 1979, gradually spread to Kharkov and Kiev and then to other cities and towns." Drachman in *Challenging the Kremlin,* 198, concludes (without giving a source, but probably on the basis of the above report) that "the Kremlin had [already] decided to curtail emigration drastically and to crack down on 'troublesome Jews' because of internal political and economic factors." There is no proof for this assumption. It rather seems to have been a localized action, perhaps to prevent a stampede from certain cities. The monthly totals of visas issued at the Netherlands embassy do not show a decrease until November.

2. Carter's former adviser Stuart Eissenstett says he now wishes that a one-year waiver had been granted by Carter. Interview, Brussels, June 8, 1994. Robert Cullen has also called it "in retrospect a questionable decision." He quotes Jerry Goodman of the National Conference on Soviet Jewry, who supported the refusal to grant a waiver on the grounds that "the Soviets might well have cut off the flow of emigration once they had gotten what they wanted." But, according to Cullen, Hyman Bookbinder of the American Jewish Congress believed that it was a "tragic mistake" not to grant MFN status to the Soviets in 1979. See Robert B. Cullen, "Soviet Jewry," *Foreign Affairs* 65, no. 2 (Winter 1986): 261.

3. Eissenstett, interview, stated he believes SALT might still have had a chance of being ratified, but he acknowledges that "the Soviets may well have calculated that from their perspective SALT wasn't going to pay off anymore." Cullen, "Soviet Jewry," writes (261) that "by the end of the year, whatever hopes the Soviets might have had for MFN- status, as well as a ratified SALT II treaty, were dead."

4. "From Hesitation to Intervention (Documentation)," *Bulletin of the Cold War International History Project* 4 (Fall 1994): 75.

5. Schifter, interview. See also his address "The Impact of the United States on Soviet Immigration Policy" at Tel Aviv University, December 28, 1993. Former Soviet ambassador Anatoly Dobrynin denies that there was a "grand strategic plan" and claims that the invasion in Afghanistan was a reaction to a local situation in which the security of the Soviet southern borders was threatened. *In Confidence*, 441.

6. "From Hesitation to Intervention," 75.

7. Drachman, *Challenging the Kremlin*, 200.

8. Embassy to The Hague, February 27, 1980.

9. Embassy to The Hague, June 3, 1980.

10. Embassy to The Hague, letter, April 14, 1981.

11. Drachman, *Challenging the Kremlin*, 97.

12. Quoted from *Position of Soviet Jewry, 1977–80*, and from reports by the Netherlands embassy.

13. The Hague to embassy, January 4, 1980.

14. Yitzhak Shamir, Israeli prime minister, to the Netherlands government, letter, October 29, 1979. See also Drachman, *Challenging the Kremlin*, 288.

15. Levin, *Jews in the Soviet Union*, 739.

16. Embassy to The Hague, January 23, 1980.

17. The Ministry of Foreign Affairs seems to have reached a similar conclusion. A few months later the embassy was instructed to intervene in behalf of several Georgian Jews who had been condemned to death for economic delicts. "Although it is realized that you will receive an answer like: 'this is interference with the internal affairs of the Soviet Union,'" cabled the ministry, "you are still requested to carry out a demarche." The Hague to embassy, June 2, 1980.

18. Interview with Vladimir Tumarkin, former staff member of the Central Committee, CPSU, Moscow, October 7, 1994.

19. Embassy to The Hague, August 18, 1980.

20. Embassy to The Hague, July 25, 1980.

21. Embassy to The Hague, May 14, 1981.

22. Embassy to The Hague, June 18, 1982.

23. Embassy to The Hague, July 24, 1981.

24. The Hague to embassy, letter, August 16, 1982.

25. Embassy to The Hague, August 31, 1982.

26. The Hague to embassy, letter, September 6, 1982.

27. Embassy to The Hague, November 2, 1982.

28. The Hague to embassy, June 16, 1983, and response, June 21, 1983.

29. Ministry of Foreign Affairs, internal memorandum, July 19, 1983.

30. Embassy to The Hague, June 26, 1984. The files do not show whether the ambassador had received specific new instructions from The Hague.

31. Embassy to The Hague, June 22, and July 2, 1984.

Chapter 10, Perestroika

1. Donald Morrison, ed., *Mikhail S. Gorbachev: An Intimate Biography* (New York: Time, Inc., 1988), 76.

2. See Peter M. E. Volten, "Prospects within the Soviet Union for Improving East-West Relations," *RUSI* (Royal Institute for Defence Studies, London), March 1985, 50.

3. Mikhail Gorbachev, *Perestrojka: Een Nieuwe Visie voor Mijn Land en de Wereld* (Perestroika: A new vision for my country and the world, Dutch translation from the Russian) (Utrecht: Spectrum, 1987), 17.

4. Jack F. Matlock, *Autopsy on an Empire* (New York: Random House, 1995), 77: "Gorbachev had to create a more benign international environment if any program of internal reform, however modest, was to be successful."

5. Eduard A. Shevardnadze was appointed foreign minister by Mikhail Gorbachev on July 1, 1985, as successor to Andrei Gromyko, who was given the largely ceremonial function of chairman of the Presidium of the Supreme Soviet (which, in fact, made him president of the Soviet Union). Shevardnadze, *The Future Belongs to Freedom* (New York: Free Press, 1991). Gromyko, *Memories*.

6. George P. Shultz, *Turmoil and Triumph* (New York: Scribner's, 1993), 531.

7. Embassy to The Hague, July 14, 1986.

8. Netherlands chargé d'affaires, Helsinki, to Ministry of Foreign Affairs, The Hague, August 19, 1986.

9. TASS press communiqué, August 19, 1986.

10. See F. J. M. Feldbrugge, "The New Soviet Law on Emigration," *Soviet Jewish Affairs* 17, no. 1 (1987).

11. Both George Shultz and Andrei Gromyko mention this meeting in their memoirs: Shultz, *Turmoil and Triumph*, 121; Gromyko, *Memories*, 387.

12. Shultz, *Turmoil and Triumph*, 165.

13. Ibid., 488.

14. Ibid., 767. Cf. Matlock, *Autopsy on an Empire*, 148. Ambassador Dobrynin points to the statement accepted by Gorbachev in the final communiqué of the first summit in Geneva in November 1985, committing the parties to "resolving humanitarian cases in the spirit of cooperation." He calls it a first sign of a Soviet shift on this question. *In Confidence*, 591. However, there does not seem to have been any follow-up. Gorbachev himself in his memoir does not mention this statement at all. *Erinnerungen* (Memories, German translation from the Russian) (Berlin: Siedler Verlag, 1995), 585–86.

15. Interview with Alexander Yakovlev, former member of the Politburo, Moscow, October 14, 1994.

16. Ibid.

17. Kovalev, interview: "Gorbachev was no radical reformer and made concessions on human rights only as a result of Western pressures."

18. Tumarkin, interview.

19. Yakovlev, interview.

20. Robert V. Daniels quoted in Volten, *Brezhnev's "Peace Program,"* 128. See also Kissinger, *White House Years*, 526: "Since Stalin no General Secretary

has had unbridled discretion." Former Soviet ambassador Dobrynin writes: "In the West many believed that the general secretary of the CPSU was a true dictator accountable to no one, and this was of course true for Stalin, but for not his successors. . . . Brezhnev . . . even as a first among equals could not always impose his views." *In Confidence*, 219.

21. Dobrynin, *In Confidence*, 616: "Gorbachev was not an authoritarian ruler and had to take into account the general mood [of the Politburo]." Matlock, *Autopsy of an Empire*, 52, concurs: "From the outside, Soviet leaders since Stalin have usually looked more powerful than they in fact were."

22. Gorbachev, *Erinnerungen*, 578.

23. Yakovlev, interview.

24. Tumarkin, interview.

25. Yakovlev, interview.

26. See *New York Times*, January 17, 1987.

27. Embassy to The Hague, February 4, 1987.

28. Embassy to The Hague, February 11, 1987.

29. Schifter, "Impact of the United States on Soviet Emigration Policy."

30. Morris B. Abram, to the secretary of state, U.S. Department of State, Washington, D.C., internal memorandum, April 7, 1987.

31. Drachman, *Challenging the Kremlin*, 490, claims that "in July 1987 the Soviet authorities decided to let Jews emigrate *to any country* for the purpose of family reunification." No source is given. If such a promise was made, it would have been practically meaningless at that time. As we have seen, there never was an official Soviet policy against Jews who wanted to go to the United States leaving on Israeli visas. If Jews would have been granted Soviet exit permits on the basis of an invitation directly from the United States or any other Western country, they would still have been able to obtain an immigration visa from that country only if they qualified as regular immigrants, which very few did. Until September 1989 entry to the United States as a refugee was granted only to those who were already outside the Soviet Union (in Rome) on Israeli visas.

32. Yakovlev, interview.

33. Netherlands embassy, Washington, D.C., to Ministry of Foreign Affairs, The Hague, March 13, 1987.

34. Quotations and details presented by Schifter in "Impact of the United States on Soviet Emigration Policy."

35. The Netherlands ambassador had the same experience. See Piet Buwalda, *Diplomatiek Dagboek Moskou* (Diplomatic diary Moscow) (The Hague: SDU, 1991), 37.

36. Altshuler, *Soviet Jewry since the Second World War*. It is to be noted that the almost automatic dismissal of applicants for emigration and the refusal to reappoint Refuseniks stood in obvious contrast to the expressed fear of a brain drain.

37. Shultz, *Turmoil and Triumph*, 986–94.

38. Gorbachev, *Erinnerungen*, 675.

39. Gorbachev did not reply to written questions on this subject submitted to him by the author.

40. Eduard Shevardnadze, quoted in Shultz, *Turmoil and Triumph*, 990.

41. Meiman, interview. See also Buwalda, *Diplomatiek Dagboek Moskou*, 58.

42. Netherlands embassy, Tel Aviv, to The Hague, April 29, 1988.

43. The arrival of the Israeli delegation was probably the direct reason for the formation that summer of a new anti-Zionist committee, the Committee of the Soviet Public against the Establishment of Diplomatic Relations with Israel. Drachman, *Challenging the Kremlin*, 101.

44. Shultz, *Turmoil and Triumph*, 1102.

45. It should be remembered that an increasing number of non-Jews left the Soviet Union with Israeli visas. See Chapter 12.

46. Embassy to The Hague, August 3, 1988.

47. U.S. Department of State, Washington, D.C., to U.S. embassy, Moscow, June 27, 1988.

48. The Hague to embassy, August 4, 1988.

49. Embassy to The Hague, October 14, 1988.

50. Andrew Crowley, in the *Economist*, April 8–14, 1995: "If the price of oil had not slumped in the 1980s, the Soviet Union might have stumbled on for a few more years." The exact opposite happened in the 1970s, when Brezhnev was able to reject the trade agreement with the United States that included the Jackson-Vanik and Stevenson Amendments partly because of the sudden increase in the oil price at that time. See Chapter 6.

Chapter 11, The Bucharest Route

1. David Ben-Gurion, quotations in Krammer, *Forgotten Friendship*, 150.

2. The number of Soviet Jewish emigrants who in Vienna obtained visas for other countries, such as Australia and Canada, always remained small.

3. "Dropout" is the English translation of the Hebrew *noshrim*. The term is considered derogatory by some Jews in the United States, who claim that Soviet Jews coming to the United States as refugees had chosen to go to that country using the only route at their disposal and should therefore not be called "dropouts." In the technical sense, however, they were en route with documents valid for Israel and deviated from that route to go elsewhere. The term "dropouts" is used here for clarity's sake in that technical sense.

4. Tom Segev, *The Seventh Million* (1993), quoted in *NRC-Handelsblad* (Rotterdam), August 7, 1993, 2.

5. Drachman, *Challenging the Kremlin*, 195.

6. Orbach, *American Movement*, 71.

7. Attorney General John Mitchell sent a letter to Congress stating: "I would exercise my discretion if the situation demanded and parole Soviet Jews who are able to leave the Soviet Union." Quoted in internal memorandum, U.S. Department of State, concerning testimony by Assistant Secretary of State Davies during hearings of the Committee on Foreign Affairs, Subcommittee on Europe, November 9, 1971.

8. Orbach, *American Movement*, 75.

9. "Leak May Endanger Israel-Soviet Accord," *Jerusalem Post*, July 21, 1985, 1.

10. Ibid.

11. Kedmi, interview.

12. Schifter, interview. See also Chapter 9. Among other American experts sharing the opinion that the dropout rate did not provide an excuse for the Soviets to stop the Jewish emigration is Professor Walter Laqueur, chairman of the International Research Council Center for Strategic and International Studies, interview, Jerusalem, March 15, 1994.

13. As noted in Chapter 9, the Netherlands embassy in Moscow reported in May 1980: "It is striking that Ukrainian emigrants, who more often go to the United States than to Israel, are suffering most."

14. The same opinion was expressed by the Netherlands embassy in Moscow in 1979: "It may be assumed that it is not regretted here that the majority opts for other destinations than Israel." Embassy to The Hague, July 19, 1979.

15. Netherlands embassy, Tel Aviv, to Ministry of Foreign Affairs, The Hague, August 21, 1987, reporting on a meeting of Genadi Tarasov with the Israeli representative Nimrod Novik held in Bonn.

16. The same opinion was expressed by Pamela Cohen, interview. Lewis H. Weinstein, "Soviet Jewry and the American Jewish Community," 610, goes even further: "The argument that the Soviet Union might reduce or eliminate future exit visas because Jews were not going to Israel was puerile. The cause of the sharp decline . . . of Russian Jewish emigrants was not the destination of emigrant Jews but the absence of détente between the Soviet Union and the United States and the cold war."

17. It should be remembered, however, that visas for Israel were an adjunct to exit permits, necessary only because the Soviets demanded this combination. Many Jews regarded the Israeli visas as permits to travel not *into* a country but *out of* a country.

18. Orbach, *American Movement*, 75.

19. Cohen, interview.

20. Embassy to The Hague, June 5, 1979, Moscow embassy archives, code 912.3: "Montreal Treaty."

21. Embassy to The Hague, August 1, 1979, ibid.

22. The Hague to embassy, May 4, 1981.

23. Ministry of Foreign Affairs, The Hague, internal memorandum to Directorate of European Affairs, December 9, 1987 (File 912.3, "Israël-Sovjet Unie," part 1).

24. Shamir, interview.

25. Shimon Peres, Israeli foreign minister, letter to Hans van den Broek, Netherlands foreign minister, December 10, 1987.

26. Ministry of Fo reign Affairs, The Hague, internal memorandum from director general for political affairs to minister, January 14, 1988.

27. Ministry of Foreign Affairs, The Hague, internal memorandum to minister, June 30, 1988.

28. The Hague to embassy, April 15, 1988.

29. The U.S. Department of State noted, however, that Vienna arrivals included non-Jews. There was reported to be an emerging flow of Pentecostals of some two hundred or more per month. See Chapter 12.

30. U.S. embassy, Tel Aviv, to U.S. Department of State, May 20, 1988.

31. U.S. Department of State, internal memorandum, May 19, 1988.

32. U.S. Department of State, to U.S. embassy, Moscow, June 27, 1988.

33. U.S. embassy, Tel Aviv, to U.S. Department of State, Washington, D.C., June 20, 1988. It is a curious habit of the Israeli cabinet not only to vote on proposals but to divulge the results. The Israeli cabinet at that time consisted of a coalition of Likud and Labor, but the vote was not along party lines.
Among the opponents in Israel were Ida Nudel and Natan Sharansky. The *olim* are those Jews who migrate (make *aliyah*) to Israel.

34. The Hague to Netherlands embassy, Tel Aviv, August 3, 1988.

35. Ministry of Foreign Affairs, The Hague, internal memorandum, July 28, 1988.

36. The Hague to Netherlands embassy, Washington, D.C., July 21, 1988.

37. Cables from Netherlands embassy, Washington, to The Hague, September 3 and 8, 1988.

38. U.S. Department of State, to U.S. embassy, Moscow, September 17, 1988.

39. Netherlands mission to the United Nations, New York, to The Hague, September 29, 1988.

40. Levanon, interview.

41. Interview with Yeshayanu Ahug, Jerusalem, March 16, 1994.

42. The Hague to embassy, October 12, 1988.

43. Netherlands embassy, Tel Aviv, to The Hague, October 11, 1988.

44. Embassy to The Hague, October 14, 1988.

45. Ministry of Foreign Affairs, The Hague, internal memorandum, October 18, 1988.

46. John M. Gosko, "Israel Fails in Plan to Divert Soviet Jews," *Washington Post*, October 23, 1988, 1.

47. Netherlands embassy, Washington, D.C., to The Hague, October 26, 1988.

48. Ministry of Foreign Affairs, The Hague, internal memorandum to the minister, November 11, 1988.

Chapter 12, Non-Jews Leave with Israeli Visas

1. Drachman, *Challenging the Kremlin,* 91, maintains that the purpose of forcing non-Jewish dissidents like Andrei Amalrik to leave the Soviet Union on Israeli visas was to "create the impression that a Jewish-Zionist conspiracy was the driving force behind the entire Soviet human rights and emigration movements." That explanation seems far-fetched. The KGB would have had to be very naive to believe that the West could have been deceived in such a way.

2. Embassy to The Hague, March 17, 1969.

3. Alexeyeva, *Soviet Dissent,* 186–87.

4. Ministry of Foreign Affairs, The Hague, internal memorandum, January 4, 1972.

5. Embassy to The Hague, March 29, 1976. Among them was the Jewish poet and later Nobel Prize winner Joseph Brodsky. It is not clear why in these cases the KGB went to the trouble of requiring an invitation.

6. Cables exchanged between The Hague and embassy, June 23, 25, and 27, 1980.

7. One of the leaders of the Uniate Church was Josyp Terelya, who was sentenced to seven years in prison, plus five in internal exile, for defending the rights of the Ukrainian Catholics in August 1985. See Matlock, *Autopsy on an Empire*, 155. Terelya was freed in September 1987 and then issued—by great exception— a visa for the Netherlands. See Buwalda, *Diplomatiek Dagboek Moskou*, 44.

8. Commission on Security and Cooperation in Europe, *On the Right to Emigrate for Religious Reasons* (Washington, D.C.: Congressional Printing Office, May 1979).

9. See John Pollock, *The Siberian Seven* (London: Hodder and Stoughton, 1979). See also U.S. House of Representatives, Committee on the Judiciary, Subcommittee on Immigration, Refugees and International Law, *Siberian Seven: Hearing on HR 2873 and S 312*, 97th Cong., 2d sess., December 16, 1982.

10. Shultz, *Turmoil and Triumph*, 169. Cf. Dobrynin, *In Confidence*, 518.

11. Dobrynin, *In Confidence*, 521.

12. The Hague to embassy, April 11, 1983.

13. Max M. Kampelman, *Entering New Worlds* (New York: Harper Collins, 1991), 238 n., 270–71; interview with Max M. Kampelman, former U.S. ambassador, Washington, D.C., December 8, 1993. Shultz, *Turmoil and Triumph*, 169, gives July 7 as date.

14. Embassy to The Hague, February 7, 1989.

15. According to Israeli law, any person with one Jewish parent or even grandparent is a Jew, but according to religious law only a person with a Jewish mother is accepted as such.

16. Cables exchanged between embassy and The Hague, April 21, 23, and 27, 1987.

17. U.S. embassy, Rome, to U.S. Department of State, Washington, D.C., September 6, 1988, concerning meeting of Assistant Secretary Richard Schifter with Pentecostal refugees.

18. Embassy to The Hague, April 12, 1989.

19. Ministry of Foreign Affairs, The Hague, internal memorandum concerning demarche made by U.S. embassy on April 17, 1989. The U.S. note stated *inter alia*: "To impose a new regime abruptly would strand many applicants. Israel incurs no burden from the present arrangement." The Netherlands memorandum noted, however, that a request from Israel to carry out a demarche in Moscow could hardly be refused. Later the U.S. embassy indicated that, based on reports from Tel Aviv, it did not expect Israel to make any more requests for such a demarche. The Hague to embassy, April 21, 1989.

20. Netherlands embassy, Tel Aviv, to Ministry of Foreign Affairs, The Hague, May 17, 1989; ambassador, Moscow, to The Hague, memorandum, May 29, 1989. Aryeh Levin, who was present, claims that the Netherlands ambassador "refused" to change the practice. *Envoy to Moscow*, 100. That cannot be correct, because the consistent Netherlands policy line was not to refuse clearly expressed Israeli wishes. The ambassador did emphasize the problems a change would cause.

21. Assistant Secretary Richard Schifter to Secretary of State, information memorandum, January 3, 1989.

22. Data from Soviet Refugee Arrivals Report provided to the author by the Refugee Data Center, New York, by letter dated February 9, 1994.

23. U.S. Department of State, Washington, D.C., to U.S. embassies in Vienna, Rome, Moscow, Tel Aviv, and The Hague, January 20, 1989.

24. According to a cable from embassy to The Hague, May 18, 1989, the head of the Department of Humanitarian Affairs of MID, Yuri Reshetov, had declared that 3,000 members of Christian sects had received permission for direct emigration, "and so did not have to pretend anymore that they wanted to go to Israel."

25. Soviet Refugee Arrivals Report, letter dated February 9, 1994.

Chapter 13, Trouble for Refugee Status in the United States

1. U.S. embassy, Rome, to U.S. Department of State, January 25, 1989.

2. Cohen, interview.

3. Schifter, interview. In *Cardoza v. Fonseca* (1987), the Supreme Court stated: "a moderate interpretation of the standard would indicate that so long as an objective situation is established by the evidence, it need not be shown that the situation will probably result in persecution, but it is enough that persecution is a reasonable possibility."

4. U.S. Department of State, to U.S. embassy, Moscow, December 7, 1988; deputy Secretary of State Laurence Eagleburger, testimony before Congress, September 15, 1989.

5. This procedure was authorized following the adoption of Public Law 101-167 on November 21, 1989.

6. U.S. Department of State, Washington, D.C., internal memorandum to Richard Moore, ambassador in charge of refugee programs, March 20, 1989.

7. Leonid Stonov had been deprived of his academic title by the Soviet Higher Attestation Committee because of his work for the Refusenik movement. Interview. Text of the relevant Soviet decision in Drachman, *Challenging the Kremlin*, 143.

8. U.S. Department of State, internal memorandum to the secretary of state, April 21, 1989.

9. U.S. embassy, Moscow, to U.S. Department of State, February 7, 1989.

10. U.S. Department of State, internal memorandum to the secretary of state, April 21, 1989.

11. U.S. Department of State, to U.S. embassy, Moscow, March 14, 1989.

12. U.S. Department of State, internal memorandum to the secretary of state, April 21, 1989.

13. U.S. Department of State, internal memorandum to Ambassador Richard Moore, March 20, 1989.

14. Acting secretary of state to Policy Coordinating Committee on U.S. Policy on Soviet Refugees, memorandum, May 31, 1989.

15. John M. Gosko, "U.S. Plans to Bar Thousands of Soviet Jews," *Washington Post*, September 7, 1989, A1.

16. Embassy to The Hague, May 10, 1989.

17. Gosko, "U.S. Plans to Bar Thousands of Soviet Jews."

18. Mark Levin, interview; Mark E. Talisman, lobbyist for Jewish organizations and former assistant to Representative Charles Vanik, interview, Washington, D.C., October 6, 1993.

19. Cohen, interview.

20. Schifter, interview; see also the statement by the assistant secretary of state for European affairs to the Netherlands ambassador: "the well-known Israeli wishes did not play a big role." Netherlands embassy, Washington, D.C., to Ministry of Foreign Affairs, The Hague, September 8, 1989.

21. U.S. Department of State, internal memorandum to participants in follow-up meeting on Soviet refugees, July 3, 1989.

22. U.S. Department of State to U.S. mission, Geneva, and U.S. embassy, Rome, August 24, 1989.

23. Gosko, "U.S. Plans to Bar Thousands of Soviet Jews"; John M. Gosko, "U.S. Eyes 50,000 Limit on Soviet Emigres in '90," *Washington Post*, September 12, 1989, A1; Netherlands embassy, Washington, to The Hague, September 13, 1989.

24. U.S. Information Service, wireless file, September 14, 1989.

25. Embassy to The Hague, September 15, 1989.

26. U.S. Department of State, to U.S. embassy, Moscow, September 26, 1989.

27. Eagleburger testimony, September 15, 1989.

28. Statement by Assistant Secretary of State Joan Clark to Netherlands ambassador, Moscow, transmitted by embassy to Ministry of Foreign Affairs, The Hague, September 19, 1989.

29. The Austrian authorities decided they would no longer issue transit visas to applicants holding Israeli visas dated after October 1, 1989. Embassy to The Hague, October 6, 1989.

30. The Hague to embassy, October 3, 1989.

31. Austrian authorities in the end decided they would no longer issue transit visas to applicants wanting to go to the United States after October 1, 1989. Embassy to The Hague, October 6, 1989.

32. U.S. embassy, The Hague, to Department of State, September 26, 1989; The Hague to embassy, September 26, 1989.

33. Embassy to The Hague, September 27, 1989.

34. Consular Section, embassy, memorandum to The Hague, November 23, 1989.

Chapter 14, The Last Years

1. Netherlands ambassador, Moscow, to Ministry of Foreign Affairs, The Hague, memorandum, December 4, 1989.

2. Josien Driessen, in *Het Onvoltooid Verleden,* ed. Gerrits and Rankema, 155: "Rumors were circulating with exact data for pogroms. Nothing happened." Cf. Zvi Gitelman, "Glasnost, Perestroika and Antisemitism," *Foreign Affairs* (Spring 1993): 145. See also the *Status Report on Soviet Jewry: Hearing before the Commission on Security and Cooperation in Europe,* 101st Cong., 2d sess., March 7, 1990.

3. Buwalda, *Diplomatiek Dagboek Moskou,* 171.

4. Gitelman, "Glasnost, Perestroika, and Antisemitism," 146; Driessen, 155.

5. Buwalda, *Diplomatick Dagboek Moskou,* 111, 159.

6. Gitelman, "Glasnost, Perestroika and Antisemitism," 141.

7. Embassy to The Hague, March 22, 1990.

8. Embassy to The Hague, April 23, 1990.

9. Gorbachev, *Erinnerungen,* 722.

10. Concluding Document of the CSCE Follow-up Meeting in Vienna, January 19, 1989, in *From Helsinki to Vienna,* ed. Bloed, 213.

11. See Schifter, "Impact of the United States on Soviet Emigration Policy."

12. Max Kampelman, quoted in Drachman, *Challenging the Kremlin,* 395. See also Van der Stoel, "Heart of the Matter," 27.

13. "The Results of the Conference on the Human Dimension in Copenhagen" (in Russian), n.d. This report was put at the disposal of the author.

14. Schifter, "Impact of the United States on Soviet Emigration Policy."

15. Embassy to The Hague, January 18, 1985.

16. Embassy to The Hague, March 29, 1985.

17. Embassy to The Hague, March 8, 1985.

18. Embassy to The Hague, May 9, 1985.

19. The Hague to embassy, June 10, 1985.

20. Embassy to The Hague, June 28, 1985.

21. Embassy to The Hague, July 26 and 29, 1985.

22. Embassy to The Hague, August 7, 1985.

23. Embassy to The Hague, August 20, 1986.

24. Embassy to The Hague, September 2 and October 10, 1986.

25. Ministry of Foreign Affairs, The Hague, internal memorandum, November 22, 1986.

26. Author was present at the meetings in Stockholm and Moscow.

27. Embassy to The Hague, January 23 and February 2, 1987.

28. Embassy to The Hague, February 4, 1987.

29. Embassy to The Hague, March 9, 1987. It was several months before the other members of Begun's family received exit permits, and Begun refused to go without them. The whole family was then given a permit in September 1987, valid for only two weeks. Begun calmly declared he could not settle his affairs so quickly and he and his family stayed on. They finally left in January 1988.

Embassy to The Hague, September 7, 1987. See also Buwalda, *Diplomatiek Dagboek Moskou*, 54.

30. Buwalda, *Diplomatiek Dagboek Moskou*, 23.

31. Hartman, interview.

32. Buwalda, *Diplomatiek Dagboek Moskou*, 33 et passim. See also Bill Keller, "For Soviet Jews, Fear of Losing a Path to U.S.," *New York Times*, June 23, 1988, A6.

33. Buwalda, *Diplomatiek Dagboek Moskou*, 36–39.

34. Embassy to The Hague, December 16, 1987.

35. The Hague to embassy, December 18, 1987. The scare of 1972 (see Chapter 5) was still working.

36. Embassy to The Hague, February 5, 1988.

37. Embassy to The Hague, December 13, 1988.

38. Embassy to The Hague, February 8, 1990: "We have handed over the cashbox to the Israeli mission on December 15, 1989, and not granted any loans since then."

39. Kedmi, interview.

40. Buwalda, *Diplomatiek Dagboek Moskou*, 97.

41. Embassy to The Hague, January 27, 1989.

42. Embassy to The Hague, June 2, 1989.

43. The Hague to embassy, September 8, 1989; embassy to The Hague, October 18, 1989. Irina Voronkevich's picture appears on the cover of this book.

44. Professor David de Wied, chairman of the Netherlands Academy of Science, letter to Foreign Minister Hans van den Broek, December 12, 1988.

45. Uspensky and Voronkevich, Jerusalem, interview, March 21, 1994.

46. Embassy to The Hague, March 27, 1990.

47. TASS press release, January 12, 1990.

48. Agence France Presse and TASS press release, September 30, and October 1, 1990.

49. Yitzhak Shamir, letter to Netherlands Prime Minister Dr. R. F. M. Lubbers, January 7, 1991.

50. Embassy to The Hague, October 16 and December 31, 1990; The Hague to embassy, February 13, and March 1, 1991.

51. Vienna Convention on Consular Relations, April 24, 1963, United Nations Treaty Series, vol. 596, 261ff.

52. Figures provided by Lishka in Tel Aviv. See table 3, p. 224.

53. On October 20, 1989, the Netherlands ambassador in Moscow reported in a memorandum to The Hague, that a list of 247 cases had been presented to him by Refuseniks. In July 1991 there were 95 cases left. Embassy to The Hague, August 10, 1991.

54. Embassy to The Hague, May 10, 1989.

55. Embassy to The Hague, May 18, 1989, reporting on a conversation with Yuri Reshetov, MID.

56. Drachman, *Challenging the Kremlin*, 393, raises the possibility that "negative reactions of Palestinians and Arab states to the record large emigra-

tion" had something to do with the delay, but this seems unlikely. Drachman himself concludes (394) that "the Kremlin needed Western aid more than Arab support." It should rather be remembered that the new Soviet Congress of People's Deputies was then hotly discussing many issues it considered more urgent than emigration and that it repeatedly refused to be rushed.

57. Gorbachev, *Erinnerungen*, 731.

58. Matlock, *Autopsy on an Empire*, 381.

59. Eduard Shevardnadze, quoted in Drachman, *Challenging the Kremlin*, 394.

60. Ibid., 397.

61. On the Procedure for Exit from the Soviet Union and Entry into the Soviet Union by Citizens of the Soviet Union, signed by President Mikhail Gorbachev, May 20, 1991, text in Russian in *Vedomosti S'ezda Narodnykh Deputatov SSSR y Verkhovnogo Soveta SSSR*, no. 24, June 12, 1991, 939–45.

62. Embassy to The Hague, August 10, 1991.

63. Kuznetzov, head of OVIR, press conference, reported in embassy to The Hague, June 1, 1991.

64. Embassy to The Hague, August 10, 1991. The reference is to visa requirements; clearly this did not apply to Israel.

65. According to the Soviet Jewry Research Bureau, National Conference on Soviet Jewry, letter to the author, November 15, 1995.

66. According to Lishka; see Table 3.

Epilogue

1. The number of Jews living in the Soviet Union had been going down continuously after the Second World War, not just because of emigration but also because of a low birthrate and many mixed marriages. In fact, the census of 1989 showed a decline of 36 percent compared to the Jewish population of 1959. See Drachman, *Challenging the Kremlin*, introd.; Altshuler, *Soviet Jewry since the Second World War*, 21, 50. By the autumn of 1995, the loss from emigration alone probably constituted about 50 percent of the Jewish population of 1959.

Glossary

Aliyah	Hebrew for, literally, "ascent"; emigration to Israel.
BBI	Dutch abbreviation for "Belangen Behartiging Israel" (Interest Representation on Israel)
CIA	Central Intelligence Agency, USA
CPSU	Communist Party of the Soviet Union
CSCE	Conference on Security and Cooperation in Europe
Final Act	The closing document of the CSCE conference, signed in Helsinki on August 1, 1975
Glasnost	Russian for "openness"; the public affairs policy initiated by Mikhail Gorbachev when he was secretary general of the CPSU
KGB	Komitet Gosudarstvenoy Bezopasnosti: Committee for State Security, Soviet Union (from 1954)
Lishka	Hebrew abbreviation for Lishkat Hakesher, or "bureau of liaison," the service in Tel Aviv, Israel, responsible for the migration of Jews from Eastern Europe
MFN	Most-favored-nation status, which gives the country in question the same rates of import duties as most other trading partners already have
MID	Ministerstvo Innostrannikh Del: Ministry of Foreign Affairs, Soviet Union
NATO	North Atlantic Treaty Organization; defense alliance among Western nations

Noshrim	Hebrew for "dropouts"; Jewish emigrants from the Soviet Union with Israeli visas who did not go to Israel
Olim	Hebrew for those Jews who migrate (make *aliyah*) to Israel
OVIR	Otdel Viz I Registracii Inostrannykh Grazdan; office of visas and registration of foreign citizens, re-sorting under the Ministry of Internal Affairs, Soviet Union
Pale	Pale of Settlement, territory in Western Russia where most Jews had to live until 1917
Perestroika	Russian for *reconstruction*; the reform policy of Mikhail Gorbachev when he was secretary general of the CPSU
Politburo	Standing committee of the Central Committee, CPSU, in fact the governing body
Priyom	Russian for a receiving hour reception held every afternoon by the Dutch consul in Moscow
Refusenik	A combination of English and Russian for a person whose application for an exit permit from the Soviet Union had been refused
SALT	Strategic Arms Limitation Talks, treaty; SALT I concluded 1972, SALT II, 1979
Samizdat	Russian abbreviation for self-publishing of books and magazines, usually clandestinely
Shtetl	Yiddish for a town in the Pale of Settlement; plural, *Shtetlekh*
TASS	The official news agency of the Soviet Union
UPDK	Upravlenye Po Obsluzhivaniyu Diplomaticheskogo Korpusa: Management Bureau for the Diplomatic Corps, Soviet Union
Vysov	Russian for, literally, "summons"; the invitation to migrate to another country
Yordim	Hebrew for those who emigrate from Israel to other countries

Bibliography

Book-Length Studies

Alexeyeva, Ludmilla. *Soviet Dissent*. Middletown, Conn.: Wesleyan University Press, 1985.

Alleluyeva, Svetlana. *Letters to a Friend*. London: Hutchinson, 1967.

Altshuler, Mordechai. *Soviet Jewry since the Second World War*. New York: Greenwood Press, 1987.

Bloed, Arie, ed. *From Helsinki to Vienna: Basic Documents of the Helsinki Process*. Dordrecht: Martinus Nijhoff, 1990.

Brutzkus, Jules. *Les origines du Judaism russe*. Geneva, 1946.

Brym, Robert J. *The Jewish Intelligentsia and Russian Marxism*. London: Macmillan Press, 1972.

Buwalda, Piet. *Diplomatiek Dagboek Moskou* (Diplomatic diary Moscow). The Hague: SDU, 1992.

Carter, Jimmy. *Keeping Faith*. New York: Bantam, 1982.

Commission on Security and Cooperation in Europe. *On the Right to Emigrate for Religious Reasons*. Washington, D.C.: U.S. Congress, May 1979.

Dagan, Avidor. *Moscow and Jerusalem: Twenty Years of Relations between Israel and the USSR*. London: Abelard Schuman, 1970.

De Jonge, Alex. *Stalin and the Shaping of the Soviet Union*. Glasgow: Collins, 1986.

Dittrich, Z. R., and A. P. van Goudoever. *De Geschiedenis van de Sovjet Unie* (The history of the Soviet Union). The Hague: SDU, 1991.

Dobrynin, Anatoly. *In Confidence*. New York: Times Books, Random House, 1995.

Drachman, Edward. *Challenging the Kremlin: The Soviet Jewish Movement for Freedom*. New York: Paragon House, 1991.

Eban, Abba. *My Country: The Story of Modern Israel*. London: Random House, 1972.

Eytan, Walter. *The First Ten Years: A Diplomatic History of Israel*. Boston: Little, Brown, 1971.

Fosdick, Dorothy, ed. *Henry Jackson and World Affairs: Selected Speeches, 1953–1983*. Seattle: University of Washington Press, 1990.

_____, ed. *Staying the Course: Henry M. Jackson and National Security*. Seattle: University of Washington Press, 1987.

Freedman, Robert O., ed. *Soviet Jewry in the Decisive Decade 1971–1980*. Durham, N.C.: Duke University Press, 1984.

_____. *Soviet Jewry in the 1980's*. Durham, N.C.: Duke University Press, 1989.

_____. *The Soviet Union and the Carter Administration*. Pittsburgh: University Press, 1987.

Friedberg, Maurice. *Why They Left*. New York: Academic Committee on Soviet Jewry, 1972.

Gerrits, A. M., and H. Rankema, eds. *Het Onvoltooid Verleden* (The unfinished past). Utrecht, 1993.

Ginsburg, George. *The Citizenship Law of the USSR*. The Hague: Martinus Nijhoff, 1983.

Gitelman, Zvi. *A Century of Ambivalence*. New York: Schocken Books, 1988.

Golan, Matti. *The Secret Conversations of Henry Kissinger*. New York: Quadrangle/New York Times Books, 1976.

Gold, Donna L. *Soviet Jewry: U.S. Policy Considerations*. Congressional Research Service report 85-88S. Washington, D.C.: CRS, April 17, 1985.

Goldberg, Benjamin Z. *The Jewish Problem in the Soviet Union: An Analysis and a Solution*. New York: Crown, 1961.

Goldman, Marshal. *Détente and Dollars*. New York: Basic, 1975.

Gorbachev, Mikhail. *Erinnerungen* (Memories; German translation from the Russian). Berlin: Siedler Verlag, 1995.

_____. *Perestrojka: Een Nieuwe Visie voor Mijn Land en de Wereld* (Perestroika: A new vision for my country and the world; Dutch translation from the Russian). Utrecht: Het Spectrum, 1987.

Gromyko, Andrei. *Memories from Stalin to Gorbachev*. London: Arrow Books, 1989.

Ingles, José D. *A Study of Discrimination with Respect to the Right of Everyone to Leave Any Country, Including His Own, and Return to His Own Country.* New York: United Nations, 1965.

Janner, M. A. *La Puissance protectrice en droit international d'après les expériences faites par la Suisse pendant la seconde querre mondiale.* Bâle: Helling et Lichtenhahn, 1984.

Kaminskaya, Dina. *Final Judgement.* London: Harville, 1983.

Kampelman, Max M. *Entering New Worlds.* New York: Harper Collins, 1991.

_____. *Three Years at the East-West Divide.* New York: Freedom House, 1983.

Khrushchev, Nikita. *Khrushchev Remembers: The Last Testament.* Translated by Strobe Talbott. Boston: Little, Brown, 1974.

Kimche, Jon, and David Kimche. *Both Sides of the Hill.* London: Secker & Warburg, 1960.

Kissinger, Henry. *Diplomacy.* London: Simon & Schuster, 1994.

_____. *The White House Years.* London: Weidenfeld & Nicolson, 1979.

_____. *Years of Upheaval.* London: Weidenfeld & Nicolson, 1982.

Kochan, Lionel, ed. *The Jews in Russia since 1917.* Oxford: Oxford University Press, 1978.

Koestler, Arthur. *The Thirteenth Tribe: The Khazar Empire and Its Heritage.* New York: Random House, 1976.

Korey, William. *Human Rights and the Helsinki Accord.* Headline Series 264. New York: Foreign Policy Association, 1983.

_____. *The Promises We Keep: Human Rights, the Helsinki Process, and American Foreign Policy.* New York: Institute of East-West Studies, 1993.

Krammer, Arnold. *The Forgotten Friendship.* Urbana: University of Illinois Press, 1974.

Lerner, Alexander. *Change of Heart.* Minneapolis: Lerner Publications, 1992.

Levin, Aryeh. *Envoy to Moscow.* London: Frank Cass &. Co. 1996.

Levin, Nora. *The Jews in the Soviet Union since 1917.* New York: New York University Press, 1988.

Litvinov, Emanuel. *Soviet Antisemitism: The Paris Trial.* London: Wildwood House, 1974.

London, Arthur. *L'Aveu: Le procès de Prague* (The confession: The Prague trial). Paris: Gallimard, 1968.

Maclean, Fitzroy. *Holy Russia.* London: Weidenfeld & Nicolson, 1978.

Maranz, Paul, and David Goldberg, eds. *The Decline of the Soviet Union and the Middle East*. Boulder, Colo.: Westview Press, 1994.

Mastny, Vojtech. *Helsinki, Human Rights and European Security: Analysis and Documentation*. Durham, N.C.: Duke University Press, 1986.

Matlock, Jack F. *Autopsy on an Empire*. New York: Random House, 1995.

Matthews, Mervyn. *The Passport Society: Controlling Movement in Russia and the USSR*. Oxford, 1933.

Meir, Golda. *My Life*. London: Weidenfeld & Nicolson, 1975.

Morrison, Donald, ed. *Michail Sergejevitsj Gorbatsjov, Een Persoonlijke Biografie* (Dutch translation from the English). New York: Time, Inc., 1988. Franeker: Van Wijnen, 1989.

_____. *Mikhail S. Gorbachev: An Intimate Biography*. New York: Time, Inc., 1988.

National Conference on Soviet Jewry, comp. *White Book of Exodus*. New York: NCSJ, 1972.

Orbach, William W. *The American Movement to Aid Soviet Jews*. Amherst: University of Massachusetts Press, 1979.

Pinkus, Benjamin. *The Jews of the Soviet Union, 1917–1923*. Cambridge: Cambridge University Press, 1988.

Pipes, Richard. *The Formation of the Soviet Union*. Rev. ed. Cambridge, Mass.: Harvard University Press, 1964.

Pockney, B. P. *Soviet Statistics since 1950*. Dartmouth, N.H., 1991.

Pollock, John. *The Siberian Seven*. London: Hodder and Stoughton, 1979.

Potok, Chaim. *Wanderings*. New York: Knopf, 1978.

Rapoport, Jakov, and Natasha. *Het Dokterscomplot* (The Doctors' Plot, Dutch translation from the Russian). Amsterdam: G. A. van Oorschot, 1990.

Rapoport, Louis. *Stalin's War against the Jews*. New York: Free Press, 1990.

Raviv, Dan, and Yossi Melman. *Every Spie a Prince*. Boston: Houghton Mifflin, 1990.

Remnick, David. *Lenin's Tomb*. New York: Random House, 1993.

Rosenfeld, Nancy. *Unfinished Journey*. New York: University Press of America, 1993.

Roth, Stephen J. *The Helsinki Final Act and Soviet Jewry*. London: Institute of Jewish Affairs, 1976.

_____, ed. *Human Contacts: Reunion of Families and Soviet Jewry*. London: Institute of Jewish Affairs, for the International Council of the World Conference on Soviet Jewry, 1986.

Sakharov, Andrei. *Mijn Leven* (Dutch translation from the Russian). Amsterdam: Meulenhof, 1990.

_____. *My Life*. New York: Knopf, 1990.

_____. *Sakharov Speaks*. New York, 1974.

Salitan, Laurie P. *Politics and Nationality in Contemporary Soviet-Jewish Emigration, 1968–89*. New York: St. Martin's Press, 1992.

Sanders, Ronald. *Shores of Refuge*. New York: Holt, 1988.

Schroeter, Leonard. *The Last Exodus*. 2d ed. Seattle: Weidenfeld, 1979.

Schulzinger, Robert D. *Henry Kissinger, Doctor of Diplomacy*. New York: Columbia University Press, 1989.

Sharansky, Natan. *Fear No Evil*. New York: Random House, 1988.

Shevardnadze, Eduard. *The Future Belongs to Freedom*. New York: Free Press, 1991.

Shindler, Colin. *Exit Visa*. London: Bachman & Turner, 1978.

Shultz, George P. *Turmoil and Triumph*. New York: Scribner's, 1993.

Stern, Paula. *The Water's Edge: Domestic Politics and the Making of American Foreign Policy*. Contributions in Political Science 15. Westport, Conn.: Greenwood Press, 1979.

Svirsky, Grigory. *Hostages: The Personal Testimony of a Soviet Jew*. New York: Alfred Knopf, 1976.

Tarnopolsky, Yury. *Memoirs of 1984*. New York: University Press of America, 1993.

Tatu, Michel. *Gorbatchev, l'URSS Va-t-Elle Changer?* (Will the Soviet Union change?). Paris: Le Centurion, 1987.

Teller, Judd L. *The Kremlin, the Jews and the Middle East*. New York: Thomas Yoschoff, 1957.

U.S. Congress, Helsinki Commission. *Implementation of the Final Act of the Conference on Security and Cooperation in Europe: Findings and Recommendations Two Years after Helsinki*. Washington, D.C.: U.S. Government Printing Office, 1977.

Vance, Cyrus. *Hard Choices*. New York: Scribner's, 1983.

Vogelgesang, Sandy. *American Dream, Global Nightmare: The Dilemma of U.S. Human Rights Policy*. New York: Norton, 1980.

Volten, Peter M. E. *Brezhnev's "Peace Program": Success or Failure?* Boulder, Colo.: Westview Press, 1982.

Werth, Alexander. *Russia at War*. London: Barrie & Rockliff, 1964.

Wiesel, Elie. *De Joden der Stilte* (The Jews of silence; Dutch translation from the French). Hilversum: Gooi & Sticht, 1985.

World Conference on Soviet Jewry. *The Position of Soviet Jewry, 1977–80.* New York: WCSJ, 1980.

_____. *The Position of Soviet Jewry, 1983–1985.* London: WCSJ, 1986.

Zaslavsky, Victor, and Robert J. Brym. *Soviet-Jewish Emigration and Soviet Nationality Policy.* New York: St. Martin's Press, 1983.

Magazine Articles

Alexander, Z. "Immigration to Israel from the USSR." *Israel Yearbook on Human Rights* 7, supp. (1977).

Cullen, Robet B. "Soviet Jewry." *Foreign Affairs* 65, no. 2 (1986).

Feldbrugge, F. J. M. "The New Soviet Law on Emigration." *Soviet Jewish Affairs* 17, no. 1 (1987).

Freedman, Robert O. "Review of *Politics and Nationality*, by Laurie Salitan." *Slavic Review* (Spring 1993).

Galey, Margaret E. "Congress, Foreign Policy, and Human Rights: Ten Years after Helsinki." *Human Rights Quarterly* 7, no. 3 (1985).

Gitelman, Zvi. "Glasnost, Perestroika and Antisemitism." *Foreign Affairs* (Spring 1993).

Korey, William. "The Future of Soviet Jewry." *Foreign Affairs* (Autumn 1979).

_____. "The Story of the Jackson Amendment, 1973–1975." *Midstream: A Monthly Jewish Review* (March 1975).

Roth, Stephen J. "Facing the Belgrade Meeting: Helsinki—Two Years After." *Soviet Jewish Affairs* 7, no. 1 (1977).

Stern, Paula. "US-Soviet Trade: The Question of Leverage." *Washington Quarterly* (Autumn 1989).

Stevenson, Adlai E., and Alton Frye. "Trading with the Communists." *Foreign Affairs* 68, no. 2 (1989).

Weinstein, Lewis H. "Soviet Jewry and the American Jewish Community." *American Jewish History* 77, no. 4 (June 1988).

List of Interviews

All interviews have been conducted by the author, who is most grateful to all those who have been willing to discuss the subject of this book with him. Some have been quoted by name in the endnotes and some have not, but all have contributed indispensable data, background information, and knowledge. Several interviews have been recorded; during others only notes were taken. Tapes and notes are in the personal archives of the author.

United States

Washington, D.C.

Alexeyeva, Ludmilla: former dissident and author, September 29, 1993.

Eissenstett, Stuart: President Jimmy Carter's former adviser, June 8, 1994 (in Brussels).

Goodby, James E.: former U.S. ambassador, October 12, 1993.

Hartman, Arthur: former U.S. ambassador to the Soviet Union and former assistant secretary of state, December 2, 1993.

Jentleson, Bruce: special assistant to the director of the Policy Planning Staff, U.S. Department of State, November 22, 1993.

Kampelman, Max M.: former U.S. ambassador and counselor, U.S. Department of State, December 8, 1993.

Laqueur, Walter: chairman of the International Research Council, Center for Strategic and International Studies, March 15, 1994 (in Jerusalem).

Perle, Richard: former assistant to Senator Henry Jackson and former assistant secretary of defense, November 8, 1993.

Reddy, Leo: former State Department officer, December 15, 1993.

Schifter, Richard: counselor at the National Security Council and former assistant secretary of state for humanitarian affairs, September 30, 1993.

Simes, Dmitri: senior associate at the Carnegie Endowment for International Peace, December 3, 1993.

Singer, Lynn: executive director of the Long Island Committee for Soviet Jewry, December 5, 1993.

Sonnenfeldt, Helmut: former personal assistant to the secretary of state, December 6, 1993.

Soyfer, Valery: former Refusenik, now professor at George Mason University, Oakton, Va., November 30, 1993.

Stern, Paula: former assistant to Senator Gaylord Nelson, former member of the International Trade Commission and author, November 17, 1993.

Talisman, Mark E.: former assistant to Representative Charles Vanik, October 6, 1993.

Vest, George: former U.S. ambassador to the European Communities, head of the U.S. delegation to Helsinki Preparatory Conference, and assistant secretary of state for European affairs, December 14, 1993.

Wise, Sam: director of the Commission on Security and Cooperation in Europe, U.S. Congress, December 15, 1993.

Zimmerman, Warren: former U.S. ambassador and director of refugee affairs, U.S. Department of State, November 10, 1993.

New York

Birnbaum, Jacob: former head of Student Struggle for Soviet Jewry, October 20, 1993.

Kissinger, Henry: former security adviser to the president and former secretary of state, January 10, 1994.

Korey, William: director of international policy research of the International Council of B'nai B'rith, November 24, 1993 (in Washington, D.C.).

Levin, Mark: executive director of the National Conference on Soviet Jewry, October 14, 1993.

Saipe, Robin: communities coordinator, National Conference on Soviet Jewry, October 14, 1993.

Samoilovich, George: former Refusenik, October 20, 1993.

Scott, Dick: International Organization for Migration, October 22, 1993.

Steinberg, A.: World Jewish Congress, October 21, 1993.

Stolov, Dale: director, overseas operations, Hebrew Immigrant Aid Society, October 20, 1993.

Wenick, Martin A.: executive vice-president, Hebrew Immigrant Aid Society, October 20, 1993.

Chicago

Cohen, Pamela: president of the Union of Councils for Soviet Jews, October 4, 1993.

Stevenson, Adlai E., III: former U.S. senator, October 4, 1993.

Stonov, Leonid, and Natasha Stonov: former Refuseniks, now on the staff of the Union of Councils for Soviet Jews, October 3, 1993.

Baltimore

Freedman, Robert: professor at Hebrew University, October 15, 1993.

Boston

Zieman, Tatyana: former Refusenik, April 2, 1995 (in The Hague).

Zieman, Yuri: former Refusenik, October 30, 1993 (in Washington, D.C.).

Israel

Jerusalem

Altshuler, Mordechai: professor at Hebrew University, March 11, 1994.

Anug, Yeshayanu: former Israeli ambassador, March 16, 1994.

Arad, Shimson: former Israeli ambassador to the Netherlands, March 7, 1994.

Bar-On, Hanan: former Israeli ambassador to the Netherlands, March 10, 1994.

Gordon, Miron: director of the Eastern European Division I, Israeli Ministry of Foreign Affairs, March 7, 1994.

Kislik, Vladimir: former Refusenik, March 1, 1994.

Lein, Evgeny: former Refusenik, March 21, 1994.

Levanon, Nehamiah: former head of Lishka, October 31, 1993 (in Washington, D.C.).

Levin, Aryeh: former Israeli ambassador to Moscow, March 22, 1994.

Mantver, Arnon: director general of the Department of Immigration and Absorption, Jewish Agency, March 18, 1994.

Ostrin, Asher: Joint Distribution Committee, Jerusalem office, March 22, 1994.

Rubin, Ina: former Refusenik, March 21, 1994.

Shamir, Yitzhak: former prime minister of Israel, March 14, 1994.

Sharansky, Natan (formerly, Anatoly): former dissident and Refusenik, now president of the Zionist Forum (Russian), March 17, 1994.

Uspensky, Igor, and Irina Uspensky: former Refuseniks, March 21, 1994.

Tel Aviv

Kedmi, Yaakov: head of Lishka, March 6, 1994.

Meiman, Naum: former Refusenik, now professor at the University of Tel Aviv, March 6, 1994.

Rehovot

Lerner, Alexander: former Refusenik, now professor at the Weizmann Institute, March 16, 1994.

Lod

Lurye, Emanuel, and Judith Lurye: former Refuseniks, March 12, 1994.

Russia

Moscow

Babenkov, Vladimir: former deputy head of the Department of Humanitarian Affairs, MID, October 6, 1994.

Bakhmin, Vyacheslav: former dissident and prisoner, head of the Department of Humanitarian Affairs, MID, October 6, 1994.

Bogaraz, Larissa: former dissident, October 10, 1994.

Bonner, Yelena: widow of Andrei Sakharov, former dissident, also author, October 6, 1994.

Daniels, Alexander: former dissident, now director of Memorial, October 10, 1995.

Kovalev, Sergei: former dissident, chairman of the Presidential Commission on Human Rights, October 10, 1994.

Landa, Malyeva: former dissident, October 10, 1994.

Lieberman, Alexander: Director of the Moscow Human Rights Bureau, Union of Councils for Soviet Jews, October 3, 1994.

Podrabinek, Alexander: former dissident, editor of *Express Khronika*, October 5, 1994.

Tumarkin, Vladimir: former staff member of the Central Committee, Communist Party of the Soviet Union, now press officer of the Gorbachev Foundation, October 7, 1994.

Yakovlev, Alexander: former member of the Politburo, Communist Party of the Soviet Union, October 14, 1994.

England

London

Roth, Stephen: former director of the Institute of Jewish Affairs, May 26, 1995.

Netherlands

The Hague

Gorp, L. V. M. van: embassy counselor and former head of the Consular Section, Netherlands embassy, Moscow, February 19, 1993.

Heinemann, H. J.: Netherlands ambassador and former head of the Consular Section, Netherlands embassy, Moscow, April 11, 1995.

Huydecoper van Nigtevecht, Jonkheer J. L. R.: former Netherlands ambassador to the Soviet Union, May 18, 1994.

Lanschot, R. E. M. van: counselor at the Netherlands embassy, Moscow, and former head of the Consular Section, January 15, 1996.

Marchant et d'Ansembourg, L. J. Count de: former Netherlands ambassador to Sweden and former head of the Consular Section, Netherlands embassy, Moscow, January 31, 1996.

Polak, P. J.: former director of European affairs, Ministry of Foreign Affairs, January 12, 1993.

Schmelzer, W. K. N.: former Netherlands minister of foreign affairs, March 2, 1995.

Soetendorp, P.: rabbi of the Liberal Jewish Congregation of The Hague, May 24, 1994.

Tammenoms Bakker, A. B.: former Netherlands ambassador to the Soviet Union, May 25, 1995 (in London).

Vliet, G. van: former head of the Consular Section, Netherlands embassy, Moscow, April 18, 1994.

Index

D

E

F

attacked exchange between Kissinger and Jackson on Soviet agreement with regard to emigration, 105; diploma tax would fade away, 96; given largely ceremonial function of chairman of the Presidium of the Supreme Soviet, 250; grudging admission that a yearly number of Jewish emigrants up to 45,000 was possible, 104; had great trouble in getting Politburo to accept freer movement provisions in Helsinki Final Act, 118; memoirs of, 229; not incorrect in claiming that the texts of Kissinger and Jackson did not reflect agreement with Kissinger, 110; personal plea on behalf of Sharansky to, 205; proposal that Netherlands foreign minister write a letter regarding Joseph Begun to, 145–6; Soviet contempt for rights of the individual, 150; trip to the United States in 1977, 132

"guardian angel of the prisoners and Refuseniks": Ida Nudel called, 143

Gudava family from Georgia, 208

H

"harassment": Kissinger definition of, 103–4

Hartman, Arthur: interview with, 269; U.S. ambassador to Moscow, 207

Hazewinkel, H. J., official, Netherlands ministry of foreign affairs: information provided by, 239

Hebrew grammars and dictionaries: distribution through Netherlands embassy of, 208

Hebrew Immigrant Aid Society, 10; disbanded and founded several times, 228; estimate of total number of Soviet Jews arriving in North America in 1990, 214; how assisted emigrants in Vienna, 59, 164; United States had neither resources nor legal authority to process and receive all Soviet emigrants, 188

Hebrew Immigrant Aid Society and Joint Distribution Committee: accused by Israel of "hijacking" Jews in Vienna, 165

Hebrew language: Soviet Union probably only country where was illegal, 231

Hebrew publications in Russia: last appeared in 1926, 13

Heinemann, H. J., Netherlands ambassador: interview with, 273

Helsinki Final Act of 1975 (also referred to as CSCE-Final Act), xvi, 117–9, 261; agreement for follow-up meetings, 119; freer movement provisions in, 117–8; generated fundamental changes that helped end the cold war, 126; Arthur Goldberg interpretation of, 122–3; impact was a surprise even to Western negotiators, 119; improvements of provisions in, 124; Max Kampelman interpretation of, 122–3; permanently established relationship between human rights and international peace, 122–3; Politburo non-compliance implied, 246; promoted cooperation between Jewish and human rights movements in Moscow, 120; regarding human rights Soviet Union had no intention of honoring, 121; U.S. position that emigration cases could be discussed under, 156

Helsinki meeting of Israel and Soviet consular officials, 149

Helsinki Process: pressure for better observance of the obligations in, 201; role in increasing issue of Israeli visas of, 122. *See also* Helsinki Final Act of 1975

Helsinki Conference on Security and Cooperation in Europe, 113–26

I

L

M

R

S

T

U

V

W